Reasonable Self-Esteem

D0153678

VCTC Library
Hartness Library
Vermont Technical College
Randolph Center VT 05061

Reasonable Self-Esteem

RICHARD KESHEN

McGill-Queen's University Press
Montreal & Kingston • London • Buffalo

© McGill-Queen's University Press 1996
ISBN 0-7735-1372-8 (cloth)
ISBN 0-7735-1373-6 (paper)

Legal deposit first quarter 1996
Bibliothèque nationale du Québec

Printed in Canada on acid-free paper

This book has been published with the help of
a grant from the Canadian Federation for the
Humanities, using funds provided by the Social
Sciences and Humanities Research Council of Canada.

McGill-Queen's University Press is grateful to the
Canada Council for support of its publishing program.

Canadian Cataloguing in Publication Data

Keshen, Richard, 1946–
  Reasonable self-esteem
  Includes bibliographical references and index.
  ISBN 0-7735-1372-8 (bound) –
  ISBN 0-7735-1373-6 (pbk.)
  1. Self-esteem. I. Title.
  BF697.5.S46K47 1996   179   C96-900689-3

Typeset in Palatino 10/12
by Caractéra inc., Quebec City

To Mary Ellen (lucky man I)

Contents

rejects competitive reasons as out of keeping with his nature and so inhibits envy in
himself. Self-evaluations involving adjec-
tives such as "poor," "good," and "excellent" are shown to be distinct from
competitive self-evaluations.

Reasons for self-esteem grounded in social
relationships are analysed. Self-evaluations
which imply that an agent has less moral
status than another entity are shown to be
out of keeping with the RP's nature. Her
ambivalent relationship to group membership is described.

Reasons for self-esteem involving qualities
we conceive as issuing from ourselves are
analysed. Such qualities are the basis for
what I call *inherent reasons* for self-esteem.
The notion of "issuing from ourself" is analysed. It is shown that appreciation of what
has *intrinsic worth* can be as much the basis
for an inherent reason as voluntary acts. The
trait of attaching importance to one's being a
unique person is analysed. It is shown that
the RP is disposed to have this trait.

PART TWO   ELEMENTS IN A WAY OF LIFE

Self-respect is distinguished from self-esteem.
It is argued that being a self-respecting
teacher, carpenter, etc., involves attributing
positive worth to a tradition or quasi-tradition.
It is shown that reasonableness, as I define it,
can be thought of as a tradition. Hence, the
RP can have the benefit of seeing herself as
self-respecting *qua* RP. It is argued that part
of the tradition of reasonableness includes
science. It is shown how the RP of a certain
temperament has meaning added to her life
through contributing to science, either by
being a scientist herself or by being a genuine
appreciator of science.

Preface

In this book I describe a moral ideal which I call *reasonable self-esteem* and argue that this ideal can be productive of a desirable life. The book is divided into two parts. In part 1, I describe how a person committed to reasonableness can analyse his self-esteem. I argue that, through this analysis, such a person is disposed to cultivate certain personality traits and to reject others. For example, he is disposed to cultivate autonomy and to reject envy; to cultivate self-esteem grounded in individual achievement and to reject relationships grounded in unequal moral status. In part 2, I argue that the relevant traits can be elements of a meaningful life. I describe how a person with reasonable self-esteem can feel herself part of a worthy tradition, acquire a sense of dignity, and contribute to the good of others. In the end, then, I aim to demonstrate the appeal of a life in which reasonableness is a central commitment.

Acknowledgments

My interest in philosophy was especially encouraged by two under-graduate teachers, Edward Broadbent and John Yolton. From my earliest undergraduate days, when I first read his book on Spinoza, I have found in Stuart Hampshire's writings a sympathetic viewpoint – a viewpoint which has helped me work toward the expression of my own thoughts. Jonathan Glover's writings and personal influence have meant a great deal. His understanding of the way moral philosophy should be done has been the most sustaining influence on my work. The University College of Cape Breton has been generous in its support. Thanks to Aaron Keshen for preparing the bibliography. The critical encouragement of my work by Stan Godlovitch, Peter Singer, Richmond Campbell, and two anonymous reviewers has been crucial to my completing the book. I am grateful to my friend Richard Mueller for the cover artwork, which speaks to our mutual interest in the relationship between reason and the emotions. Peter Blaney, Elizabeth Hulse, and Joan McGilvray have been a great help through the publishing process.

PART ONE

Reasons for Self-Esteem

1 Self-Esteem and the Reasonable Person

> ... it is no wonder that languages should not be very precise in marking the boundaries between virtues and talents, vices and defects; since there is so little distinction made in our internal estimation of them. It seems indeed certain, that the *sentiment* of conscious worth, the self-satisfaction proceeding from a review of a man's own conduct and character; it seems certain, I say, that this sentiment, which, though the most common of all others, has no proper name in our language.   David Hume[1]

A: SELF-ESTEEM

1.1 This chapter constructs a model which I apply in the rest of the book. My model focuses on those experiences in which we feel our self enhanced or diminished, and I shall use the term *episodic self-esteem* to refer to such experiences. As I define the concept, episodic self-esteem extends but does not distort our notion of self-esteem as it is ordinarily used.[2]

Here are examples of the experiences I mean to capture: (a) Jones feels a momentary glow of self-satisfaction upon making a witty remark at a party; (b) Jones feels ashamed when Adams criticizes him for not being able to cook; (c) When painting, Smith, an artist, has a sense of being at one with her work; (d) Smith sometimes wonders whether she is spending too much time on her painting, to the detriment of her family; these thoughts are accompanied by feelings of guilt.

There are, of course, significant differences between the experiences described in (a) and (c) on the one hand and those described in (b) and (d) on the other. But (a) and (c) have in common the fact that the agent experiences an enhancement of his* self, and (b) and

---

* My way of dealing with male and female pronouns in this book is to alternate them chapter by chapter, beginning with the male pronoun in this chapter.

(d) have in common the fact that the agent experiences a diminution. As important as it is, for some purposes, to understand the differences between the ways our self can be enhanced or diminished,[3] it is the general categories which are useful for my purposes. Let us therefore refer to the pleasure or satisfaction a person experiences when his self is enhanced as *feelings of enhancement*. And let us refer to feelings such as humiliation, guilt, shame, and mortification as *feelings of diminution*. We may call these two types of feelings, taken together, the *self-esteem feelings*. It is important to note that such feelings do not necessarily assume the form of strong agitations in a person's mind. Smith's sense of being at one with her painting, for example, counts as a feeling of enhancement, even though it does not agitate her mind.

1.2 We understand the experiences in our examples as self-esteem feelings, I want to say, because we see implicit in these feelings *beliefs* of the agent.[4] Jones's self-satisfaction is not something which happens to him like a back spasm. Rather, it is connected to some such thought as "I am admirable insofar as I have made people laugh at my witticism." Of course, such a belief need not be articulated by Jones in order for it to be true that it plays a part in his feeling. We accept that unarticulated thoughts and beliefs may be active in people's minds. I may rightly infer, for example, that Smith believes it is going to rain by the way she looks at the grey sky and goes into the house to get her umbrella, even though she has not explicitly formulated the thought "It is going to rain" to me or to herself. (Later in the book, it will be useful to speak, when a person's belief that p is unarticulated, of his *taking it for granted* that p, rather than of his believing that p in the full sense; but for now it is not misleading to use the concept of belief to cover the wider category.)

Many feelings and emotions are incomprehensible apart from the beliefs with which they are connected. For example, people could not be said to experience fear, in the standard case, unless they had some notion of being in a dangerous situation. The self-esteem feelings must similarly be defined in terms of the beliefs with which they are connected. In examining these defining beliefs, we shall clarify the concept of a *reason for self-esteem*.

1.3 I cited the belief which helps us understand Jones's feeling of enhancement as "I am admirable insofar as I have made people laugh at my witticism." Now it further clarifies Jones's feeling if we see this belief as consisting of two component beliefs. First, there is Jones's belief that he exemplifies some property or characteristic, namely, the property of his having made people laugh by his witticism. Then there is his belief that his having made people laugh in this way is admirable. These components are separable parts of the original thought, since it is conceivable that a person could believe he had made a witticism but not regard his having done so as admirable. That the two component beliefs are implicit in Jones's self-esteem feeling is further evident from the fact that if he were to deny that he had either of the beliefs, or some such beliefs which serve the same function, then neither he nor we could regard his feeling as rationally comprehensible. Of course, we are often enough struck by emotions which do not make complete sense to us. But we understand these irrational or non-rational emotions only against the standard case in which there is an appropriate match between feelings and beliefs. It will be useful now to introduce the following semi-technical terms.

Let us say that when a person ascribes some property or characteristic to himself, he thereby has a *self-ascription*. Let us further say that when a person believes some self-ascription is worthy of praise or admiration, he thereby attributes *positive worth* to the self-ascription. A parallel structure applies to the case of diminution. Let us say that when a person believes some self-ascription merits blame, disapproval, or contempt, or is in some way shameful or repugnant, he thereby attributes *negative worth* to that self-ascription. If, then, Jones is going to make rational sense of his diminution, he must see the feeling as related to his having attributed negative worth to his self-ascription of having been criticized by Adams for not being able to cook.

The notions of positive and negative worth allow us to distinguish those self-feelings which do not involve our self-esteem from those which do. For example, there is a difference between the person who merely regrets his being an incompetent cook and Jones, who attributes negative worth to this self-ascription. Only Jones suffers feelings of diminution. Similarly, there is a difference between the person who is happy about his painting simply because it will bring him money and Smith, who attributes positive worth to her painting and so experiences enhancement.

When we ask someone what his reason is for self-esteem, we are usually referring to some specific instance in which the agent experiences enhancement or diminution. So it is the self-esteem feelings for which we ask, and expect to hear, reasons. Now when someone produces reasons, what he typically offers are precisely the belief components of his self-esteem. So, for example, if we ask Jones why he feels ashamed, he could appropriately reply, using my terminology, that he has attributed negative worth to his self-ascription of being criticized by Adams for not being able to cook. Let us say that when some set of beliefs stands in the relation of being the agent's own reason for a feeling, those beliefs *rationalize* the feeling for the agent.[5]

As I indicated earlier, we sometimes have self-esteem feelings for which we judge there to be no appropriate match in our beliefs. When this occurs, we can say that a person's feelings are *unrationalizable* from his point of view. It is also worth noting that we may have the belief components of episodic self-esteem but lack the appropriate feelings. For example, a person may believe that his activity has positive worth and yet find himself incapable of feeling enhancement on that account (a common experience of people suffering from depression: "I see, not feel, how beautiful they are," writes Coleridge of an analogous mental state in "Dejection: An Ode"). Here too a person's mental state does not make complete sense to him.

Because our self-esteem is grounded in reasons, we can ask what are good or bad reasons and hence *evaluate* our own and others' grounds for episodic self-esteem. In the next part of the chapter, I examine the criteria I shall use in this evaluation.

B: THE REASONABLE PERSON

1.4 My purpose now is to introduce what I call the *critical guidelines*. In my model, these guidelines help set the standard for *reasonableness* in scrutinizing and revising our grounds for self-esteem. I call these rules "guidelines" (rather than the stronger "principles," for example) because I do not want to suggest that rational scrutiny, in this area at least, involves the application of an algorithm which mechanically produces a definitive answer as to whether some reason for self-esteem is reasonable or not. Such is far from the case. My analysis leaves scope for reasonable people to disagree, and also for the exercise of judgment not governed by definitive rules.[6] The view of critical inquiry I am proposing sees this activity as dialectical and ever evolving. In formulating his beliefs about self-esteem, a reasonable agent does not start from the question *simpliciter* "What, as a person committed to the guidelines, should my reasons for self-esteem be?" Rather, the agent *finds himself* with certain reasons and then directs questions to himself as suggested by the critical guidelines or as a result of dialogue with others (very often the guidelines will be implicit in a question or discussion, rather than consciously applied). Depending on how he answers these questions, the agent either revises his reasons or feels justified in continuing to hold them.

Thus the guidelines, initially at least, provide a test for *eliminating* inadequate reasons.

Although I shall describe the critical guidelines with specific reference to self-esteem, it will be clear that they are applicable to our beliefs in general (though in some cases, depending on the context, a guideline would have to be expressed differently). Now I am going to introduce the semi-technical concept *Reasonable Person* (or RP) to refer to a person who, to begin with, cares deeply about having reasonable beliefs through an application of the critical guidelines. This concern I call the RP's *defining commitment*.

Reasonableness is a rich concept.[7] It includes epistemic, prudential, and moral dimensions. As the book unfolds, my concept of the Reasonable Person comes to incorporate all three of these dimensions. My strategy, however, is to start from what is essentially the epistemic dimension and then to see how the other two dimensions are congruent with it. In the end, I show how, in the life of the RP, the three dimensions can be mutually supporting. Let us turn now to the critical guidelines.

1.5 In order to examine critically an experience of episodic self-esteem, the RP must be able to articulate or describe that experience. Attention to this process of articulation gives rise to the first two guidelines.

We often articulate our self-esteem experiences in terms of the beliefs which rationalize them. For example, Smith may describe her experience of enhancement as the feeling of having created this good painting. At the same time, there is the more purely "felt" aspect of an experience of self-esteem, which is constituted by pleasurable or displeasurable sensations. These sensations we may articulate as being intense or weak, long-lasting or fleeting. We may also describe such sensations by means of metaphor. Smith, for example, may say that when she is painting she feels on top of the world, or Jones may say that he felt like crawling into a hole when he was criticized by Adams.

To articulate one's sensations in either of the above ways is to describe, in part, how *seriously* one finds oneself taking the related reason for self-esteem. Now this opens up space for critical scrutiny. For the question arises as to whether the strength of one's feelings are commensurate with the weight one believes, on reflection, to be appropriate, given the reason which rationalizes the feelings. Jones, for example, may decide that, although his being criticized by Adams for not being able to cook justifies some diminution, nevertheless his wanting to crawl into a hole gives too much weight to this reason for diminution. This accommodation of feeling to reason presupposes criteria of appropriate weighting, and that in turn presupposes some overall theory of what constitutes good or bad grounds for self-esteem. To provide such a theory, at least from the perspective of a Reasonable Person, is one purpose of this book. Therefore, we cannot now answer specific questions about weighting. However, we can formulate the following general guideline:

1 *Weighting Guideline*   A Reasonable Person attempts to bring the feeling component of his self-esteem experience into accommodation with the weight he believes appropriate, given the reason which rationalizes the feeling.

We shall see the importance of this guideline for the RP in the final chapter.

Another component of the self-esteem experience to be articulated is the self-ascription itself. The self-ascription is a belief, and, as I said earlier, most often people's beliefs are implicit in their behaviour, emotional expression, or other mental states. This means that inference and interpretation, even by the agent himself, are required to make self-ascriptions explicit. Consider the following example. While Smith is painting, she notices, out of her studio window, her daughter playing with the babysitter, and she immediately feels diminution. Now to articulate the self-ascription which partly rationalizes her feeling, she must propose a hypothesis to herself and then test the hypothesis against her own sense of what the self-ascription was. Smith, say, proposes that she has ascribed to herself the characteristic of being an irresponsible mother. But, having made this hypothesis, she may then decide she does not have it quite right and may propose another, more specific hypothesis: say, that she has ascribed to herself the characteristic of not spending enough time with her daughter (which need not itself amount to being an irresponsible mother). Moreover, even if Smith believes that she now has it right, she may later change her mind when she sees how she reacts in other contexts, or in discussing her experience with a friend, or through seeing her experience reflected in a novel or film. From such sources may come concepts or ways of seeing which, though not actually implicit in Smith's self-esteem experience, nevertheless give her a deeper understanding of that experience. Relevant to this point is the way an account of how we have acquired the concepts used in our self-ascriptions may then cause us to change the way we make those self-ascriptions, as when a woman comes to see (rightly or wrongly) her concept of good mother as the product of an oppressive ideology.

The effect of the above analysis is to show that describing the self-ascription component of an episodic reason for self-esteem is far from a simple introspective process. On the contrary, the person who wants to describe his self-ascriptions accurately and deeply, as the RP will want to do, must keep himself open to refining and revising the sense he makes of his experience; which in turn means keeping himself open to the good ideas of other people. We can now encapsulate this discussion in the following guideline and corollaries:

2 *Adequacy and Truthfulness Guideline*   In evaluating his reasons for self-esteem, the Reasonable Person seeks to have as adequate and truthful descriptions of his self-ascriptions as possible.

Corollary 1   The RP revises a reason for self-esteem if he can be shown a more adequate way of describing his self-ascription. This means that he must keep his mind open to, indeed seek out, the criticisms and ideas of others.

Corollary 2   The RP revises a reason for self-esteem if he can be shown that he has not, where appropriate, followed the canons of sound inductive and deductive reasoning, for experience shows that following such canons *makes it more likely* that a person acquires adequate and truthful beliefs.

Corollary 2.1   The RP strives as far as possible not to permit wishful, lazy, or biased thinking to pull his mind away from following the canons of sound inductive and deductive reasoning.

1.6 In turning now to guidelines for evaluating the attribution-of-worth component of a reason for self-esteem, we note first that the RP must be sensitive to inconsistencies:

3 *Consistency Guideline*   A Reasonable Person revises or gives up one of two, or possibly even both, attributions of worth upon discovering that they are inconsistent with each other.

Note now that two people may each make self-consistent attributions of worth, but attribute worth to different characteristics or assign different weights to the same characteristics. For example, whereas Smith greatly admires being an artist, Jones may be indifferent to this property. Attributions of worth usually involve a disposition to be emotionally moved when one sees people who exemplify the relevant characteristic. But our emotional dispositions reflect our cultural and home environments, as well as our individual temperaments. This is common sense, but it is common sense supported in interesting ways by empirical research. For example, Erik Erikson has documented how widely hunting and fishing cultures may differ in the personality traits each admires. He describes, for example, how impetuous ferocity, fighting spirit, and generosity in sharing spoils of the hunt are highly approved traits in the hunting culture of the Sioux, whereas in the fishing culture of the Yurok, patience, absence of ferocity, and a certain shrewdness are the most admired traits. Erikson also describes how raising children in the two societies is structured to produce just those traits which each culture admires.[8]

Granted all this, the RP nevertheless recognizes that he can step back from his attributions of worth in order to evaluate them. Then, through this evaluation, he may cause this component of his reason for self-esteem to be either sustained or weakened. One guideline for this evaluation is the consistency guideline just mentioned. I now consider two others.

In evaluating an attribution of worth, the RP must determine whether he can attribute either *intrinsic worth* or *derivative worth* to the relevant self-ascription. I say that a person attributes intrinsic worth to a self-ascription if he can sincerely say, after dispassionate reflection, that the self-ascription has either positive or negative worth for what the characteristic is in itself, or on account of its being an integral constituent of an intrinsically admirable or contemptible way of life. This is not to imply that attributions of intrinsic worth embody self-evident universal truths or are unrevisable; for people may sincerely differ over what they find has intrinsic worth, and they also may revise such attributions through further experience or thought. Nor, however, is it to say that attributions of intrinsic worth are freely chosen starting points for justifying reasons. To make a sincere attribution of intrinsic worth, a person must be *struck* by the worthiness of the characteristic in question or feel deeply the worthiness of a way of life in which the characteristic plays an integral role. We often express our attributions of intrinsic worth in the language of vision: we say that we *see* a trait, situation, or way of life in a given light (I discuss this language of vision further in 9.4). It is clear, then, that a person cannot simply will that he find a characteristic intrinsically worthy (though will-power may be required to apply the attribution consistently, a topic to which I return in a moment).

I say, on the other hand, that a person regards a self-ascription as having derivative worth if, after dispassionate reflection, he can say sincerely that the self-ascription has worth, but only because it is subsumable by another self-ascription to which he attributes intrinsic worth. It will be useful now to see how the concepts of intrinsic and derivative worth can be applied in a concrete example of a person's reasoning about his self-esteem.

Say that Jones feels diminution on account of his being unemployed. Then, if Jones is a Reasonable Person, he must be able to say sincerely, and after cool reflection, that being unemployed itself has intrinsic negative worth, or that it is subsumable by another self-ascription which has intrinsic negative worth. If he cannot make either of these attributions, then he has discovered that his feelings of diminution have no foothold in beliefs to which he can commit himself; therefore, *qua* RP, he must judge his feelings to be unreasonable. To carry the example further, assume now that Jones comes to believe that being unemployed does not *per se* have intrinsic negative worth, but that not-making-a-contribution-to-society does have intrinsic negative worth and that being unemployed can be subsumed by this self-ascription. He now has, from his point of view, a reasonable reason for his feeling diminished (at least so far as this guideline goes). It is easy to see, however, that Jones could be made to revise his reason after further thought or discussion with others. For example, someone might convince him that being unemployed does not mean, necessarily, that one does not make a contribution to society. Jones then has to look again to see whether his being unemployed means that he is not making a contribution to society (here guideline 2 must be brought to bear). If he determines that he is in fact making a contribution to society, even though unemployed, either he must find another self-ascription to which he can attribute intrinsic worth and which subsumes being unemployed, or he must conclude that his feeling diminished is unreasonable.

Taking now a different approach, someone might convince Jones that there is a valid distinction between not-making-a-contribution-to-society-when-there-is-nothing-one-can-do-about-it versus not-making-a-contribution-to-society-when-there-is-something-one-can-do-about-it. On reflection, Jones might realize that he attributes intrinsic negative worth only to the latter characteristic, but that it is the former characteristic which subsumes his being unemployed. So, again, he must revise his reasoning and must realize that his feeling diminished is unreasonable. (I am not saying, it is important to emphasize, that to judge a feeling unreasonable automatically means that one ceases to undergo the feeling. There are powerful non-rational forces which bring about or sustain feelings. I discuss this issue at several points in the next two chapters.)

Following from the above discussion, we have the following guide-line:

4 *Sincere Assent Guideline*   The Reasonable Person revises a reason for self-esteem if he cannot sincerely say, after due reflection, that the relevant self-ascription has either intrinsic or derivative worth. Here again, as we see from the above example, entering into dia-logue with others is necessary if a person is genuinely going to take a given guideline to heart.

The next guideline extends the previous one so as to include attributions of worth to other people's characteristics. Smith, say, rationalizes her feeling of enhancement by determining that she attributes positive worth to her being a good painter. Assume further that she comes to believe that MacLeod (or any other person) is also a good painter in essentially the same way that she is. Then Smith, if an RP, must be willing sincerely to say that MacLeod too merits positive esteem on account of his painting. If she were not able or willing to do this (and we are dealing here with a combination of capacity and will), then it would be as if she were saying that good painting both does and does not, from her perspective, have positive worth; that is, she would be inconsistent. (This form of inconsistency is not fully explained until the next paragraph.) I will refer to this extension of the consistency guideline under the following guideline:

5 *Universalizability Guideline*   The Reasonable Person strives to uni-versalize his attributions of worth when appropriate. The RP, then, commits himself to seeing the same worth in others' attributes as he sees in his own (the converse also holds).

The application of this guideline hinges on Smith's recognizing that it is being a good painter that has the worth and not the fact that *she*, Smith, is the one doing the painting. The principle at work here is that our esteem for a person, to be intelligible, must in the first instance be directed at a universalizable property of that person. If Smith were to say, for example, that her painting is praiseworthy for no other reason than that "I am the individual I am" or "I am me" or "I am Smith," then we would regard her as unreasonable. We would properly want to know *what it is* about Smith or her paintings which makes them esteem-worthy. But once she cites the property which justifies her attribution of worth, then she must grant, in consistency, that any other paintings which have this property also possess worth.

To move from a self-referential attribution of worth to an attribution not tied essentially to a particular individual is to adopt an impartial perspective. A commitment to adopting, when appropriate, an impartial perspective on the worthiness of characteristics is implicit, therefore, in the ideal of being an RP. There are now three clarifications to make in relation to this guideline. The first one I consign to an endnote[9] since it is not directly relevant to my argument in the rest of the book. The two others, however, are relevant.

1.7 *First Clarification*   The RP commits himself to seeing the same worth in others' characteristics as he sees in his own. But it is surely unrealistic to think that the *feelings* connected to attributions of worth, as opposed to the judgments themselves, could be impartially directed. It would be natural, for example, for Smith sometimes to dwell with more intense admiration on her own paintings than on those even of a Rembrandt (while fully recognizing that Rembrandt is the superior artist). Now I should not want to say that Smith is necessarily being unreasonable, especially if she is a good painter and being a painter plays a big part in her life. But then is not Smith contradicting guideline 1, which says that the RP should try to bring his feelings into balance with his reasons for attributing worth? There is, then, an issue to resolve here regarding both the universalizability and the weighting guidelines.

We are granting that Smith recognizes that *qua* painter Rembrandt merits more admiration than she does. So she *does* universalize the purely cognitive component of her attribution of worth, and in that important sense she is not being unreasonable (her judgment *per se* is not skewed by bias or self-deception). Nor does Smith believe there is something magical about being this individual, Smith, which justifies giving greater weight to her paintings. Her feelings, however, are clearly influenced by the fact that these are *her* paintings. To make sense of this situation we must distinguish between internal and external criteria for judging the appropriateness of our self-esteem dispositions.

Internal criteria utilize the five critical guidelines so far adduced. These guidelines arise out of the fact that self-esteem is grounded in beliefs and that beliefs are meant to be true or adequate to reality. But we can also judge our self-esteem dispositions from the (external) point of view of how they contribute to other things we value, such as healthy personal relationships, a dignified existence, and promoting others' good. Now I assume the RP, *qua* human being, has such values and interests. Given this, he cannot ignore the question of how his defining commitment coheres with these other values. Indeed,

I want to say that it would be unreasonable for him to do so. We must therefore expand our notion of the RP's defining nature to include this consideration. I shall deal in general terms with this issue in a moment, but first I briefly show its application to the specific question of the partiality of our feelings.

There are understandable biological reasons why people dwell longer or more intensely on self-related achievements (or the achievements of their children) than on those of strangers. After all, such feelings help motivate us to achieve things (and to further the interests of our children). Of course, we often become preoccupied with ourselves to an unhealthy degree. Nevertheless, things would go less well overall if people did not have the disposition to dwell on their own achievements. Moreover, so deeply rooted is this partiality of our feelings, it would be counter-productive to try wholly to suppress the disposition. In the light of these considerations, we can understand why the RP's self-esteem feelings would not always universalize in tandem with his judgments of worth. But he need not consider this fact out of keeping with his reasonable nature, given that it would be counter-productive to try to make things otherwise. There is then a reasonable balance which has to be struck between self-attention and attention to others, and finding that balance will be part of the reasonable life (a topic central to chapter 9). Our discussion here can be encapsulated in the final critical guideline:

6 *Harmonization Guideline*   As far as possible, the RP tries to bring his reasons for self-esteem and his overall values into harmony. This balance may be brought about either by revising his overall values or by revising his reasons for self-esteem.

This guideline may suggest that the RP has a higher commitment than to have reasonable beliefs, as defined by guidelines 1–5. This, however, would be a misconstrual of my approach to the Reasonable Person. As I conceive him, he starts from a powerful commitment to apply critical guidelines 1–5. Then, after seeing where this commitment leads, he is in a position to weigh it against his other values. When we have put the situation this way, it is true that we admit the conceivability of the RP's having to give up his commitment to guidelines 1–5. But in fact what we shall find, as our study proceeds, is that this commitment is strongly congruent with other important values, and that therefore an application of guideline 6 gives the RP *further* reason to sustain reasonable self-esteem as defined by 1–5.

Second Clarification   Once the RP judges good painting to be esteem-worthy, then his commitment to the guidelines tells him to judge good painting esteem-worthy in any relevantly similar situation. But the guidelines *per se* cannot dictate that the RP should find good painting esteem-worthy in the first place. Now an analogous point, I want to say, holds regarding moral concern; that is, being committed to guidelines 1–5 does not *in itself* lead the RP to have moral regard for others. "I am going to pursue my own interests, whatever the consequences for others" is not itself an inconsistent position, for a person may pursue his interests without necessarily believing that they are praiseworthy or admirable. An analogous point could be granted even by R.M. Hare, who is the strongest contemporary defender of universalization as a tool in moral thinking.[10] Hare grants that in order for universalization to gain a rational foothold, a person must first be using words such as "ought" or "right" in a specific fashion. But it is conceivable, as others have emphasized, that a rational person would not use "ought" and so on in the required fashion.[11] It is a mistake, then, to build moral concern into guidelines 1–5 from the start. But this conclusion still leaves open the question whether the RP's nature is *supportive* of moral concern, once he has a base of such concern to begin with (as derived from sources external to his commitment to guidelines 1–5). In the second part of the book, we will see that the answer to this open question is yes.

C: MOTIVATION

1.8 It is important that we understand how the RP's defining commitment enters into his motivation. The key to this understanding lies in the relationship between the self-esteem feelings on the one hand and desires or dispositions to act on the other hand. I begin, then, with this relationship.

Feelings of diminution are forms of displeasure, and feelings of enhancement are forms of pleasure. Now if a person experiences, or anticipates experiencing, diminution in making some self-ascription, he thereby *desires* (at least to some degree) that the self-ascription *not* be true of him. Let us apply this principle to the case of the Reasonable Person. If Smith experiences, or anticipates experiencing, diminution in failing to meet the guidelines, then she thereby desires that she not fail to meet them. But the way to satisfy this desire is to make it true that she meets the guidelines, that is, she is an RP. In a parallel way, if Smith experiences, or anticipates experiencing, enhancement through being a Reasonable Person, she thereby desires (to some degree) to be an RP. The self-esteem feelings and their anticipation thus give rise to what we can call *self-esteem desires*. And desires dispose us to act. We have here the beginning of an account of what I call the *ideal self*. Before filling out that account, however, we must expand our understanding of self-esteem desires in two important respects.

1 *The Object of Self-Esteem Desires* The self-esteem feelings give rise to self-esteem desires. But it would be a mistake to think that self-esteem desires are normally desires *for* self-esteem feelings. Thus, the object of Smith's desire to be an RP is distinct from the quite different (and rather strange) desire to feel enhancement for being an RP. As well as generating desires, the self-esteem feelings are related in other ways to the self-esteem desires; but none of these ways implies that the self-esteem feelings are objects of these desires. For example, self-esteem feelings are often a by-product when self-esteem desires are satisfied (thus reinforcing or inhibiting the desire in question). As well, anticipated self-esteem feelings partly constitute the felt part, when it is felt, of a self-esteem desire – the anticipation of pleasure being itself pleasurable and the anticipation of displeasure being itself displeasurable. But these sensations of anticipation are not the object of the desires. If, then, self-esteem feelings are not the object of self-esteem desires, what are their objects?

The object of a self-esteem desire is best thought of as a fact, or possible fact, as described by a self-ascription. For example, the object of one of Smith's self-esteem desires is that-I-be-a-good-painter, another is that-I-be-a-good-mother, and yet another is that-I-be-a-Reasonable-Person. We see here the intrinsic connection between the capacity for self-esteem and being a language user, for we cannot desire to exemplify a characteristic unless we can formulate the concept of the characteristic in language, that is, ascribe the characteristic to ourselves. When a cat wants food, we cannot say that the object of the cat's desire is that the words "I get food" truly apply to him (nor would this ordinarily be true when a human desires food). Rather, the object of the desire is the food itself. But we cannot understand Smith's self-esteem desire, that she be a good painter apart from her desire, even if unarticulated, that the sentence "I am a good painter" truly apply to her.

This consideration about self-esteem desires helps us understand why it is a mistake to see human motivation essentially in terms of either pleasure or self-preservation. Our self-esteem desires motivate us *to be* things or, in other words, to make certain facts true of ourselves. But these desires would not be satisfied even if we had the pleasure of falsely believing they were satisfied.[12] So we see that, in terms of satisfying our self-esteem desires, it is not the pleasure we are after. Similarly, if people were mainly motivated by self-preservation, highly demanding or risky activity, which does not have some pay-off in terms of self-preservation, would have to be explained away as irrational or mad. But of course it seems perfectly sane to us that people sometimes choose what is arduous and risky over what is easy and safe. This is because we implicitly recognize that people are powerfully motivated to satisfy their self-esteem desires – to see themselves as worthy on account of their self-ascriptions. I turn now to the second point regarding self-esteem desires.

2 *Secondary Desires*   A desire may influence a person's behaviour and yet not be the desire which defines the purpose of the act for the agent. Let us call such a desire a *secondary desire*. Now self-esteem desires are typically secondary desires. When Smith, for example, buys a birthday present for her child, her conscious purpose may simply be to bring pleasure to the child. At the same time, it may be correct to see a self-esteem desire, such as the desire not to be a poor mother, as an influence in her behaviour. We might believe, for example, that she would not have been as strongly motivated to buy the present if not for her self-esteem desire. Such a conjecture would be difficult to establish with certainty, but there is evidence which could reasonably be brought to bear, evidence based on what we know both about human nature in general and about Smith's past pattern of self-esteem feelings in particular. She herself, of course, might happily acknowledge the influence of such a desire. Secondary desires, then, are not ordinarily unconscious in the Freudian sense.

Once we have the concept of a secondary self-esteem desire, we are better able to understand the great amount of human activity which would be incomprehensible if we did not see in people the active and pervasive presence of these desires. Take, for example, the evident facts that we generally engage in activities in which we are competent rather than incompetent; that we associate with people who respect us rather than disrespect us; that we typically compare our talents and situation to those with whom we compare favourably rather than unfavourably; and that we generally take responsibility for our successes but look to excuse our failures.[13] One side-effect of all these behaviours is that we gain enhancement and avoid diminution. These behaviour and thought patterns – and a great many others – would not be so deeply ingrained if self-esteem desires were not a powerful subconscious presence in our psyches. (This account is supplemented in 9.9, where I discuss self-esteem as a human need.)

1.9 We gain deeper insight into the connection between self-esteem and motivation by seeing how self-esteem desires give rise to the *ideal self* and, through the ideal self, to mental conflict. It will be best to introduce these considerations through examples which do not initially make reference to the Reasonable Person. In the end, however, their application to the RP will be clear.

Smith attributes negative worth to her not being a good mother, and so to-be-a-good-mother is the object of one of her self-esteem desires. Imagine now, contrary to my earlier description, that her desire to paint, though powerful, arises solely from the intense enjoyment she derives from painting. In particular, she does not attribute negative worth to her not being a painter. If she believes she cannot be both a good mother and a painter, then her desires will pull her in contrary directions and she will experience conflict. It is clear, however, that Smith's two desires are not on the same footing. Given her attribution of negative worth to her not being a good mother, it is inevitable that she should see her conflict as between a "higher" and a "lower" course of action.[14] The attribution of negative worth, then, not only gives rise to desires, but also serves to assign moral priority, from the agent's (perhaps unreflective) point of view, to one course of action over another. This does not mean, however, that Smith's desire to be a good mother need be stronger than her desire to paint, for people's strongest desires are not necessarily those which, all things considered, they prefer or believe they ought to satisfy. We are now in a position to define the ideal self and its relation to mental conflict.

Most people would experience diminution if they were to murder someone, but few people derive enhancement from the self-ascription of not being a murderer. Smith, on the other hand, not only experiences diminution from her not being a good mother but, as we may imagine, derives enhancement when she judges herself to be a good mother. Thus she is motivated to be a good mother by *both* negative and positive reasons for self-esteem. Now self-ascriptions with this dual source of motivation play a central part in our life; and it is these self-ascriptions which I define as constituents of our ideal self. This analysis highlights, then, how once to-be-an-RP is the constituent of some person's ideal self, motivational energies, arising from his self-esteem desires, are set in motion. This lesson will prove important later in the book. We may now distinguish several forms of mental conflict or unhappiness connected to the ideal self.

First, Smith's desire to be a good mother is part of her ideal self, but her desire to paint is not (as we are imagining it for the moment). If now her desire to paint is persistent, she will experience this desire as a force external to her own will and so be disposed to attribute negative worth, not only to her actually painting, but even to her desire or wish to paint. This kind of mental conflict, when severe, leads to the sense of being dissociated from one's own mental states and is one of the deepest kinds of unhappiness related to our self-esteem.

A second form of mental conflict occurs when the constituents of a person's ideal self conflict with each other. Such would be the case, for example, if to-be-a-good-mother and to-be-a-good-painter were both constituents of Smith's ideal self, while it remained true, in her mind, that she could not properly satisfy both. This kind of conflict, if severe, leads to incapacitating anxiety, which can be resolved only when the agent assigns priority to one constituent of his ideal self and comes to terms with the loss of what he cannot pursue.[15]

To have an ideal self is to be susceptible to the above forms of mental conflict. At the same time, it is not as if we could do without an ideal self. When people do not internalize norms of ideal behaviour, their actions and feelings can form no meaningful pattern from their point of view.[16] Moreover, such people lack sufficient self-esteem desires to give forward thrust to their lives. An attenuated ideal self, therefore, inevitably leads to apathy, anxious confusion, and a sense of emptiness. It is not surprising that this form of unhappiness should be found in people whose cultures are in the process of disintegration.[17] The risk of mental conflict as described in the two previous paragraphs, therefore, is the price we pay for possessing an intact ideal self and thereby avoiding a more irremediable unhappiness.

The RP's commitment to reasonableness, as defined by the guidelines, is incorporated into his ideal self. In the following four chapters, I analyse how he evaluates commonly experienced reasons for self-esteem in terms of the guidelines. My argument will be that through this evaluation the RP is led to see certain personality traits, or character ideals, as consonant with his defining commitment. A commitment to these ideals is in turn incorporated into his ideal self.

Throughout the ensuing discussion, I apply the model introduced in this chapter. But given that reasons for self-esteem play such a variegated role in our lives, we might wonder whether it is realistic to think of evaluating these reasons – where would we start? However, most reasons for self-esteem fall into four broad categories. In the next four chapters, I evaluate each of these categories in turn.

2 Reflected Reasons

Karenin had seen nothing peculiar or improper in his wife sitting at a separate table and talking animatedly with Vronsky but he noticed that the rest of the party considered it peculiar and improper, and for that reason it seemed to him, too, to be improper. He decided he must speak to his wife about it.

Tolstoy[1]

Friday, March 12th: Oh the relief! L. brought the *Lit. Sup.* to me and said it's quite good. And so it is; and *Time and Tide* says I'm a first rate novelist ... to think then [*The Years*] is *not* nonsense ... But now, my dear, after all that agony, I'm free, whole; round: can go full ahead ... *Friday, April 2nd*: E.M. says *The Years* is dead and disappointing. So in effect did S. James. All the lights sank; my reed bent to the ground. Dead and disappointing – so I'm found out and that odious rice pudding of a book is what I thought – a dank failure.

Virginia Woolf[2]

By our continual and earnest pursuit of a character, a name, a reputation in the world, we bring our own deportment and conduct frequently in review, and how they appear in the eyes of those who approach and regard us. This constant habit of surveying ourselves, as it were in reflection, keeps alive all the sentiments of right and wrong, and begets, in noble natures, a certain reverence for themselves, as well as others, which is the surest guardian of every virtue.

Hume[3]

2.1 In order to appraise the impact of others' evaluations on her self-esteem, the Reasonable Person must first, in accord with guideline 2, *articulate* the relevant self-esteem experiences. Now this articulation requires that the RP attend to what I call the *reflected self-evaluation*.

I say that a person makes or undergoes a reflected self-evaluation if a direct cause of her experiencing a self-esteem feeling is her occurrent belief that some other person has evaluated her in a positive or negative way. The notion of a *non-reflected self-evaluation*, on the other hand, is defined simply as a self-esteem experience which is not directly caused by a person's occurrent belief that she is evaluated by another person.

One may try to dismiss this distinction on the grounds that *all* our self-evaluations are, at bottom, reflected ones. For do we not learn to make attributions of worth in the first place through seeing ourselves reflected in the evaluations of our parents and peers? And is not this early learning a continuous influence on us?

I do not deny that our disposition to make attributions of worth is influenced in the above way. But the distinction between a reflected and non-reflected self-evaluation hinges on whether the reflected belief is a *direct* cause of the self-esteem feeling and, further, whether it is occurrent in our self-esteem experience. And I believe it is evident that many self-esteem experiences do not in this way involve reflected self-evaluations. Take the difference, for example, between Jones's feeling diminution because he is disapproved of by Adams and Smith's feeling enhancement as she paints. Jones's experience fits the definition of a reflected self-evaluation (as we shall see in more detail in a moment). In Smith's case, however, we need not imagine that her enhancement involves an occurrent belief that some other person evaluates her positively on account of her paintings. If her experience is best articulated without reference to such a belief, then her self-evaluation is a non-reflected one – even if her wanting to be a painter has been shaped by the evaluations her parents or others made of her in the past. In the end, a distinction such as this must prove its worth through its capacity to elucidate our moral experience; and in this regard the distinction between reflected and non-reflected reasons is, as we shall see, of great value.

Note that many of our self-esteem experiences are compounded of reflected and non-reflected self-evaluations, in which one kind of feeling supervenes on the other. (That this compounding occurs no more undermines the distinction between reflected and non-reflected self-evaluations than the existence of water undermines the distinction between hydrogen and oxygen.) This compounding is important, and I shall return to it in the final section of the chapter. However, for the purpose of critical examination, it is important that the RP learn to abstract out the components of her experience and evaluate them separately. To clarify further the notion of a reflected self-evaluation, then, let us return to the relatively simple case of Jones and to how he might evaluate his reason for self-esteem (assuming him to be an RP).

Jones, we recall, felt diminution when he believed that Adams disapproved of him for not being able to cook (i.e., attributed negative worth to his not being able to cook). Now if A disapproves of B, then B has the characteristic of being disapproved of by A. If, then, Jones is going to rationalize his feeling of diminution, he must see himself as attributing negative worth to his being disapproved of by Adams for not being able to cook. Now he may judge from the start, perhaps even as he is undergoing the experience, that he does not attribute negative worth to this self-ascription. In this case, there is a sense in which Jones does not in fact have a reason for self-esteem, even though, from his point of view, he finds himself irrationally experiencing feelings of diminution. Let us assume, however, that this is not the case. He has a reason, we may assume, at least in the weak sense that there is nothing in his belief system, so far as he recognizes, which excludes his making this attribution of worth. Jones, we can say, *takes it for granted* that this attribution is justifiable.[4] Given this, he now has a reflected self-evaluation which he can critically analyse. (This taking-for-granted that our reasons are justifiable is often our situation in the first stage of evaluation. It seems to capture, for example, Virginia Woolf's vacillating mental state about her new novel in the passage at the head of the chapter.)

The key to analysing the reflected reason is to understand the relationship between Jones's attitude to his self-ascription of being disapproved of by Adams for not being able to cook and his attitude to the self-ascription of not being able to cook. Clearly, these self-ascriptions are logically distinct in the sense that he could exemplify one without exemplifying the other (Adams might even have falsely believed Jones could not cook, and then Jones would have had the former self-ascription, but not the latter). Although these self-ascriptions are logically distinct, there is, in a reflected self-evaluation, a close connection between them. As I am imagining Jones's situation, for example, had he not believed he was disapproved of by Adams, then he would not have experienced diminution for not being able to cook.

Now it is important here to keep two possibilities distinct. One is that, although Jones believes his not being able to cook has negative worth apart from the attitude of Adams, nevertheless he does not experience diminution, or as intense diminution, until he realizes he is disapproved of by Adams. The other possibility is that he neither experiences diminution nor believes (or takes it for granted) that his not being able to cook has negative worth until he recognizes that he is disapproved of by Adams. In the latter case, it is as if Jones reasons, "My not being able to cook has negative worth because Adams believes my not being able to cook has negative worth." It is this second, purer reflected self-evaluation that I shall be concerned with in what immediately follows, and I shall refer to it simply as *the* reflected self-evaluation. Near the end of the chapter, however, I shall return to the mixed form, which is one subspecies of the compounding to which I earlier referred.

It bears emphasis in this context, following what I said about beliefs in chapter 1, that one need not have the description of the reflected self-evaluation explicitly in mind as one sets out to ratio-nalize one's feeling. (Few people are as self-consciously articulate about, or as self-satisfied with, a reflected self-evaluation as is Kare-nin in the passage quoted at the head of the chapter; I am assuming there is an element of diminution in his mental state as he recognizes he is disapproved of by others.) But it may be that as one attempts to understand one's experience, it is the reflected reason, with the implicit train of thought mentioned above, that best explains, or partly explains, the feeling. Indeed, I believe that *many* of our self-esteem experiences would have to be articulated as containing ele-ments of reflected reasons (as is evidently true of Virginia Woolf's mental states, for example).

2.2 My argument will be that the very attempt to justify a reflected self-evaluation leads the RP to have *her own* reason for self-esteem, with the result that essential reference to the evaluator drops out of her rationalization. In other words, the reflected self-evaluation is undercut by the very attempt to justify it in terms of the guidelines. Why this is so we can see by examining the justificatory strategies open to Jones *qua* RP.[5]

Jones feels diminution on account of the self-ascription Adams-attributes-negative-worth-to-my-not-being-able-to-cook, and it is this self-ascription which gives rise to the train of thought which defines the reflected self-evaluation. Now following from the sincere assent guideline, and as the first step in the justification, Jones must ask whether he himself can sincerely say that this self-ascription has negative worth, that is, merits blame, disapproval, or is in some way shameful or repugnant (1.2). Further, and following from the univer-salizability guideline, Jones must recognize that this self-ascription cannot possess negative worth simply in virtue of the fact that Adams is the individual he is. He must then be led to see that being-disapproved-of-by-Adams-for-my-not-being-able-to-cook could have negative worth only because of some further property of Adams himself or because of some further feature of my-not-being-able-to-cook of which Adams is aware and disapproves. But whichever of these two paths Jones pursues, he must be led to undercut his reflected self-evaluation. We can see why this is so by examining each path, starting with the latter one.

In pursuing the second path, Jones must find out why Adams attributes negative worth to my-not-being-able-to-cook. Let us assume he does so because this means that Jones is, from Adams's perspective, an unliberated male who practices unfair household work-sharing and that Adams attributes intrinsic negative worth to being an unliberated male in this sense. Following again from the guideline for sincere assent, Jones must now ask whether he himself believes that his not being able to cook means he is an unliberated male, and also whether being an unliberated male in the relevant sense has intrinsic negative worth. But then whether or not he gives his assent to these propositions, he undercuts the reflected self-evaluation. That is, if Jones does not give his assent to these propositions, then he undercuts his reflected self-evaluation; for it hardly makes sense to attribute negative worth to being disapproved of by a person for reason X and at the same time to reject reason X. On the other hand, if Jones does give his assent to these propositions, he may then have a reasonable reason for his feeling diminution. However, he again undercuts his reflected reason, since his reason now is no longer grounded in the train of thought which defines the reflected reason; that is, Jones no longer believes his not being able to cook has negative worth on the grounds that Adams disapproves of him for not being able to cook. Rather, he now has his own reason for self-esteem, apart from any essential reference to Adams.

We now turn to looking for some property of Adams himself which Jones could cite as a justification of his reason for diminution. If he is Jones's friend (or father, etc.), then we can imagine that Jones would be made uncomfortable or even anguished by Adams's disapproval. But these feelings must be distinguished from Jones's feelings of diminution; it is only with the latter feelings that our argument is concerned, and *their* justification requires an attribution of negative worth. Now it is clear that the RP cannot simply reason, "Because Adams is my friend and believes my-not-being-able-to-cook has negative worth, therefore for this reason alone I sincerely accept that my-not-being-able-to-cook has negative worth." This rationale begs the question of why being a friend gives Adams any special insight into a characteristic's worth (could not one be a friend and yet not have this insight?). It is possible, perhaps, that Jones attributes special wisdom or insight to Adams and for this reason regards his disapproval as justified.

Now this consideration may provide a route to a successful justification, but it will not be one based on the train of thought implicit in the reflected reason. If Jones is sincerely to assent to the proposition that Adams has special wisdom, then he must have a reason why Adams (as opposed to, say, MacLeod) has this wisdom. This reason could only be based on the way he has judged Adams's attributions of worth in the past and then on the further judgment that the present circumstances are analogous to those past situations. But if Jones takes this route, then again, essential reference to Adams drops out of Jones's justification. Rather, it is Adams's *reason* for attributing worth to which Jones commits himself; a commitment made on the grounds that Adams's reason is likely to be a good one, since in the past his reasons in analogous situations have, in Jones's *own judgment*, proven to be good ones. So in pursuing this path, too, the purely reflected self-evaluation is undercut.

The above argument can be approached from a different angle. A person who makes a reflected self-evaluation treats another person as the source of her beliefs about a self-ascription's worth. But note that my analysis shows that each reflected self-evaluation presupposes a non-reflected self-evaluation. For example, in order for Jones to experience diminution on account of Adams's evaluation, he *himself* must attribute negative worth, as we have seen, to his being evaluated negatively by Adams. And this attribution is not itself grounded in a reflected self-evaluation. Therefore a person who said, "I derive all my attributions of worth from A," would be contradicting herself, since there is at least one attribution of worth she could not get from A, namely, the attribution which leads the agent to take A's attributions of worth to heart. It follows that to fully justify his reason for self-esteem, Jones must ask why he attributes negative worth to being negatively evaluated by Adams. "Because he's Adams" begs the question, as does "Because Adams evaluates me negatively." Rather, Jones must cite some property of Adams which makes him a justifiable source of reasons for self-esteem, and he must pass his own judgment on the relevance of this property. This in turn means, as we saw in the previous paragraph, that Jones's final justification involves a commitment of his own to Adams's *reasons*, and so reference to Adams *per se* again becomes redundant.

I believe the above are the main routes any attempted justification of a reflected reason would have to take, and we have seen that such routes are blocked by an application of the critical guidelines. Given my analysis of the Reasonable Person in chapter 1, we can now say that *not* to ground one's self-esteem in reflected self-evaluations becomes part of the RP's ideal self and thereby subject to the causal force of her self-esteem desires. But now the RP, as I am depicting her, is not a "pure will," unaffected by the forces which move the rest of us. And it is far from true that our seeing an experience of self-esteem as unreasonable prevents that experience from recurring. The RP's desire to be reasonable, then, can be outweighed by other forces. It is appropriate that I now briefly sketch some of these countervailing forces. Though what I describe here has specific reference to the reflected reason, it will be easy enough to generalize this discussion to the categories of reasons analysed in the next three chapters.

2.3 Our disposition to make reflected self-evaluations runs very deep, and this fact makes it reasonable to believe that the disposition has biological roots. It makes sense that natural selection would favour entities for whom the approval of others brings immediate pleasure and for whom disapproval brings immediate displeasure; for pleasant feelings reinforce behaviour, and unpleasant feelings inhibit behaviour. And if a species of social animals is going to survive (or the genes of the individuals within the group are going to survive), then it is necessary that the group be capable of reinforcing and inhibiting the behaviour of its members. Evolutionary scenarios cannot be tested to the degree many other scientific hypotheses can, but I believe my scenario at least suggests a plausible reason why the disposition to make reflected self-evaluations has become rooted in our nature. That it is so rooted cannot be denied, and evolution must have had something to do with it.

The connection between the self-esteem feelings and pleasure or displeasure suggests how other causes might reinforce a biologically rooted tendency to make reflected self-evaluations. One psychologist has plausibly argued, for example, that this disposition is partly explained by the fact that, when we are infants and children, we can get what we need or want only by pleasing others. Through association (or, more technically, secondary reinforcement), we come to develop an intrinsic and generalized desire to please others and avoid their displeasure.[6] In this way, our susceptibility to make reflected reasons is strengthened.

Sociological considerations suggest a further cause of our disposition to make reflected self-evaluations. Differences in status, prestige, and power characterize almost all social groups. It is a further feature of most larger social groups that with status, prestige, and power go mystique. To experience someone as having mystique is to feel a certain awe and befuddlement regarding that person and, especially when the mystique is due to power, an element of fear. Now when a person experiences another as having mystique – whether child to parent, student to teacher, employee to employer, fan to star, parishioner to priest, or citizen to politician – then the former is apt to be susceptible to reflected self-evaluations whose source lies in the latter. Because mystique is so pervasive in our social relations, it must be listed as an important factor in deepening our disposition to make reflected self-evaluations.

A final cause which weighs against our desire to have reasonable self-esteem has to do with our cognitive faculties. These faculties serve us well for many purposes. But we know that they do not serve us adequately for all purposes, and in some cases they have a natural tendency to mislead (I am talking here about human beings as a species, rather than as individuals). We know this fact from common experiences, such as mirages; but psychologists who study perception and rational choice have discovered many more subtle examples.[7] From the point of view of natural selection, there is no reason why our perceptual and cognitive faculties should be "wired" to detect easily all forms of irrationality, since in our primitive pasts this capacity need not always have had survival value, and in some cases may even have had disvalue.[8] Now we have seen that to understand how the reflected self-evaluation is self-defeating requires us to make some fine distinctions, which are not necessarily easy to hold in the mind's grasp. Yet in order to counteract an unreasonable disposition, a person must be capable of seeing clearly what it is about the disposition that is unreasonable. The limitations, therefore, of our cognitive faculties are another factor which must be counteracted if the reasonable person is to bring her feelings and beliefs into harmony with her defining nature.

Given these factors which may reinforce unreasonableness, a question I must deal with is whether the RP has resources at her disposal strong enough to overcome these forces. I deal with this issue in part 2 of the book.

2.4 In this section, I show how a strong disposition to make reflected self-evaluations grounds the trait of *other-dependency*, and in the next two sections, how the non-reflected self-evaluation allows for the growth of *autonomy* in the RP.

I begin with the definition of a psychological tendency which I then apply in the next paragraph. A person, A, is apt to feel dependent on a person, B, if the following three conditions hold: (1) A needs or wants something; (2) A lacks the capacity, or believes she lacks the capacity, to provide what she needs or wants; and (3) A believes B has the capacity and is in a position to provide A with what she needs or wants. Clearly, the more urgent are A's needs or wants, the more dependent she is apt to feel toward B.

I showed in chapter 1 that self-esteem desires are a pervasive and deeply rooted part of our life. Given this fact, a person whose self-esteem is grounded in reflected self-evaluations must feel herself dependent upon others; for the satisfaction of some of her most important desires hinges on how she believes others react to her, or might react to her (recall here the importance of *anticipated* self-esteem feelings discussed in 1.8).[9] Moreover, a person with a disposition to undergo reflected reasons tends not to differentiate amongst her evaluators. To make a reflected self-evaluation is, as we have seen, to be affected by the evaluations of others apart from any clear sense of the reasons which might justify their evaluations. But from this point of view, one evaluator is little different from another. Given this understanding of the other-dependent trait, we can further describe three of its key properties. These properties emerge when the trait is deeply rooted in a person's character.

First, the other-dependent person is disposed not to question the judgments of others, and her actions therefore bend easily to others' will (I shall call this property *pliancy*). This characteristic follows from the fact that, in the first place, the other-dependent person derives from others many of her beliefs regarding which characteristics have worth and, in the second place, from the fact that she is deeply averse to risking others' disapproval, since to do so is to risk the loss of her own self-esteem. Second, the other-dependent person is apt to suffer from that lack of self-confidence in which a person, even if she believes she has the ability to accomplish a task, nevertheless flounders for fear of others' disapproval. Third, implicit in the other-dependent person's way of gaining self-esteem is the sense that between herself and her evaluators there is a significant inequality. It is as if she acquiesces to the notion that others have the capacity, but she does not, to determine which characteristics have worth. This sense of inequality may lead in turn to feelings of inferiority and to behaviour which is exceedingly deferential.

2.5 In order to understand the trait allowed for by the disposition to make non-reflected self-evaluations, we must first understand the notion of an *autonomous reason*. Recall that the non-reflected self-evaluation is defined simply as the contrary of the reflected one. This means that a person could have a non-reflected reason and yet not have influenced her reason through critical reflection. Jones, for example, may simply take it for granted, without reference to another's disapproval, that not being to cook has negative worth. On the other hand, it is an implication of our earlier argument that if a person successfully undercuts a reflected reason, then, by virtue of this fact, she comes to have a non-reflected reason. A non-reflected reason gained in this way would consist in beliefs the agent has brought about or sustained through critical reflection. To focus on this latter kind of non-reflected self-evaluation allows us to formulate the concept of an autonomous reason.

I begin by briefly reviewing an aspect of Jones's case. He starts by making a reflected self-evaluation. Then, applying the appropriate guidelines, he asks whether he himself can attribute intrinsic negative worth to being an unliberated male (in the sense of entailing unfairness). If, after dispassionate reflection, he answers yes, then he has his own reason for attributing negative worth to his not being able to cook. In ideal terms, Jones could now reason as follows: "(1) Being an unliberated male has, for me, intrinsic negative worth; (2) my not being able to cook means (or is reliable evidence that) I am an unliberated male; (3) hence, my not being able to cook has derivative negative worth; (4) therefore, the diminution I feel, or might in the future feel, for not being able to cook is reasonable." One could imagine that Jones gives his clear-headed assent, after applying the guidelines, to each step in the justification. Now in order for a reason to count as autonomous, this process of justification must be causally responsible for the reason being held or sustained.

When we say that a justification is causally responsible for a reason, we imply the following conditions to hold: (1) if the agent judges the reason to be unjustifiable, then the reason would cease to be held; and (2) if the agent judges the reason to be justifiable, the reason would continue to be held. To these two, we must add a third, more complex condition: (3) a justification is causally responsible for a reason being held only if the agent would give up the reason if she were presented with considerations which, given her own standards of reasonableness,[10] would ordinarily be good enough to overthrow the reason. This element in the meaning of "autonomous" allows us to focus on the fact that sometimes beliefs are so fixed in people's minds that it is impossible to give them up. Now when a person cannot give up a belief, we cannot say that her reason for self-esteem occurs autonomously, even if she hits upon an adequate justification for continuing to hold the reason. In this case, it would not be the process of justification which sustains the reason, since the person would have gone on holding the reason even if the justification had not been found (at most, the process of justification over-determines the existence of the reason). An unalterable belief, then, excludes autonomy, however thorough or assiduous is the process of justification.[11]

The RP aims to have autonomous reasons. But now it is an implication of the above discussion that she cannot justifiably believe that her reasons *are* autonomous except by keeping herself open to dialogue with others.[12] It is only in dialogue that a person can ultimately test, even if indirectly, the fixity of her beliefs. Why is this? Note, first, that a person cannot believe that a reason is justifiable (after subjecting it to rational scrutiny) and at the same time occupy a viewpoint which puts the reason in question. This would be like believing a proposition is true (after critical reflection), while holding some reason to believe it false. It follows that a person can only test the fixity of such a reason through opening herself to the contrary viewpoints of others; and so it is literally only in dialogue that a person can approach the ideal of being an RP. In chapter 9 we shall see the significance of this point.

From the above analysis, we can see what an autonomous reason is, but also what it is not.[13] It is not, for example, a reason which an agent necessarily invents for herself. On the contrary, it is likely that an autonomous reason is constituted by beliefs, or at least suppositions, which at the outset the agent has absorbed from others. Nor therefore is an autonomous reason necessarily out of keeping with beliefs current in the agent's society (though it might be). Nor, finally, should we think that an autonomous reason is one which the agent reaches by paying attention only to her own thoughts. It is indeed, as we have seen, just the opposite.

An autonomous reason, rather, is constituted by those beliefs a person has made her own by testing them (in the case of the RP) against the guidelines and in dialogue with others. It is as if a person, say Jones, has inherited a house with a great many things in it. In one sense all the objects in the house are his, but in another sense they are not. Say that Jones then goes around the house asking himself of each item whether it meets his own standards of taste or usefulness. He then proceeds to discard those items which do not meet these criteria and to keep those that do. The remaining items belong to Jones, are his, in a deeper sense than they were when he first inherited them. So it is with our beliefs: the RP can come to hold them autonomously and so make them her own in a deeper sense than they would otherwise be. I must now make two clarifications.

It could be argued that an account such as mine is too intellectualistic.[14] Steadfastness in the face of hostility is one paradigm of autonomy. But people who exemplify such steadfastness sometimes have deeply fixed beliefs, beliefs which are unrevisable through open-minded dialogue with others. An example of this phenonemon is the way that Jehovah's Witnesses stayed true to their values in Nazi concentration camps, when the values of so many others collapsed.[15] The Witnesses remained their "own person" and in this sense were autonomous, even though it seems justifiable to say that their beliefs were acquired through indoctrination. (There is much literature which demonstrates how thoroughgoing such indoctrination can be, and how different it is from ordinary learning.)[16]

The proper way to deal with this point is to recognize that there are distinct senses to the meaning of autonomy.[17] A person whose ideas are fixed through indoctrination lacks autonomy because she cannot make her beliefs her own in the deeper sense open to the RP. But clearly such a person may have autonomy in the sense of steadfastness in the face of hostility. That there are these distinct senses of autonomy is no reason to downplay one sense at the expense of another. The RP's self-understanding leads her to encompass autonomy of belief as following from her defining nature. Nevertheless, as we shall see in the following section and more fully in chapter 8, autonomy in the form of steadfastness is a good which, in the life of the RP, may supervene upon autonomy of belief.[18]

A further clarification arises through recent discussions of autonomy by feminist and black philosphers.[19] People can be socialized into subservient roles and thereby ground their self-esteem in the fulfilment of such roles. Now sometimes this socialization may encompass, or at least deeply influence, the very criteria by which the agent judges what is reasonable. In this case, even when a person's beliefs are not fixed through indoctrination (and most socialization falls far short of indoctrination),[20] it is nevertheless unlikely that such a person would ever revise her beliefs, even after self-reflection and dialogue with others. For the standards by which the agent judges relevant considerations would tend always to reinforce her original judgments. Such a person's beliefs hardly seem autonomous, even if they have been sustained through critical reflection.

The above consideration has given rise to important debates about autonomy.[21] I will confine myself, however, to comments directly relevant to my analysis of the Reasonable Person. The RP commits herself to testing her beliefs against the critical guidelines. These guidelines exclude beliefs which are inconsistent or contrary to empirical evidence. Now all subservient socialization, I believe, is founded on false and inconsistent assertions. Therefore, the RP is likely, on this count alone, to resist subservient socialization. Moreover, as we shall see in 4.6, a commitment to the guidelines opens her to a certain imaginative disengagement from her social roles. This fact is a further antidote to subservient socialization. Finally, the traits congruent with the RP's nature run deeply counter to subservient socialization. Given these facts, we can conclude that a commitment to the critical guidelines, in the manner of the RP, is incompatible with that narrow and self-reinforcing circle of beliefs which characterizes subservient socialization. With these clarifications in mind, we are in a position to understand the trait, or character ideal, related to autonomous reasons.

2.6 The first point is that the person whose reasons for self-esteem are autonomous does not undergo, to that degree, reflected self-evaluations. This fact in turn means that the RP is not likely to be other-dependent. Therefore, we can expect her not to be so averse to risking the disapproval of others, or to fear nonconformity in her attitudes, or to suffer from that lack of self-confidence which flounders under the gaze of others. As well, we saw how the other-dependent person suffers from feelings of inferiority grounded in her sense that she lacks the capacity to determine for herself which self-ascriptions have worth. Now let us see how a contrary way of seeing herself is open to the Reasonable Person.

The RP must recognize that she has the capacity to justify reasons for self-esteem and so to discover, from her own point of view, which characteristics have worth. The way a person exercises this capacity can be evaluated in terms of speed, thoroughness, or depth; and in these terms, one person will outscore another. But there is one respect in which any person who successfully justifies a reason for self-esteem may regard herself as the equal of any other: she has made her reason for self-esteem autonomous. Analogously, two people may be unequal in the time it took them to finish a marathon, but equal in the fact of having finished the marathon. Now in talking about equality to this point, I mean to suggest nothing more than that people who are equal in some respect have some characteristic in common (having made a reason autonomous, having finished a marathon, etc.). The question of what significance to attach to any given equality is a distinct question. In chapter 8, I shall show that being able to make reasons for self-esteem autonomous is an important ingredient of the RP's self-understanding. The points I briefly make in the following paragraph are reinforced in that chapter.

In the first place, a person with a strong and settled disposition to make her reasons autonomous is not subject to those feelings of inferiority to which the other-dependent person is subject, for she does not share the other-dependent person's sense of inequality between herself and others. In the second place, in exercising her capacity to make her beliefs autonomous, the RP lessens the effect of mystique. In order to have autonomous reasons, an RP must push from her mind factors which are irrelevant to the adequacy of the beliefs she is considering. Now, as I previously mentioned, mystique most often arises through inequalities of status, prestige, wealth, and power. But these inequalities, except in rare circumstances, are irrelevant to the adequacy of a belief or an argument. The Reasonable Person must try, therefore, to make herself immune to the befuddling effects of mystique. She is aided in this task by her capacity to produce for any other person, whatever the inequalities between them, an adequate justification for those of her beliefs that involve attributions of worth. As well, the less one experiences others as having mystique, the weaker is the disposition to make reflected self-evaluations; and therefore the easier it is to have autonomous reasons, which in turn lessens the tendency to experience others as having mystique. We see, then, how these aspects of the autonomous trait are mutually supporting.

In describing the relationship between self-esteem and autonomy (or the other traits I shall discuss in the following chapters), I do not wish to suggest that we are dealing with invariable connections. There are always factors unrelated to a person's self-esteem which enter into the formation of any personality trait; moreover, contrary traits usually coexist in the same person. (As an antidote to thinking in simplistic terms, one may read Virginia Woolf's diaries. There we see a person with a very powerful disposition to make reflected self-evaluations, who at the same time possesses many of the qualities indicative of autonomy.) What I do say, however, is that having autonomous reasons for self-esteem provides one possible foundation, both psychological and philosophical, from which it is natural for the autonomous trait to grow.

My analysis of an autonomous reason applies so far only to reasons for self-esteem, which include, of course, attributions of worth. Attributions of worth, however, are moral beliefs, and as such, they eventually have to cohere with the Reasonable Person's other values (as discussed in the harmonization guideline). Now I believe it is easy to see that my analysis of an autonomous reason applies equally to any moral belief; that is, a person who has the capacity to make her attributions of worth autonomous has equally the capacity to think through and make autonomous her other moral beliefs. This fact means that even when the justificatory process moves to the stage of the harmonization guideline, what I have said about the RP's capacity to make her reasons autonomous continues to apply.

2.7 In concluding this chapter, I return to compound self-evaluations and make an important clarification. To be admired by others is generally a source of great pleasure, while to be disrespected is a source of intense displeasure. If someone were indifferent to the attitudes of all others toward herself, we would justifiably regard this person as arrogant, mad, or falling prey to the kind of self-protective hypocrisy which has its roots in fear of rejection. It is important to see, therefore, that my arguments do not in the least require that the Reasonable Person be indifferent to the admiration or disrespect of her fellows.

To begin, we saw that the RP can be made to think in a novel way about a self-ascription through being evaluated positively or negatively by others. Through such a re-evaluation, the RP might come to accept, in her own terms, the reasoning of those who have evaluated

her. Now this self-evaluation is clearly not a reflected one and therefore is not out of keeping with the RP's nature. This possibility points
to a type of compound self-evaluation which I introduce through the
following example.

Say that Jones had never thought of his not being able to cook as
having negative worth, but that through Adams's evaluation he is
made to think about this inability. Then through this thinking, he
comes, in his own terms, to attribute negative worth to the self-
ascription (my analysis of this example is easily translatable into our
experience of enhancement). When others, including Adams, now
evaluate him negatively on account of this inability, Jones can judge
that their reason corresponds to his own. Given this correspondence,
it may well be that his self-esteem feelings are intensified, especially
if he respects or otherwise cares about those doing the evaluating.
There are, in this situation, reflected *feelings*, since Jones would not
be feeling so intensely if it were not for the influence of others. On
the other hand, this influence is radically different from the pure
reflected self-evaluation, which the RP finds unreasonable; for in the
compound case, the reflected feelings occur as confirmation of an
already autonomously held reason. It is easy to see that an application of the guidelines need not undercut the compound self-esteem
experience, for this experience does not contain implicit in it the train
of thought blocked by the guidelines. (One may imagine, however,
cases in which this kind of compound reason has the same significance as an unmixed reflected self-evaluation. I am thinking of how
a person might have an autonomous reason for self-esteem, but
nevertheless be incapable of experiencing any – or hardly any – self-
esteem feelings unless her self-evaluation is confirmed by others. In
this situation, we might doubt the sincerity or depth with which the
person holds her reason for self-esteem. As well, this person would
likely find herself with the other-dependent trait, since she is dependent upon others to experience the enhancement of her self-esteem
to a satisfying degree.)

The central case in the above paragraph typifies experiences of self-
esteem which are not grounded in pure reflected reasons, but in
which we nevertheless take to heart the evaluations of others – most
happily, of course, when the evaluations are positive. The RP's self-
understanding does not exclude the appropriateness of such experiences. We may conclude, therefore, that the Reasonable Person need
not labour, on account of her defining commitment, under a false and
inhuman self-sufficiency. I return to this topic in 4.6, where I discuss
recognition.

3 Competitive Reasons

> Now in all his social and worldly ambitions, in all his strivings to catch good fortune and trap propitious luck, man moves in an atmosphere of rivalry, of envy, and of spite. For luck, possessions, even health, are matters of degree and comparison, and if your neighbour owns more cattle, more wives, more health and more power than yourself, you are dwarfed in all you own and all you are. And such is human nature that a man's desire is as much satisfied by the thwarting of others as by the advancement of himself.   Malinowski[1]

> With the wise man, what he has does not cease to be enjoyable because someone has something else. Envy, in fact, is one form of vice, partly moral, partly intellectual, which consists in seeing things never in themselves, but only in their relations.   Russell[2]

3.1 Common sense and psychological theory agree that how we compare ourselves to others is important to our self-esteem. Indeed, it is often said, as Malinowski does above, that comparisons *must* predominate in the way we ground our self-esteem. On the other hand, there is the view, as expressed by Russell, that the better life is one which rises above competitive comparisons. In this chapter, I argue that the Reasonable Person is disposed, through his defining commitment, to undercut competitive self-esteem of a certain kind. In part 2 of the book, we see that this fact about the RP is congruent with a desirable life (and thereby we side with Russell).

In articulating his experience of self-esteem (in line with guideline 2), the Reasonable Person must distinguish two ways his reasons for self-esteem may involve competition with others. These I call *direct comparisons* and *proportionate comparisons*. The person who has a strong disposition to undergo either of these reasons, I say has the *competitive trait*. Let us now describe each of these reasons in turn.

In a direct comparison, the self-ascription makes explicit reference to some *specific* other individual or individuals. For example, if I feel diminution for not being as good a pianist as Sam, then my reason involves a direct comparison. It is as if I picture my self on a scaled line measuring piano-playing ability, with Sam farther along the line than I am. (Because of the vagueness inherent in our attributions of traits to people, the image of a scaled line becomes misleading if interpreted too literally.) Direct comparisons may also be non-scalar, as when I feel diminution for not owning a piano whereas Sam does. In this case, since (generally) one either owns or does not own a piano, there is no scaled line presupposed; but there is a direct comparison.

In the proportionate comparison, an agent compares the proportion of people who share some characteristic he possesses with the proportion of people who do not. The most common species of the proportionate comparison involves a judgment regarding the relative rarity of some characteristic. Say, for example, that I feel diminished for being unemployed and that part of my diminution is the result of my recognizing that being unemployed is rare relative to the rest of the people in my society (or relative to some other comparison group). Or say that I feel enhanced for being given an award and that part of my feeling is explained by my belief that to receive this award is relatively rare. Of course, the proportionate comparison can work the other way round, as when I feel *less* diminished when I realize that being unemployed is common in my comparison group.

Direct and proportionate comparisons constitute what I call *competitive reasons for self-esteem*. Now it is important to distinguish, for the purpose of evaluation, competitive reasons from what I call *grading reasons for self-esteem*. I make a grading self-ascription if, for example, I ascribe to myself the characteristic of being a good (or poor or fair or brilliant) pianist. Many people are inclined to assimilate grading reasons and competitive reasons, but to do so is a serious mistake. I shall argue that when the RP undercuts competitive reasons in himself, he need not on that account undermine grading reasons. This argument occurs in several stages through the chapter and is not complete until the final section. The first stage, however, occurs in the next section, where we see one reason why people are so prone to run together the two types of reason.

Before turning to that issue, however, I wish to emphasize a point mentioned in chapter 1. I said in 1.4 that we should not expect an application of the critical guidelines to yield a definitive answer, along the lines of an algorithm, to the question whether a reason for self-esteem is unreasonable. There are grey areas, I said, in which thoughtful judgment is required (indeed, it is sometimes through making such judgments that the guidelines themselves are clarified, or even made to evolve). Now we shall find a number of such grey areas in what follows, and I do not wish to hide this fact from the reader. Nevertheless, I believe most Reasonable People (i.e., those with a commitment to the critical guidelines) would find, even if they were to disagree with me on one or two specific points, that the weight of argument is strongly in favour of rejecting our two types of competitive reasons. This is especially clear when we take into account the non-rational forces which incline us to undergo competitive self-evaluations.

3.2 I turn first to the direct comparison reason and take for analysis the example of my feeling diminished when I compare my piano playing to Sam's. To rationalize my feeling, I must attribute (or take for granted) that my-not-being-able-to-play-as-well-as-Sam has negative worth. Assume further that I judge myself to be a good player, only not so good as Sam. Let us now note that my grading self-ascription of being-a-good-player is logically distinct from the direct-comparison reason. This we may easily see from the fact that, even if Sam allows his playing to deteriorate so that it falls below my level, it would nevertheless be true, all other things being equal, that my grading self-ascription of being-a-good-player remains the same. The RP must be aware, therefore, that in evaluating his direct comparison reasons, he must keep distinct any associated grading reasons. He is aided in this task if he understands why people have a tendency to run together the two kinds of self-ascriptions. Let us, therefore, briefly consider one aspect of this question.

Though what I wish to say applies as much to enhancement as to diminution, the point is most easily made regarding diminution. Say then, contrary to the previous example, I judge myself to be a poor pianist and feel deep diminution on that account. Now when I see other pianists who are better than I am, such as Sam, then this is likely to bring forcibly to mind the poor quality of my own piano playing. In this way, the diminution I feel for my playing ability *per se* (the grading self-ascription) becomes strongly associated with the direct comparisons I draw between others and myself. This is one significant factor, I believe, which make us run together grading and direct comparison reasons for self-esteem. However, it is important, as I have said, that the RP learn to keep the two reasons separate. We can further help him in this task by describing another aspect of the relationship between the two.

The thought that I am less good than Sam, as we have seen, causes me to think of the state of my own playing. Now this causal relation is mirrored, in converse form, at a more abstract level. For my not being as good as Sam is a fact about the world which holds in virtue of, or as an effect of, the quality of my own piano playing together with the quality of Sam's playing. This relation further strengthens our tendency to run together the one self-ascription with the other in specific self-esteem experiences. It is especially worth emphasizing, therefore, that there is no rational principle which allows one to infer that an effect has some moral quality simply on the grounds that its cause does. From the fact, for example, that my making Jones happy is good, it does not follow that my making Jones's enemy sad, an event caused by Jones becoming happy, is good. Similarly, the attribution of worth I make to the quality of my piano ability does not flow, without some separate justification, to my being a lesser pianist than Sam. Later in the chapter, I consider the argument that grading self-ascriptions presuppose, in a more subtle way, direct comparisons. But for now I have said enough about the distinctness of the two to allow us to continue with the evaluation of the direct-comparison reason.

3.3 In applying the universalizability guideline, I recognize, assuming I am an RP, that I cannot attribute *intrinsic* negative worth to having less ability than Sam just because he is the individual he is. Why, this guideline leads me to ask, does having less ability than Sam merit intrinsic negative worth, but having less ability than someone else, say Jim, not merit it? The universalizability guideline tells me, moreover, that to justify my attribution of intrinsic worth to my direct comparison, I would have to commit myself to holding that anyone who is relevantly like me must also merit negative worth because he has less ability than Sam, and that this is true no matter how good a pianist the other person is, so long only as he is a lesser pianist than Sam. So if Sam is in fact a pseudonym for Vladimir Horowitz, and Glenn Gould is a lesser pianist than Horowitz, then this principle would tell us to attribute negative worth to Gould simply on the grounds that he is not the pianist Horowitz is. Such an attribution of intrinsic worth, it is evident, cannot be reasonable as it stands.

As an RP, then, I must ask *what it is about* Sam which can justify the attribution of negative worth. If I could find a relevant characteristic of Sam's, then my justification would have the following structure: (1) to have less piano-playing ability than a person with characteristic X has intrinsic negative worth; (2) Sam has characteristic X; (3) therefore, to have less ability than Sam has derivative negative worth; (4) I have less ability than Sam; (5) therefore, my feeling of diminution is justifiable.

The difficulty facing this strategy is to find an "X" which is at all relevant to the attribution I want to make. Sam may be a businessman, a father, and a long-distance runner; but it hardly makes sense to attribute intrinsic negative worth to having less piano-playing ability than someone else simply on the grounds that this person is a businessperson and so on.

Perhaps the one place to look for the relevant X is in the quality of Sam's piano-playing ability. Say I perceive Sam as rating a "very good," whereas I rate myself as only a "decent." In attempting to justify the direct comparison, I might then consider accepting the proposition "Falling lower than another person who rates a 'very good' merits an attribution of intrinsic negative worth (or perhaps is subsumable by another characteristic which merits such an attribution)." A commitment to this proposition might give me the beginning of an adequate justification. However, adopting this strategy would undercut my reason for self-esteem which has direct reference to Sam. For in terms of this justification, there is no more reason for feeling diminution when I compare myself to Sam (who, let us say, is in my piano class) than there is for feeling diminution when I compare myself to George (who also rates "very good," but lives at the other end of the country). This line of thought, which arises naturally from the strategy we are analysing, must make the RP realize that his competitive reason with reference to Sam results mainly from the fact that Sam is near at hand; but proximity in space or time, as I shall shortly argue, is usually irrelevant to an adequate justification in circumstances such as these. However, first consider the following.

To carry one's justification to the level mentioned in the previous paragraph is to come very close to eliminating the direct-comparison, or competitive, component of the self-esteem reason altogether. For to attribute intrinsic negative worth to rating less than *any* other person who rates a "very good," when no specific individual is mentioned, is not significantly different, upon reflection, from attributing negative worth to rating less than "very good" *per se* (which is a gradable, not a competitive, self-ascription). Moreover, this in turn is hardly different – focusing now on my specific case – from my attributing negative worth to my being merely a decent pianist (a self-ascription I recognize myself to have and which had become intermixed with the competitive reason). In other words, this strategy must take me in the end away from focusing on the comparison to Sam and lead me to focus on the question of whether I ought to attribute negative worth to the gradable self-ascription of being a decent pianist (as opposed to being a very good pianist). So, in this sense as well, the RP finds that the direct-comparison self-evaluation is undercut.

3.4 Once the RP recognizes that this type of reason is undercut through applying the critical guidelines, then not-to-undergo-direct-comparisons becomes part of his ideal self. However, the disposition to make such self-evaluations has deep roots and is a force which works against the RP's desire to realize this component of his ideal self. To understand the causes of this disposition can help him to overcome it. A complete categorization of these causes would have to encompass – as well as our tendency to run together competitive and grading reasons – biological, psychological, and sociological considerations analogous to those I raised in chapter 2 regarding the reflected self-evaluation. I shall leave the reader to ask himself how such analogous considerations can be applied. There is, however, another important non-rational factor, not yet discussed, which deepens our disposition to undergo competitive self-evaluations, and it is necessary that I say a few words about it.

Proximity in space or time to some entity can cause us to act, or to undergo an emotion, contrary to our best judgment – as when we overeat and so allow the smaller, but closer pleasure to overcome the more distant, but greater pleasure of returning to a healthy weight. Now this source of irrationality is a factor in our disposition to undergo comparison self-evaluations.

Consider, for example, the following situation. I rate myself a decent historian. I know that George, who lives in a different city from me, is a better historian than I am, but this comparison does not affect my self-esteem. However, George gets an appointment in my department, and now I find that the comparison self-ascription results in my feeling diminished. Rather than believe that I have all of a sudden found a justifiable reason for attributing negative worth to-not-being-so-good-a-historian-as-George, it is more reasonable to believe that my feelings are simply affected by the fact that George is nearer to hand – where I and others in my reference group notice him more. But his being closer in space to me, with the result that the comparison between himself and myself is more forcibly impressed on my mind, hardly seems a rational consideration out of which a justifiable attribution of worth could be constructed. Proximity in time can have similar counter-rational effects. For example, it would be unusual for a present-day historian to feel diminished because he rates himself a lesser historian than Herodotus. Yet the same person might feel diminished by believing himself a lesser historian than his contemporary George, even though he ranks George as a lesser historian than Herodotus.

In the next section, I evaluate the second species of competitive reason, the proportionate comparison. After seeing how it too is undercut through the process of justification, we shall consider a further non-rational factor which deepens our disposition to undergo competitive reasons.

3.5 In the proportionate comparison, the fact that a characteristic is rare relative to some comparison group enters into the reason for self-esteem. To begin the evaluation, say that I feel diminished on account of having a cleft lip and that I trace part of this diminution to my recognizing that this is a relatively rare characteristic. (My diminution will have other sources, which I shall discuss later, but for now I am isolating the rarity component.) One route to justify this aspect of the self-esteem experience might be to consider attributing intrinsic negative worth to having a self-ascription simply on the grounds of its rarity. It is clear, however, that it is absurd to attribute intrinsic worth, whether positive or negative, to a characteristic simply on account of its rarity. My telephone number, for example, is extremely rare; but having the telephone number 564–4401 could hardly in its own right constitute a justifiable reason for self-esteem.[3]

Even once we grant that relative rarity cannot in itself bestow worth on a self-ascription, could we not say that if a characteristic has positive or negative worth in the first place, then its worth is *further* enhanced or diminished on account of its rarity? In order to evaluate this strategy, we must distinguish two main ways that relative rarity can enter into our self-esteem. One way points to a possibly valid justification; but the RP, in following this strategy, is led away from the purely comparative element in his experience. The second way points to a non-rational force which deepens a self-esteem feeling, but cannot serve as a good justification. With regard to the cleft lip case, it is more likely the non-rational factor that is at play. Before considering this factor, however, let us examine how relative rarity may point to a possibly valid justification.

3.6 When the rarity of a self-ascription enters into our self-esteem, we may take the rarity as a sign for something else; it is then this something else which we see, or can come to see, as a valid focus for our self-esteem feelings. This point can be made most clearly in cases of enhancement. Say that Smith feels enhanced on account of a house she has designed and that part of her enhancement has to do with the fact that, in terms of construction and aesthetic qualities, the house has certain admirable features which make it stand out – make it relatively rare. Now, on reflection, we can see that the reason rarity plays a role in Smith's self-esteem is that she is taking the rarity as a sign that she is a good designer. She may then come to have a possibly justifiable reason grounded in the self-ascription of being a good designer; but now the proportionate comparison *per se* is no longer the focus of her reason (again assuming, what I shall argue for in more detail later, that grading self-ascriptions are logically distinct from competitive self-ascriptions).

Nor would it be reasonable to say that the rarity of Smith's achievement can acquire derivative worth through connecting the rarity to the achievement. There is perhaps a natural movement of the mind such that if X is a sign for Y and we attribute worth to Y, then we are inclined to attribute worth to X. There is, however, no rational justification for such an inference. Indeed, we are dealing with precisely the same point I made earlier regarding the illegitimacy of automatically transferring an attribution of worth from a cause to its effects. Often, if X is a sign for Y, then X is an effect or consequence of Y. This principle holds when we take the rarity of a characteristic as a sign of some further characteristic. For example, the rarity of Smith's design is a consequence of her talent or achievement. But then we know from our argument in 3.2 that from the fact Smith attributes positive worth to her talent or achievement, it does not follow automatically that she can with justification attribute positive worth to one of the consequences of her talent, which in this case is the rarity *per se* of her achievement. That would require a separate justification.

Returning now to my cleft lip, and looking for some further justification, I might try to see my disfigurement as a sign for some other self-ascription to which I attribute worth. Such would be the case, for example, if I held the superstitious belief that my cleft lip was a sign that in a previous life I had committed great sins. Once we dismiss this sort of strategy, however, I must consider the possibility that the deeper diminution I feel on account of the rarity of my cleft lip is due to non-rational causes. And there is, in fact, an evident one to hand.

For understandable reasons, we take notice of things that stand out from their backgrounds. This principle clearly applies to the notice we take of people's characteristics. So, for example, we find our eyes drawn to the person in a crowd who is abnormally tall; and that a person has been to Tibet does not soon drop from our minds, for no other reason than that it is rare to meet someone who has been to Tibet. To have our attention drawn to something because it stands out from its background is itself neither rational nor irrational. Clearly, however, this factor can contribute to irrationality if it continually causes us to give emphasis where, upon reflection, we determine emphasis is not due. Now to give emphasis to something is a form of intensifying our perception of it, and it is the workings of this same principle which may operate to intensify our self-esteem feelings when we have a self-ascription which is relatively rare. This is especially true when this principle combines, as it often does, with a reflected self-evaluation. Let us now see how this consideration can help me, *qua* Reasonable Person, think through my attitude toward my cleft lip.

Say I determine that I do not attribute negative worth to my having a cleft lip in itself, but I still find myself feeling diminution. In part, I can trace my feelings to reflected self-evaluations, which, as an RP, I will reject as unreasonable since I myself, on my own, do not attribute negative worth to the self-ascription. I can also see other people's reactions to me, and my own susceptibility to reflected self-evaluations, as the result of our feelings being intensified by the relative rarity of my disfigurement. And this is a factor I can also seek to discount, given the argument of the previous paragraph. Even if we assume, contrary to the original assumption, that I do determine that having a cleft lip has negative worth, I can realize that its rarity is not an *additional* reason for feeling diminution; and so the intensity of my diminution, on account of this consideration, might be mitigated.

3.7 We have seen that the process of justification disposes the RP to inhibit competitive reasons in himself. Now I want to say that a strong disposition to undergo competitive reasons underlies attitudes such as envy. Given this fact, the RP sees envy, as well as other forms of invidious comparisons, as out of keeping with his defining nature. The connection between self-esteem and envy has often been noticed, though how best to interpret the connection is controversial.[4] For my present purposes, we may note the following connection.

All envy, whether benign or malicious, involves a comparison self-ascription. If Adams envies Jones for his sexual attractiveness to women, for example, then he ascribes to himself the characteristic of not-being-so-sexually-attractive-as-Jones (a scalar direct comparison) or the characteristic of my-not-being-attractive-whereas-Jones-is (a non-scalar direct comparison).[5] Adams's envy may simply take the benign form of idly fantasying that he is like Jones in being attractive to women. But now when envy involves ill will, it is usually because the comparison self-ascription damages the envier's self-esteem. If Adams's envy involves ill will toward Jones, for example, it is plausible to believe that his self-esteem is hurt on account of the comparison he draws between himself and Jones. We may therefore see Adams's envy as grounded in the fact that he attributes negative worth to the self-ascription of not-being-so-attractive-to-women-as-Jones. A parallel analysis applies to other forms of invidious comparisons, such as begrudgingness. This attitude looks with ill will on others who reach, or might reach, some equal state to ourselves.[6] Here too the ill will usually arises because the agent's self-esteem is damaged through his attributing negative worth to a comparison self-ascription. But given this connection between competitive self-esteem and envy (begrudgingness, etc.), and given that the RP inhibits competitive self-esteem in himself, then he must also inhibit his being envious (begrudging, etc.) My claim is not that it is easy for him to realize this constituent of his ideal self. In the next part of the book, however, we shall see that the RP has resources implicit in his nature which lend support in this regard.

3.8 In recognizing that competitive self-esteem is out of keeping with his nature, the RP nevertheless need not take a puritanical view of competition in general. The key is to understand that not all competition need involve competitive *self-esteem*. In order to clarify our views on this topic, we must first return to the distinction between competitive and grading self-ascriptions.

If it were true, as is often thought, that grading self-ascriptions necessarily bring our self-esteem into competition with others, then the RP would have to consider rejecting reasons for self-esteem grounded in grading self-ascriptions. However, not only would this be wholly unrealistic, but, as we shall see in chapter 5, grading self-ascriptions play an important role in the RP's way of life. It is worth analysing, therefore, the most common line of thought which seeks to establish that grading self-ascriptions necessarily bring our self-esteem into competition with others. A good instance of this line of thought is found in a discussion by Robert Nozick, which revolves around the following example.[7]

A person living in some remote area believes he is an excellent basketball player (physicist, etc.) and derives self-esteem from this belief. But then he comes into contact with Michael Jordan (Einstein, etc.) and on the basis of this new comparison must revise downward his estimate of his ability. The conclusion we are to draw is that grading self-ascriptions, and the self-esteem we derive through them, must inevitably rest on direct comparisons to others. This perspective on grading self-ascriptions, however, glosses over important distinctions. For example, there is clearly a difference between making a grading self-ascription, on the one hand, and revising the criteria in terms of which one makes the self-ascription, on the other hand. The people in this remote community are led to do the latter, and yet the conclusion Nozick wants us to draw has to do with the former. There is a gap, then, in his argument. In a moment, I will consider this question of revising criteria. But first I examine more closely the making of a grading self-ascription itself.

In ordinary circumstances, to make a grading self-ascription is not directly to compare oneself to specific others. Take, for example, the case of grading one's performance in some social role. To know (or believe with justification) that one is a good doctor, one must be able to apply the criteria which govern the concept of good doctor, such as having concern for one's patients and keeping up on the medical literature. Now there are accepted standards for judging whether one meets these criteria, and these standards do not require making direct-comparison self-ascriptions (compare this fact to the person who is concerned with being the best doctor in his community, which does, of course, require that he make direct comparisons to others). This same point holds when we judge ourselves to be a good basketball player or a good physicist. I know, for example, that a basketball player is good if he can regularly hit sixty per cent of his three point shots in a game: no direct comparison with specific others is required.

The distinction between meeting accepted standards and directly comparing oneself to others is important in evaluating a position such as Nozick's. Nevertheless, we are apt lose sight of this distinction if we do not have regard to some further distinctions.

We must realize that implicit in grading self-ascriptions there is a kind of comparison, but not one which threatens the distinction between grading and direct-comparison self-ascriptions. This is the comparison which arises from the fact that a grading characteristic is a scalar one and that therefore to make a grading self-ascription is implicitly to place oneself along a line with other *degrees* of the same characteristic. When I judge myself to be a good doctor, I implicitly see myself along a line which has "awful doctor" at one end and "brilliant doctor" at the other. However, I could in principle know that I am a good doctor without knowing any specific doctors who are either awful or brilliant. And it follows that I could want to be a good doctor without wanting to be a better doctor than any other doctor. Of course, it may happen that Jones is a poor doctor and I know this fact. In wanting to be a good doctor, then, there is a sense in which I want to be a better doctor than Jones. But this latter want is an incidental side-effect of my wanting to be a good doctor, and as such, it need not enter into my motivation at all. Similarly, if I derive enhancement through the self-ascription of being a good doctor, the comparison self-ascription of being a better doctor than Jones need not enter into the self-esteem experience at all.

If Nozick's examples do not show that grading self-evaluations, as we ordinarily make them, presuppose direct comparisons, what do they show? One thing they demonstrate is that through coming into contact with others, we may be led to *revise* the criteria we employ in grading self-ascriptions. This outcome in turn suggests a deeper way in which these judgments might bring in comparisons to others. That is, it makes obvious sense to believe that, in the *original* growth of criteria for any grading self-ascription, direct comparisons must have played a central role. For example, the criteria for what counts as a good basketball player, whether in a remote community or in our own, must have arisen in the first place through making comparisons among basketball players. Then, once the criteria were established, one can see that they would take on a life of their own and be applied apart from mentioning specific others. Given this fact, one might then say that the original comparisons are present *implicitly* whenever the grading self-ascription is made. I would not disagree with this analysis, as far as it goes. What conclusion, however, are we to draw regarding competitive reasons for self-esteem?

In order to have a direct-comparison self-ascription, there must be explicit reference to specific others. Now even on the above analysis, this is not the case with grading self-ascriptions. Reference to specific others is long past and forgotten, and so does not constitute part of any person's self-esteem experience as he makes a grading self-ascription. On the other hand, the above analysis might seem to make grading self-ascriptions into proportionate comparisons, with the comparison group constituted by all those individuals whose characteristics originally went into development of the criteria (recall that proportionate comparisons need not refer to specific others). However, although this is a justifiable way to conceive some self-ascriptions, it is misleading to assimilate most grading self-ascriptions to proportionate comparisons. To see why this is so, we must distinguish two ways that comparing people's characteristics can go into constructing or revising criteria.

Consider first the scalar, but non-grading characteristic of physical stature, whose degrees are marked in terms of short, medium height, and tall. These labels can be applied without direct comparison to specific others. One can know that a five-foot man is short and a seven-foot man is tall without directly comparing these people to specific others. But, of course, these criteria must have been established, however informally, through comparisons among people. This is shown by the fact that the relevant criteria would automatically change if people all of a sudden grew taller. "I am short" is in fact a type of proportionate comparison which fits the suggestion mentioned in the previous paragraph. What we must see, however, is that it is highly misleading to assimilate most grading or even scalar self-ascriptions to this simple model.

Take, for example, the characteristic whose degrees are marked in terms of underweight, proper weight, and overweight. A proper weight is one which is most conducive to a person's health and is partly a function of the ratio of a person's weight to his frame. What counts as proper weight is not determined by calculating averages and would not be affected if everyone's weight were suddenly to change. This is because what counts as good health is not itself a question of calculating averages. If that were so, it would be logically impossible to have a universe of perfectly healthy people.[8] Of course, examining specific people contributes to the data which help us construct criteria for what counts as good health and so for proper weight. But these facts about people do not actually constitute the criteria, as the corresponding facts, once the averaging is done, do in a sense constitute the criteria for what counts as short or for what counts as relative rarity (the paradigm of a proportionate comparison). I cannot present here a positive theory as to how we do construct criteria for characteristics such as good health. But it is clear to me that such a theory would have to analyse how we use empirical data to construct, in our imaginations, ideal types, and then how we subject these ideal types to revision through further examination of empirical data. This process, I would argue, is crucially different from the way we use data to determine the relative rarity of a property, or to construct criteria for a concept such as shortness.

Now, regarding how their criteria become established, most grading characteristics resemble proper weight or good health, rather than physical stature or relative rarity. This is clearly true of those characteristics which have to do with fulfilling social roles. The criteria for being a good doctor must be determined in terms of what best contributes to patients' welfare. The actual behaviour of doctors, past and present, is relevant as data for suggesting the criteria, but these criteria are not directly defined in terms of this behaviour. There are additional things which would have to be said about talents, such as those of an artist, which are not as tightly tied to established norms as is the role of a doctor. But here again the important point is that the criteria which govern the use of the relevant grading characteristics are not determined by means of a direct comparison amongst people, living or dead, along the model of physical stature or relative rarity. If I am short, I am so for no other reason than that I have less height than the average person. If I am a good painter, on the other hand, it is because my paintings have certain qualities (however difficult it is to say what these qualities are).[9] In other words, how I compare with others is what makes me short; but it is in virtue of being a good painter that I compare in various ways with others. Once we attend, then, to the way comparisons amongst people go into forming the criteria for applying grading self-ascriptions, we can see that, in most cases, there is no intrinsic connection between a grading self-ascription and a proportionate comparison.

Grading self-ascriptions are amongst those central to people's self-esteem. The distinctions we have been thinking through show that it is improper to assimilate grading self-ascriptions to either direct or proportionate self-ascriptions. These distinctions, then, help us see the inadequacy of a theory, such as Nozick's, which pictures grading reasons as necessarily involving competitive self-esteem. Our discussion will stand us in good stead when we analyse achievement in chapter 5. Moreover, we are now in a position to see that competition *per se* need not be out of keeping with the RP's ideal self. I shall elaborate briefly on this point.

3.9 Competition sometimes allows us to explore how well we exercise a talent or perform a task. Thus, for example, a person may learn that he has talent for the piano through entering contests. Now when competition plays this role, we can always separate out the competitive component of our experience from the grading component; we can then ground our self-esteem in the latter, rather than the former – and indeed, this often happens. There is nothing in my argument, then, which implies that the RP ought to forego competition which allows him to explore his talents. Moreover, it is sometimes through competition that we clarify for ourselves the relevant standards and are then motivated to meet these standards. My arguments do not suggest that the RP must reject competition for these purposes, nor for the purpose of simply getting on in the world (as in competing for jobs). Note, too, that competitive self-esteem is only one of the possible pleasures associated with competitions. There are as well the distinct pleasures of companionship, the enjoyment of exercising one's skills, and the exhilaration of pushing one's will to the limit. It is true that the Reasonable Person, on my analysis, must see self-esteem feelings associated solely with outcompeting others as out of keeping with his ideal self. But even here we must distinguish between the person for whom outcompeting others is central to his self-esteem and the person for whom outcompeting others is a peripheral part of his self-esteem. It is only the former who has the competitive trait, and it is with this trait that my arguments have been mainly concerned.

3.10 In concluding this chapter, I want briefly to outline the relationship between competitive self-esteem and a contrary trait. I shall say that a person has the trait of *cooperativeness* if he has a well-developed disposition to enjoy shared goals. Let us take a simple example in which we can note the connection between this trait and competitive self-esteem. A necessary condition for a choir to perform well is that its members enjoy singing together, that is, being cooperative in this regard. But for such to be true, the choir members must not be highly envious (or begrudging) of one another,[10] since such ill will must inevitably lead to dissension. Now, as we have seen, competitive self-esteem underlies envy. It follows that absence of competitive self-esteem is a necessary condition for cooperativeness. This absence, however, is not a sufficient condition, since it is possible for people to be non-envious, but still not *enjoy* cooperating. At the same time, once envious comparisons are undercut and thereby inhibited, people often find that a desire for shared enjoyments is awakened. If then the RP values cooperativeness, he can understand that, in virtue of his defining nature, he has something to build on. Later in the book we shall see how this potential is realized.[11]

4 Identification Reasons

> In the Middle Ages both sides of human consciousness – that which was turned within and that which was turned without – lay as though dreaming or half awake beneath a common veil ... Man was conscious of himself only as a member of a race, people, party, family, or corporation – only through some general category. It is in Italy that this veil dissolved first; there arose an objective treatment and consideration of the State and of all the things of this world, and at the same time the subjective side asserted itself with corresponding emphasis. Man became a spiritual individual, and recognized himself as such.
>
> Burckhardt[1]

4.1 In this chapter, I analyse how the Reasonable Person evaluates reasons for self-esteem involving social relationships, in particular, that of group membership. In the course of this chapter and the next, we see one way to interpret Jacob Burckhardt's important claim[2] that there is an association between critical scrutiny ("an objective treatment ... of the State and of all the things of this world") and individuality ("the subjective side asserted itself").

In order to articulate how social relationships enter into her self-esteem, the RP must understand what I call the *identification reason*. Here are examples of identification reasons: (1) Smith is a Canadian artist; in touring the National Gallery for the first time, she feels enhanced when she realizes that Canada has a rich tradition of painting; (2) Jones feels diminution upon discovering that his deceased grandfather was a Nazi. Now a person who wishes to rationalize self-esteem experiences such as these must see herself as believing or taking for granted the following: (a) that she stands in the social relationship mentioned in the self-ascription (citizen of Canada, grandson of X); (b) that she attributes worth to the entity in question on account of some property it possesses (so Smith must see herself as attributing positive worth to Canada's tradition of painting, and Jones must see himself as attributing negative worth to his grandfather's having been a Nazi); and (c) that she attributes positive or negative worth to *belonging* to the group in question or being related to the person in question on account of the relevant worth-making property (so Smith must see herself as attributing positive worth to her being a citizen of Canada, which has this rich tradition of painting, and Jones must see himself as attributing negative worth to his being the grandson of a Nazi). This analysis makes it clear that identification reasons require two distinct moral evaluations, as represented in steps (b) and (c). It follows, then, that a person could belong to a social group and believe that the group has some worthy or unworthy property; but not undergo an identification reason regarding the group, since she does not make the second attribution of worth. I shall return to the significance of this point when we see how the RP evaluates her membership in social groups.

In an identification reason, it is as if the value inherent in some group or other person flows to the agent via her own attributions of worth, thereby enhancing or diminishing her self-esteem. Note now that the agent's enhancement may be intensified through the thought that she herself contributes to the entity with which she identifies. For example, Smith may believe that she contributes to the tradition of Canadian painting (if only by being an intelligent appreciator). On the other hand, Jones, even though he feels diminution, does not believe he contributed to his grandfather's having been a Nazi. This suggests a distinction between two types of identification reasons, which we may call *contributory* and *non-contributory*. There are distinct ways these two reasons enter into our self-esteem. Since, however, the contributory reason is the more important for my purposes, I shall focus on it and bring in the non-contributory reason as required by the argument.

4.2 Some contributory (and also non-contributory) reasons have implicit in them the sense that the agent has less moral status than the entity with which she identifies. This subset of identification reasons I call *a derived reason*, and I shall also speak of *derived self-esteem*. (My use of "derived" here is not meant to beg any moral questions. Whether the RP views these reasons as good or bad is a question I take up later.) Now Smith's reason for self-esteem regarding Canadian painting is unlikely to be a derived one. But take the case of someone whom we may call the *Servile Employee*. The Servile Employee feels enhancement through serving the interests of her employer, in part precisely because she regards her employer as having a higher moral status than herself. A clear example of a Servile Employee (though not, it is true, one who grovels) is found in the character of Denner in George Eliot's novel about eighteenth-century rural life *Felix Holt, the Radical*: "There were different orders of beings – so ran Denner's creed -and she belonged to another order than that to which her mistress belonged ... Denner identified her own dignity with that of her mistress."[3] In experiencing enhancement through contributing to her mistress's interests, Denner has a (contributory) identification reason for self-esteem. Furthermore, her enhancement hinges on regarding her mistress as having a higher moral status than herself. Hence, Denner's contributory reason is a derived one.

I shall be analysing the concepts of equal and unequal moral status in part 2 of this book, but it is necessary to give an initial account of the latter notion in the present context. I shall say, then, that A believes B has higher moral status than herself if A believes or takes it for granted that B's interests merit more intrinsic consideration than her own interests.[4] What would be some signs that Denner accords greater intrinsic importance to her mistress's interests than to her own? In the first place, we would expect her not to resent it if her mistress is not as solicitous of Denner's interests as Denner is of her mistress's interests (even apart from the conventions associated with their distinct social roles). Second, and related to this first point, we would expect Denner to see it as appropriate that, in certain circumstances, she sacrifice for her mistress, but not expect her mistress to sacrifice for her. Third, we might expect Denner to believe it justified that her mistress have certain basic rights not accorded to herself – rights, that is, more basic than those defined simply by their respective social positions.

Relations of moral inequality express themselves more subtly today than they did in the society Eliot was describing. Nevertheless, it is easy to see how the notion of derived self-esteem elucidates other, contemporary relationships – relationships such as those which sometimes occur between a student and her teacher, a follower and her guru, a devotee and her political leader, or a wife and her husband. In each case, we are familiar with circumstances in which a person derives enhancement through contributing to the interests of the other, and derives enhancement in part precisely because she regards the other's interests as counting for more than her own. Now when an agent grounds *a great deal* of her self-esteem in derived reasons, we expect her to exemplify certain further traits. For example, we expect her to be absorbed in how she can contribute to the other's interests; to rely uncritically on the beliefs of the other person; and to undergo reflected self-evaluations which take the other person as their source. It would be possible to work out in detail the correlation between derived self-esteem and traits such as these insofar as these traits affect personal relationships. But rather than do so, I shall turn now to the relationship of group membership, where we shall see that many of the same issues arise and where I shall pursue the relevant correlations in more depth. My first task is to clarify derived self-esteem as it applies to group membership.

4.3 As I shall understand the concept, a social group (or entity) is a number of people united by a common bond such as citizenry or family connection. It is because people share such bonds, and recognize that they do, that we are led to think of social groups as having a unity of their own. And it is in virtue of this unity that we have names for groups and attribute characteristics to them. For example, we say that Canada came into being in 1867, is composed of two major linguistic groups, is economically dominated by foreign companies, has strong traditions of civil liberties, and so on. Canada, linguistic groups, business companies, and traditions are examples of what I am calling social groups (or entities). Insofar as we refer to social groups, we must have criteria which enable us to distinguish them from other types of entities and from each other. This in turn means that we are generally able to make judgments regarding whether a social group is flourishing, growing, and thriving; or, on other hand, whether it is floundering, degenerating, or perishing.

Because we think of social groups in the above terms, it also makes sense to talk of contributing to a group's interests, by which I simply mean contributing to the group's maintenance or flourishing. For example, the person who defends her country in war is contributing to the interests of that country, and the person who keeps good accounts for her local astronomy club is contributing to the interests of her club. Now these two people might well derive enhancement on account of their contributions. But neither of them, so far as I have described them, has a *derived* reason, since nothing I have said indicates that they think of their respective social groups as having higher moral status than themselves. How then are we to understand this feature of derived self-esteem with reference to social groups?

We need to understand what it means for a person to see the interests of a group as meriting more intrinsic consideration than her own interests. The clearest indication that a person has this attitude might appear to be that she considers it appropriate to sacrifice her own interests for the group. There are evident examples of this: a person puts her life at risk in war to defend her country; an employee sacrifices her health through voluntarily overworking on behalf of her company; or, to take a less extreme example, a person donates money to help her astronomy club survive, even though, consulting her own interests alone, she would prefer to spend the money on a holiday. Yet before we can adopt such cases for the purpose of analysing the derived reason, there are ambiguities which must be clarified.

4.4 There is a metaphysical question whether a group is properly regarded as having existence over and above the individuals who constitute it. I mention this issue in order to set it aside, since the clarifications I wish to make do not necessarily hinge on how this question is resolved. Rather, the key issue, I maintain, rests on whether a person is willing to raise and take to heart certain questions about the group of which she is a member.

Our membership in social groups is important for our identities and the fellow-feeling it engenders. At the same time, we can step back from our involvement in a group and ask whether its norms and practices are good for the individuals affected by the group, where each individual is counted as having equal moral status; and also ask whether the group allows for the protection of basic individual rights. Once we recognize that we can take this reflective stance, then we can distinguish two fundamental attitudes toward social groups. One attitude sees the value of groups as ultimately lying in the contribution they make to the good of individuals regarded as moral equals, and thus as always open to criticism and revision from this perspective. (One might occupy this perspective and yet believe that social groups have a non-reducible *existence* over and above the individuals who participate in them – it is just that groups, from within this perspective, do not have any ultimate *value* over and above these individuals.) The contrasting attitude sees the existence and norms of the group as in some way possessing value in their own right, a value which can properly supersede the interests of the individuals affected by the group. Let us call these opposing attitudes the *distributive* and *corporative* attitudes respectively.

Now holding the distributive attitude does not imply a *crassly instrumental* attitude toward social groups.[5] A person with this latter attitude lacks feelings of loyalty toward her fellows, and sees her group membership mainly as a way to meet her own self-interested ends. But the distributive attitude, I want to emphasize, is compatible with feelings of deep loyalty, with a willingness to sacrifice for the group, and with a recognition of how social goods are essential for a fulfilled life. To understand this compatibility, we have further to distinguish two levels of thinking or response to social groups.[6] At the level of her day-to-day thoughts and actions, a person with the distributive attitude may have the feelings and dispositions I have just mentioned. What characterizes the distributive attitude, however, is the commitment to reflect, at a second level, on whether one's feelings and dispositions toward the group, as well as the group's own norms and practices, are contributing on the whole to the good of individuals regarded as moral equals. By contrast, what characterizes the corporative attitude is an unwillingness or incapacity to adopt and take to heart this second level of reflection.

Once we distinguish between the distributive and corporative attitudes, we can clarify two ways in which an individual may sacrifice for a group. A person with the distributive attitude sees her sacrifice as ultimately for the sake of individuals, present and future, who constitute or are affected by the group. In this case, a person's sacrifice would not entail believing that the interests of the group, taken as a unity, merit more intrinsic consideration than her own; and therefore she would not regard the group *per se* as having higher moral status than herself. (Sacrificing one's interests for the sake of other individual sentient beings raises distinct questions.) Such a person, then, in experiencing enhancement through an identification reason, nevertheless does not undergo derived self-esteem. By contrast, an individual with the corporative attitude, since she regards the group taken as a unity as having higher moral status than herself, *is* open to derived reasons.

Self-esteem feelings connected to groups are amongst the most difficult to sort out of all our experiences; and such feelings, as we are undergoing them, are not likely to be clearly delineated in terms of distributive or corporative attitudes. Regarding the corporative attitude in particular, people often act or feel in terms of this attitude without formulating it in words. Nevertheless, the distinctions I have drawn should aid the Reasonable Person, in reflection, to clarify her self-esteem experiences and finally to evaluate them. At the same time, she is helped when she sees the attitudes crystallized by others. There are explicit statements of the corporative attitude, for example, in fascist writings. (Not that all who seem to adopt the corporative attitude are fascists. Democratic communitarians sometimes talk the language of corporativeness;[7] whether they can do so consistently is another matter.) In glorifying dying for one's country, for example, the fascist thinker Alfredo Rocco writes that the good of the state may conflict with the well-being or rights of its citizens; and in that case the citizen must sacrifice for the state. People must realize, he writes, that

For fascism, society is the end, individuals the means … The State therefore grounds and protects the welfare and development of individuals not for their exclusive interests, but because of the identity of the needs of individuals with those of society as a whole … Individual rights are only recognized as they are implied in the rights of the State. In this preeminence of duty, we find the highest ethical value of fascism.[8]

As an expression of the distributive attitude, on the other hand, consider the following statement by Willy Brandt during an interview about why he returned to Germany after the Second World War:

Brandt: ... Oh, the morale of the Berliners was never so high as in the first postwar years. Even during the blockade it was never to be so high. And so my process of identification ...
Interviewer: What do you mean by identification? What they call one's country?
Brandt: No. It wasn't the country that drew me back. It was the case of a people who, having passed through dictatorship and war and destruction, were trying to rebuild for themselves a life based on freedom. Yes, it was this that induced me to become a German again. It was the fantastic will to work that was in each of them, it was that capacity to accomplish something, that desire to help one another ... Do you see what I mean? A question of human and moral values rather than a nationalistic fact ...[9]

Brandt is expressing feelings, rather than making a philosophical statement in the manner of Rocco. So his words are not an explicit expression of the distributive attitude, but I believe this concept helps us understand his state of mind. Brandt does not see the value of being German as lying in something over and above the value of individual Germans, and therefore he is not disposed to undergo derived reasons regarding his membership in the German nation. At the same time, he recognizes that being German is an important part of his identity and motivation, and so his attitude toward his nationality is far from crassly instrumental.

4.5 A person with a strong disposition for derived self-esteem, with reference to some group, has the trait I call *corporativism*. The essence of this trait is that a person defines her identity mainly in terms of group norms and relationships. I shall now describe five correlative features of this trait.

1 *Pliancy regarding Group Norms*   The corporative attitude, I have said, is characterized by an unwillingness or incapacity to subject group norms to an appropriate form of critical scrutiny. Now several other features of derived self-esteem serve to emphasize this defining feature of the trait. In the first place, when a person regards an entity as having higher moral status than herself, especially an entity with

which she identifies, then she is disposed to make reflected self-evaluations with reference to that entity (in the case of group membership, the source of reflected self-evaluations lies in the authorities who promulgate or enforce the group's norms.) But, as we saw in 2.4, to be disposed to make reflective self-evaluations causes a person to be pliant toward the relevant entity. In the second place, a person who strongly identifies with a group jeopardizes her own self-esteem if ever she doubts the worthiness of the group. Hence, such a person is disposed to be uncritical or pliant toward the group's norms.

2 *Exclusive Concern*   The corporative person is apt to focus *exclusive concern* on the group with which she identifies. I explain this point as follows. A person has *concern* for another entity if she attends to that entity without direct or immediate thought for her own interests. It makes sense that the corporative person would have concern for her group. At the same time, her concern is apt *to exclude* concern for those outside her group. In particular, the corporative person is not likely to possess a well-developed capacity for what I shall call *impartial concern*. One form of impartial concern occurs when an agent acts for the sake of a person even though that person has no special relationship to the agent; that is, the agent does not think of the other person in terms of "*my* compatriot," "*my* neighbour," "*my* child," and so on. A second form of impartial concern occurs when a person gives equal consideration to the interests of all who are affected by her acts. A final form occurs when a person judges people fairly regardless of how these people are related to herself. Impartial concern contrasts with *self-referential concern*. This latter characteristic, though genuinely other-regarding, is nevertheless focused on entities which the agent understands to have some special relationship to herself.

Now self-referential concern does not necessarily block the capacity for impartial concern. A person may have a deep regard for her children or her country, for example, and at the same time be strongly disposed to express impartial concern. On the other hand, self-referential concern can be so all-absorbing that it stultifies the capacity for impartial concern. This is precisely what must occur, I believe, with regard to a person in whose life derived self-esteem plays a central part.

3 *Role and Status Entrenchment*   Social roles and status hierarchies are defined by the norms and conventions of a given social group. In order for a person to question what is demanded or expected of her in virtue of her role or status, she must be able to disengage

herself in thought from the norms of the group. The self-esteem of the corporative person, however, is so tied to some social group that, as we have seen, she is unwilling or unable to achieve this disengagement. In this sense, I say that she is entrenched in her roles or status.

4 *Group-Related Emotions*   Because the corporative person's self-esteem is so dependent on the group, she attaches great significance to emotions which further deepen her identification. This happens in several ways. First, she is attracted to relationships which emphasize public, as opposed to private, emotional expression. As a consequence, she attaches relatively little importance to friendships which are grounded in non-group feelings. In the extreme, such a person feels most at home in a society in which there is hardly any individualized emotional expression. There is a powerful description of such a society in William Prescott's book *History of the Conquest of Peru*. Concluding his discussion of the rules which regulated husband-wife relationships in Inca society, he says:

The extraordinary regulations respecting marriage within the Incas were eminently characteristic of the government, ... which penetrated into the most private recesses of domestic life ... [The Inca's] very existence as an individual was absorbed in that of the group. His hopes and his fears, his joys and his sorrows, the tenderest sympathies of his nature, which would naturally shrink from observation, were all to be regulated by laws. He was not even allowed to be happy in his own way.[10]

A person who feels at home with this feature of the corporative personality would be inclined to believe it right to sacrifice relationships grounded in "mere private emotions" for the good of the group. (Such a tendency explains why a major theme in both *Brave New World* and *1984* is that totalitarian regimes try to inculcate a large balance of public, over private feeling and so discourage non-group loyalties.)

A second feature of the corporative person's emotional life is the importance she attaches to *pooled emotions*.[11] A pooled emotion is one felt in unison with others toward some common object. Pooled emotions are an important ingredient of fellow-feeling, and a life without such emotions would lack something of the highest importance. However, in the life of the corporative person, such feelings predominate and become addictive. These emotions then have the effect of shutting her off from friendly feelings towards those outside her group. In this way, a person's disposition for exclusive altruism is deepened. Moreover, such a person is open to the well-known turn which pooled emotions can take, leading to acts of group violence and sadism: "You get enough people together, you're not just a person in the crowd, you *are* the crowd. You're *invincible*" (emphasis in the original), says a gang member explaining the phenomenon of "swarming" innocent pedestrians.[12] Writ large, this is a major factor in nationalistic and ethnic fervour, and so in war.

5 *Mystification*   The distinction I drew in 4.1 between contributory and non-contributory identification reasons helps us understand a further feature of the corporative personality. To have one's self-esteem focused on a group through derived contributory reasons must be to attach great importance to the achievements or other valued properties of the group (remembering the structure of the identification reason described in 4.1). Now when these achievements, etc., are mainly produced by others, such as star athletes, artists, politicians, or warriors, then the corporative person is disposed to undergo *non-contributory* derived reasons regarding these others. That is, she derives enhancement from the mere fact that she and these others are members of the same group. In the extreme, the corporative person does not even understand the nature of the achievements through which she derives enhancement. Such was the case, for example, with a farm-hand who, as reported in my local paper, had a consuming pride in being a distant descendant of the Bach family and at the same time admitted to being completely unmusical – though his sister, he said, could yodel. A person whose self-esteem focuses in this way on non-contributory reasons tends to mystify the producers of the valued achievements. Doing so in turn deepens her sense of having a lower moral status than the group or person with whom she identifies.

(My analysis casts the corporative trait in a negative light, and the evaluation in the next part of the book deepens this perspective. It is important to note, however, that sometimes admirable qualities, such as courage and of course loyalty, are aspects of the corporative personality. To attain a balanced view of this trait, one has to have regard for social and historical context. As an aid to this balanced view, I recommend Chinua Achebe's novel *Things Fall Apart*, in particular, his portrayal of the African tribal hero Okonkwo.)

4.6 Derived self-esteem and corporativism are integrally related. Indeed, the two are integrated to such an degree that it is misleading to think of derived self-esteem as *grounding* corporativism; rather, it is more accurate to picture the two traits as growing in tandem and as sustaining each other. This in turn means that to undercut one is to undercut the other, and this undercutting can take place in either direction. I turn, then, to describing ways the RP's defining commitment leads her to inhibit derived self-esteem and corporativism in herself. None of these ways is itself definitive, but together they strongly support the notion that the RP's nature is incompatible with both derived self-esteem and corporativism. I begin in this section by discussing two ways the RP's defining commitment runs counter to corporativism.

In the first place, exclusive concern must to some extent be countered when the RP takes to heart the attempt to justify any identification reason. Say, for example, that Jones feels enhancement through seeing himself as a Canadian on account of Canada's great hockey tradition. If he is an RP, then the universalizability guideline tells him that he must be willing to esteem non-Canadian hockey traditions for relevantly similar reasons. Moreover, even if Jones does not recognize other nations as having such traditions, he must at least acknowledge that there could be such nations. If he takes this part of his evaluation seriously and can bring his feelings into line with his beliefs, then he must be less disposed to the kind of exclusivity characteristic of the corporative person.

Secondly, we saw that the corporative person is entrenched in her social roles and status, and we connected this to the fact that she has no foothold outside group norms from which to survey her position. Now the critical guidelines give the RP just such a foothold, for she must see the validity of these guidelines as ultimately lying outside the purview of group norms. Why is this?

Standards of rational criticism, such as the guidelines are meant to be, cannot logically gain their validity simply from the fact that some social group, including the RP's, has adopted the standards. The question can always be asked, once the RP has the concept of rational justification, why *this* group's, rather some other group's, judgment is especially sacrosanct; and any adequate answer to this question must finally make reference to standards whose validity is accepted as independent of any particular group's commitment to the standards. For example, it does not make sense to say that consistency counts as a standard of rational criticism and then to give as one's reason that social group X accepts consistency as one of its norms. For then the question can be asked why group X's norms should count as the standard for rational criticism. And in order to answer *this* question, we must move in our thought beyond group X's norms. (This logical point is compatible, it should be noted, with the undoubted fact that standards of rational criticism originate within social contexts; but origin and validity are clearly distinct.) The RP's understanding of rational criticism, therefore, leads her to realize that her ideal self is constituted by a commitment which cannot be reduced to the norms of the groups to which she belongs.

In committing herself to the critical guidelines, then, the RP comes to have a concept of herself from which she can survey group norms and thereby question the expectations inherent in the roles or statuses she occupies. Her defining commitment affords her a route, we can say, to *imaginative disengagement* from her social roles and statuses. Given this, she must recognize that in principle her critical thinking might show the inadequacy of any given norm attached to her roles or statuses. This fact is a powerful antidote to entrenchment, and therefore to the disposition to develop the corporative trait.

A related point concerns the RP's attitude toward social status in particular. A status hierarchy may be defined as a group of titles or positions which relate to each other in terms of higher and lower. Thus, for example, within a business company, there may be a status hierarchy which runs from the president to the vice-presidents, on to the bookkeepers and secretaries, and finally down to the office gofers. To take seriously a status hierarchy is to be inclined to accord respect and deference in keeping with a person's position in the hierarchy, and to think it right that others should do the same. Now it is group norms which define a status hierarchy, and hence how much deference or respect each position up the ladder ought to be accorded. Because of the corporative person's entrenchment in her social groups, she is apt to have a rigid and unquestioning attitude toward status hierarchies. The RP, however, adopts a different attitude, which may be explained as follows.

Positions along a status hierarchy are supposed to be signs for some *other* respect-worthy qualities (unless the positions are moribund, in which case they are often said to have great symbolic value). So, for example, the president in a company is supposed to have more business acumen or leadership ability or experience than do the vice-presidents. We may call the attributes which ground and justify positions in a status hierarchy *grounding qualities*. Now unless we mystify status positions, we know from experience that those who occupy such positions do not always have the relevant grounding qualities. It follows that it is always fitting to ask whether a person who occupies a position does in fact possess the relevant grounding qualities; and then to accord deference or respect only if, and to the degree, that the qualities are indeed present. This, I believe, would be the attitude of the Reasonable Person, since she will want to be able to justify the deference and respect she accords. Therefore she in turn is not disposed to accord deference or respect to a person simply because she occupies some position in a status hierarchy. In keeping with this attitude, moreover, the RP must try to make herself immune to the mystification which is so often a feature of status hierarchies. Such dispositions of the RP run counter to entrenchment, and therefore counter to her acquiring the corporative trait.

4.7 We saw in 4.5 how non-contributory reasons, and the mystification they give rise to, are often an important correlative of derived reasons. A further way the RP undercuts her acquiring the corporative trait has to do with her evaluation of non-contributory reasons. We can clarify our thoughts on this topic by seeing how she would look at an evident case of a non-contributory reason, such as that of the farm-hand, mentioned earlier, who derives enhancement through thinking of himself as a remote descendant of the Bach family.

The rationalization of the farm-hand's enhancement would, one assumes, have to do with the Bach family's musical greatness. But neither does this greatness inhere in the farm-hand, nor does he make any genuine contribution to its continued recognition (if the farm-hand were intelligently to promote the Bachs' music, then he would have a contributory, rather than a non-contributory, reason). My intuition, and I believe many people's, is to say that, although the farm-hand's feelings are innocent of harm, nevertheless he has no good reason to feel enhancement. This intuition is reflected in our conceptual practices. Pride is perhaps the most common feeling of enhancement. But the very concept of pride requires that a person who has this feeling should be able to show how the object of her pride has some close relationship to herself, or is something to which she has contributed. A feeling of pride which does not satisfy this principle seems as nonsensical as a feeling of fear directed toward something which the agent admits to be harmless. Now it appears reasonable to extend this principle to all self-esteem feelings. (This principle, however, has to be understood along with recognizing how subtle some genuine contributions to social entities can be. What might appear at first to be non-contributory reasons are sometimes really contributory ones. I shall have more to say about this issue in chapter 6.)

To extend the principle in the way I am suggesting helps us make sense of our attitude toward other purely non-contributory reasons. For example, although we understand why Jones might feel diminution over his grandfather's Nazi past, nevertheless it seems appropriate to tell him that he has no good reason to do so. Or, to take another example, if someone feels ashamed over some barbarous act her country has committed, there is usually implicit in the agent's shame some thought to the effect that there is *something* she could have done to try to prevent the act. I must admit, however, that we are dealing here with a question over which there could be legitimate and ultimate disagreement: this is one of those grey areas I said we must learn to expect in this field of inquiry.[13] If the farm-hand were to insist that being a remote descendant of the Bach family is sufficient to justify enhancement, we would perhaps be at a loss to find some universally accepted principle with which to refute him. Nevertheless, there are a number of further considerations which the Reasonable Person could press.

The farm-hand can be asked, for example, whether he attributes intrinsic or derivative worth to being the descendant of the Bachs. If he takes the former route, then he can be asked why being a remote descendant of the Bachs in itself has worth, but being the remote descendant of some other family does not. He could say, and indeed would have to say, "It just does." But then, even apart from going contrary to the intuition I adduced in the previous paragraph, the farm-hand would be contravening the universalizability guideline, which asserts the illegitimacy of attributing intrinsic worth to an individual *per se* (in this case, an individual family). Does the farm-hand then want to take the option of attributing derivative worth to his self-ascription by subsuming it under some property which does not mention the Bach family? Is, say, being the remote descendant of any great musical family cause for enhancement? Or the descendant of any famous family at all? By means of such questions, we might shift the farm-hand's perspective, or the perspective of any other person for whom non-contributory reasons are at the core of her self-esteem.

We could also ask the farm-hand whether he has understood the real cause of his self-esteem feelings. For example, might it not be that it is the attention drawn to him, when people discover his Bach connection, which is the real cause of his feelings? In this case, if he tries to justify his reason, he would see that his feelings are the result of reflected self-evaluations. And indeed this is, I believe, often a major factor in the disposition to attach importance to purely non-contributory self-ascriptions.

There is a further factor which may hide from an agent the true cause of her self-esteem feelings. It sometimes happens that a person feels so inadequate regarding her own inherent characteristics that she compensates by identifying her self-esteem with another person or group. This kind of motive is especially likely to be a factor in non-contributory derived reasons. Of course, it would be difficult to establish the presence of such a motive with certainty. But if it is reasonable to believe that this can be a significant factor, then the RP who is trying to justify her non-contributory reasons must ask herself whether this motive is clouding her judgment.

In themselves, non-contributory reasons for self-esteem are usually harmless. At the same time, they are often a key ingredient of the corporative trait. In this section, we have seen that the RP is likely to regard the non-contributory reason as unreasonable. Here, then, is further reason to believe that the RP, through the process of evaluation, inhibits her having the corporative trait.

4.8 A fundamental way derived self-esteem is out of keeping with the Reasonable Person's ideal self is that she is little disposed to regard any other entity as having a higher moral status than herself. Granted this, derived reasons are ruled unreasonable from the start. The full argument for this claim is substantiated only in chapter 8, where I show why the Reasonable Person is strongly disposed to possess what I call *egalitarian self-respect*. Nevertheless, enough can be said here to support the argument of this chapter, so long as the reader keeps the promise of a fuller argument in mind.

We saw in chapter 2 that the RP undercuts any disposition in herself to make reflected self-evaluations and that in the process she comes to have autonomous reasons for self-esteem. I further argued (2.7) that she is disposed to see herself as the equal of any other person in her capacity to form autonomous moral beliefs. This is an important way to see oneself as the equal of others, for this self-perception must partly dissipate the mystique which otherwise might attach to people in virtue of their greater social status or achievements. This dissipation of mystique makes it less likely in turn that the RP would be pliant regarding the views or dictates of others. Now the person who has autonomous self-esteem, who has the sense of equality I have been describing, who does not regard others with mystique, and who is not pliant – such a person is not apt to develop, or accommodate herself to, the belief that another entity has higher moral status than herself. Given this pattern of dispositions and beliefs, then, we may conclude that the RP inhibits in herself derived self-esteem.

As a final point, we should note that there are deep currents in the spirit of our age which support the RP's disinclination to see her interests as meriting less intrinsic consideration than the interests of others. Legal doctrines of equal rights, for example, must help her to discount factors such as social status, race, gender, and even achievement as relevant grounds for determining moral status. Talk of the "spirit of the age" is not a reasoned argument. At the same time, we must recognize that there are non-rational factors which go into determining both egalitarian and non-egalitarian points of view. In other words, it is easier, even apart from reasoned arguments, to adopt an egalitarian set of attitudes in some social settings than in others. That a moral ideal, or set of psychological dispositions, has such cultural support can be a point in its favour, *assuming* the ideal is justifiable in the first place. Again, this is a topic to which I shall return.

4.9 In seeing how the RP inhibits corporativeness in herself, I have emphasized that she is able to distance herself from group norms. At the same time, I was at pains to argue that she need not, on account of her nature, be crassly instrumental in the way she expresses her group membership. In concluding this chapter, I want to reinforce this latter point by describing more fully how the RP is likely to experience group membership.

In analysing the identification reason in 4.1, we saw that a person might be a member of a social group, believe that the group has some worthy or unworthy property, and yet not undergo an identification reason; for example, Smith, herself a painter, could recognize that her country has a great tradition of painting, but not feel enhancement on that account. If a person's self-esteem is going to be affected through an identification reason, then she must make the appropriate attribution of worth to the self-ascription which *relates* her to the group (as *per* condition (c) in the structure of the identification reason). Now the most common reason a person would *not* make such an attribution is that, though a member of the group, she does not have *a sense of belonging* to the group. A sense of belonging, then, is distinct from having identification reasons (and indeed, the latter presupposes the existence of the former). I want now briefly to consider this dimension of group membership as it relates to the RP.

There are various causes which can generate a sense of belonging. For example, one superficial cause occurs when other people continually make us aware of our membership in some group (when this is the cause, perhaps "sense of belonging" is too strong, but no harm is done extending the concept to this context). Thus we often experience our nationality more intensely when travelling in foreign lands, since other people naturally want to talk to us about our country. Accordingly, we are also more prone to experience identification reasons regarding our nationality in such circumstances, though reflected self-evaluations also have a lot to do with it. Usually, however, our sense of belonging goes deeper and results from what I shall call *attachment*.

Attachment is characterized by a positive regard for another entity which develops, not only from coming to appreciate the other's worthy qualities, but also, and necessarily, from a psychological bond which arises through a shared history. This means that our attachments are not wholly grounded in beliefs about the worth-making properties of the entities to which we are attached. Love and friendship are other relationships involving attachment. If I am someone's friend, for example, there must be characteristics of her which I admire and would find admirable in any other person. But I do not automatically become the friend of anyone who has these characteristics, for friendship is something which grows on an individual through doing or undergoing things together, and through shared memories.

The above features of attachment mean that reasoned criticism, based on impersonal standards, can go only so far in leading us to revise or give up an attachment. This does not mean attachments are irrational; it means only that reason-giving, of the kind applicable to our self-esteem, is incapable of explaining completely why we possess or change our attachments. Of course, attachments can weaken and wither. But they must be grown out of as much as into, and reasoned changes in belief can never provide the complete explanation for either process.

Let us now see how the above applies specifically to our attachment to a social group, say to one's country. Take a person's enjoyment of a particular landscape, her interest in events or characters in history, or her pleasure in a style of music, all of which can be part of a person's shared attachment, and hence sense of belonging, to her country. One acquires dispositions for specific enjoyments and interests partly through a kind of osmosis: through being in *this* place at *this* time and being provided with *this* education and *this* background. I may enjoy wandering through a particular countryside, for example, mainly because I have often wandered through it in the past. It is, moreover, this bonding, with its remembered sensations and feelings shared with others, which must somehow be lost or forgotten if I am to lose this aspect of my attachment. (In explaining his decision to move back to Germany twenty years after the Second World War, a German Jew said he missed desperately the sound of the German language.) Critical reflection in terms of impersonal standards may initiate the loosening of the bond, but it cannot complete it.

Another factor in our attachment to social groups is feelings of gratitude. These feelings, too, arise from a shared history, and thus their rationale cannot wholly lie in universalizable worth-making considerations. I have feelings of gratitude, let us say, toward group X, which I recognize as having helped shape my identity in ways I consider healthy. I would not have had this identity if I were not a member of this group. Notice now a difference between reasons for gratitude and reasons for self-esteem. If I esteem myself on the grounds that my group has valuable property A, then I am committed, as an RP, to believing that any other group which has property A is equally esteem-worthy. But if I feel justifiable gratitude toward group X, then of course I am not thereby committed to regarding with gratitude other groups which may have admirable qualities equal to my group's. (I am perhaps committed to believing that other people ought to feel gratitude toward the groups from which they have benefited, but this is different from universalizing *my* gratitude, which of course it would be absurd to think of doing.) Moreover, when our attachment to a group is deepened through feelings of gratitude, we do not believe these feelings should wax and wane with our judgments about the group's overall worth-making properties. In understanding gratitude, therefore, we further grasp how the sense of belonging can be neither wholly rationalized nor revised in terms of the critical guidelines.

What now are the implications of this for the Reasonable Person's self-understanding? I wish to say that the RP must see herself, as she relates to social groups, always as that of a self-in-potential-conflict. On the one side, she has what I have called a route to imaginative disengagement from the roles and norms of the group, and also from the identification reasons which enhance or diminish her self-esteem. Her very concept of herself as an RP causes her, therefore, to be at some intellectual and emotional distance from her group membership. On the other side, there is that part of the RP rooted in attachment for which there is no complete route to imaginative disengagement in terms of the guidelines. She, therefore, must find it natural to see her group membership as always open to pulls from opposing parts of her self. We need not think, however, that this is a harmful feature of the RP's character, or something about her nature that she ought to regret, for intellectual and emotional ambivalence, when not extreme, may be fruitful and enriching (as I discuss further in 5.9).

In my view, this picture of the self-in-potential-conflict is a more philosophically accurate way to picture the self of someone for whom reasonableness is important than either Rawls's detached self behind the veil of ignorance or the communitarian's self as constituted "all the way down" by its group membership. My picture would grant the communitarian's point that there is a part of our self from which, in some sense, we cannot detach our self-understandings (though most communitarians want to go further than I regarding what cannot be detached). At the same time, my analysis, I believe, gives Rawls all he needs, as against many communitarians, in order to ground the Rawlsian values of the "free and equal person."[14] Though my interest here is not political theory, my analysis is in keeping with the spirit of William Galston's comments regarding the proper way to picture the self in liberal theory:

Liberalism, I suggest, rests not on the unencumbered self ... but rather on the *divided* self ... On the one side stands the individual's personal and social history, with all the aims and attachments it may imply. On the other side stands the possibility of critical reflection on – even revolt against – these very commitments.

   At the heart of the liberal vision is the consideration that individuality is not only shaped but also threatened by the community.[15]

In the next chapter, we examine this "individuality" as it relates to reasonable self-esteem.

5 Inherent Reasons

5.1 Reflected, competitive, and derived reasons are powerful forces in our lives. At the same time, a life which centred itself on these reasons would appear, in the eyes of many, morally deficient. The intuition behind this judgment, I believe, is that such a life lacks dignity, and it does so because it derives its self-esteem mainly from sources outside itself. It is this (admittedly vague) intuition, for example, which C.P. Snow draws upon in his novel *In Their Wisdom*, when he describes Jenny Rastall's decision to marry Lord Lorimer:

It would be nice [Jenny mused] to have someone beside her at parties. It wasn't good for anyone's self-esteem, particularly one who had as little as she had, to go about alone ... (... he had his own presence, she had seen people respecting him, she could hold on to that.) She would enjoy having a title, anyone like herself would be a hypocrite to pretend not to. (... going along to the peeresses' gallery and having notes addressed to the Lady Lorimer – that would be a distinct improvement ...)[1]

If we find Rastall morally wanting, it is because she seems willingly to accept that she has nothing in her own right upon which to ground her self-esteem. The other side to this judgment is that it is morally better, more in keeping with a person's dignity, that he ground his self-esteem in qualities which issue from himself. In the next part of the book, I interpret these moral judgments from the point of view of my theory. The present chapter lays the groundwork for this discussion by exploring the RP's attitude to what I call *inherent reasons for self-esteem.*

There is a negative and a positive component to my definition of the inherent reason. The negative component states that it is a necessary condition for a reason's being inherent that it *not* be a reflected, competitive, or derived reason. Each of these latter reasons, in its distinctive way, requires that a person look to an entity outside himself in order to rationalize his reason for self-esteem. However, there is no common definition to these three reasons which could distinguish them as a group from every inherent reason: many inherent reasons also bring us into relation with things outside ourselves. The best I can do, therefore, is to list this subset of non-inherent reasons and say that this contrastive group enters into my definition of the inherent reason. At the same time, we will see that there are sometimes overlaps between specific occurrences of these non-inherent reasons and the positive component of the inherent reason.

The positive component lies in the notion suggested by the phrase "issues from oneself." Take, for example, the enhancement a person might feel because he has built his own house, or his diminution when he breaks a promise. House building and promise breaking are voluntary acts, and we think of most voluntary acts as issuing directly from the agent in a way that, say, reflected and derived characteristics do not. (Competitive characteristics are more likely to be tied directly to voluntary acts, but in this case the negative condition of the previous paragraph excludes the competitive reason from counting as an inherent reason.) What more do we mean by "issues from oneself"? Partly it is a question of direction. In the reflected and derived reasons, the agent sees value or disvalue as flowing from an external source to himself, whereas in the case of a voluntary act, what is valuable (the house) or disvaluable (the broken promise) flows from the agent to the world. "Direction," however, is not all that we need to make sense of; there is also the idea of "flowing." A person who grounds a reason for self-esteem in his blue eyes, for example, does not derive it from external sources, at least in the sense of the reflected or derived reason. Nevertheless, such a reason does not count, in my terms, as inherent, for the property of having blue eyes does not "flow" from the agent: it is, we might say, a static characteristic. These concepts of direction and flow help us a little toward understanding the notion of "issuing from oneself." In a moment, I shall offer a more comprehensive analysis. But first we must realize that the category of inherent reason encompasses more than voluntary acts.

5.2 To act voluntarily is generally to act on the basis of a desire with which the agent identifies, as when, in building a house, Smith acts on her desire that her family has a place to live. Now there are some voluntary acts which do not issue from desires, as when a person mindlessly twiddles his thumbs. In this case, the act does not tell us anything at all about the agent's self (I am assuming that the twiddling is not the result of boredom). We may conclude, therefore, that it is not the voluntary act *per se*, but rather the desire from which the act issues, which gives us a key to understanding the concept of "issuing from oneself," and so of the inherent reason.

To have a desire to see some state of affairs realized is, I shall say, to *manifest interest* in that state of affairs. One reason we attach importance to voluntary acts, even apart from their effects on the world, is precisely that they are ways of our manifesting interest in the world and of learning how other people manifest interest in the world. But having or acting on desires is only one way of manifesting interest. If I go to a bullfight, for example, I might enjoy it, find it repugnant, or be totally indifferent to it. Enjoyment and repugnance are other forms of what I am calling manifesting interest. Now it is manifesting interest which is properly said to issue from ourselves, and therefore it is self-ascriptions involving manifestations of interest which may enter into inherent reasons. (I shall call self-ascriptions involving manifestations of interest *inherent self-ascriptions*. To have an inherent reason for self-esteem, a person must attribute worth to an inherent self-ascription.) How, then, are we to understand the concept of manifesting interest?

5.3 The essence of manifesting interest is to be either favourably or unfavourably disposed toward some entity (there are a few exceptions to this rule, but they do not affect the main line of my analysis).[2] We may form a clearer picture of our subject, therefore, by first citing other modes of being favourably or unfavourably disposed toward things:

Favourably Disposed	*Unfavourably Disposed*
want	fear
enjoy	resentment
love	jealousy
respect	envy
gratitude	anger
feel affection for	shame
believe praiseworthy	revenge

Favourably Disposed	*Unfavourably Disposed*
attracted to	guilt
show preference for	hatred
admire	contempt
happy about	mortification
sympathize with	indignation
pride	repugnance
wish	regret
like	bored with
appreciate	dislike
find amusing	annoyance
find beautiful	believe blameworthy

(I have not ordered these examples so that concepts under one heading are matched by contrary concepts, e.g., love-hate, since it is not true that for every way of being favourably disposed towards something, there is a correlative way of being unfavourably disposed toward it.)

Compare now my finding the bullfight repugnant with my being detested by others for finding the bullfight repugnant, or, on the other hand, with my having blue eyes. These latter characteristics are just as much genuine characteristics of me as is that of finding something repugnant, and they can equally, through becoming self-ascriptions, enter into my self-esteem. But I want to say that finding something repugnant issues from my self, whereas my being detested by others or my having blue eyes does not issue from my self. What is the basis for this distinction?

Most importantly, there is an experiential element to "issuing from ourself," which can only be grasped by introspection (as P.F. Strawson has said, our sense of self is in the first place a feeling, not a belief).[3] The fact is that when we manifest interest, as we are doing in one form or another most of our waking lives, then we at the same time feel ourselves to be active, rather than ever purely passive. This is true even when our manifesting interest is least connected to voluntary action, such as when we react to pain. For insofar as we *dislike* the pain, there is a component in our experience which reflects active response. We are not often, it is true, self-consciously aware of this feeling of being active, for our minds are always focused on the objects in which we are manifesting interest, rather than on the manifesting interest itself. But we can become aware of the feeling by reflecting upon our experiences after they have occurred (in which case we would be manifesting interest in the recollected experience). Another way I shall describe this active element in our experience is to say that we feel ourselves to be *subjects* of the manifestations of our interest. It is this sense of being subjects, I maintain, which denotes the experiential content of "issues from ourselves." And it is our implicit grasp of this experience which makes us judge there to be a significant distinction between self-ascriptions which involve manifestations of interest and those which do not.

Now the fact that we are subjects of our manifestations of interest does not imply that there is some subject, self, or ego which stands *apart* from our experiences and to which our experiences are attributable. That kind of metaphysical entity is not part of our experience, and my interest is not to hypothesize the existence of such an entity. Our experience of being active, when we analyse it introspectively, is largely traceable, as William James says, to subtle physiological motions in "the head or between the head and the throat."[4] Think for example, to follow James's descriptions, of the "fluctuating play of pressures, convergences, divergences, and accommodations in [our] eyeballs" which occur when we manifest interest in some visual object; or of the subtle "contractions of the jaw-muscles" which accompany any sort of effort; or of the "constant play of furtherances and hindrances, of checks and releases, tendencies which run with desire, and tendencies which run the other way."[5] It is our implicit awareness of such sensations which initially gives us the sense of being an active subject.

I have distinguished manifestations of interest as those qualities which we conceive as issuing from ourselves. This notion of issuing from ourselves I have in turned explained, to begin with, in terms of the *experience* of being an active subject. But this latter notion is itself liable to analyses even more obscure than the notion of issuing from oneself. For this reason, and before I had reread James, I was reluctantly going to bypass in my analysis this experiential element of "issuing from oneself." But James's descriptions, even though they are not the whole story, do capture, I believe, an important element in the felt experience of being an active subject. Moreover, because the descriptions are in physiological terms (and probably for this reason "by most men overlooked"),[6] we are led to the notion of an active subject without being pulled, at this level of the analysis, into metaphysics. (However, I should not want to deny that ultimately our understanding of being an active subject does require deeper metaphysical understanding: the experiences James cites could never be *sufficient* to define completely the concept of an active subject.)

5.4 I shall now describe three contrasts applicable to manifestations of interest, but not to other self-ascriptions. I maintain that in thinking of inherent self-ascriptions as issuing from ourselves, it is often these three contrasts which lie implicit in our understanding. These contrasts, we might say, *frame* manifestations of interest for us. I shall deal with each one in turn.

There is first the contrast between a non-defective awareness of something on the one hand and an individual or characteristic *response* to that thing on the other hand. We believe, for example, that any person with normal faculties must necessarily see a bullfight, if he is present at one and looking in the right direction. At the same time, two individuals may respond to the bullfight in different ways, even though both see more or less the same thing. Nor can we say that when two people respond differently, one person lacks normal faculties or is outright mistaken, as we would if one of them denied that he was seeing a bullfight. (We might want to say that one of the two is morally mistaken; but then the contrast I am pressing, far from being lost, would have to be reintroduced at a deeper level.) This same contrast applies to all forms of manifesting interest, but not to other self-ascriptions.

The second contrast is that between forced and unforced responses. We do not ordinarily choose what form our interest takes. It is often, indeed, a case of *discovering* how one responds to the object of our interest. Thus, for example, a person might be surprised, on going to his first ballet, to discover how much he enjoyed it. But although we usually do not choose what form our interest takes, we still feel that when, for example, we enjoy a ballet, feel affection for a friend, or desire to write a novel, the enjoyment, affection, and desire are unforced. The reason it makes sense to say this is that we can imagine how these same ways of responding could be forced. We know, for example, that in the extreme case, people can be brainwashed, hypnotized, or otherwise induced to enjoy or desire things which they would not normally have enjoyed or done. We also sometimes feel that our responses move us against our will, even when there is no imposition of another's will – as in the case of the alcoholic. Here too we think of our responses as forced, or as having been imposed from the "outside." And so we see how this contrast between forced and unforced helps us understand our sense that, in the usual case, our manifesting interest issues from our own self. On the other hand, this is not a contrast applicable by us to ourselves when we think of having blue eyes or of being detested by others.

The final contrast has to do with the fact that we can choose to make (or not make) manifestations of interest autonomous through the process of justification. For example, if I find the bullfight repugnant, I can ask myself why I find it so and then evaluate my reason; similarly with my finding the book boring or with my wanting to write a novel. In evaluating my reasons for manifesting interest, I must face the possibility that I may not have an adequate reason. It should be clear, then, that we are dealing here with a more general instance of what I analysed in chapter 2 as autonomy. That is, a person who justifies some way of manifesting interest and then continues to manifest the interest, due in part to this justificatory activity, has made his response to the world more his own. Because there is this possibility of either rejecting a manifestation of interest or making it more one's own, it is proper to say we are *responsible* for the manifestations of our interest, and so for our inherent self-ascriptions.[7] But we are not responsible, in this sense, for other people finding us detestable or for our blue eyes.

These three contrasts help distinguish manifesting interest from other characteristics. It is important to be clear that the distinctions I am pressing are between different forms of characteristics or self-ascriptions, rather than different forms of reasons. The self-ascriptions of being detested by others and having blue eyes are not themselves open to justification by me; they are simply characteristics I have or do not have. Of course, how I *respond* to these self-ascriptions is open to evaluation by me. But then these responses, which will often take the form of attributions of worth, are themselves manifestations of interest and thereby inherent self-ascriptions. In other words, that attributing worth to a self-ascription is a reason for self-esteem does not negate the fact that this same attribution of worth also constitutes a (second-order) self-ascription. Indeed, all attributions of worth, whatever self-ascriptions they take as their objects, are properly regarded as inherent self-ascriptions in their own right. It follows that a person may attribute positive or negative worth to the inherent self-ascription of attributing positive or negative worth to a non-inherent self-ascription. It is in such terms, for example, that a person might rationalize his disposition to experience diminution on account of feeling enhancement for attributing positive worth to his self-ascription of having blue eyes (i.e., he feels shame for taking pride in his blue eyes).

In the next two sections, I examine the most important species of inherent reason: those we undergo when we believe we are enjoying or appreciating what has intrinsic worth (5.5) and those related to achievements (5.6). Although these two reasons often overlap in the activities of ordinary life, it is important to understand them as distinct reasons.

5.5 Consider first the case of my enjoying or appreciating a ballet. It is conceivable that I enjoy the ballet at a purely sensual level, in the way one enjoys a back rub. But in addition to this reason, there are several ways my self-esteem could become engaged. One way borders on the self-conscious and snobbish. I might find myself, for example, attributing positive worth to my enjoying a ballet on the grounds that it is the kind of thing done by people with proper sensibilities. On the other hand, my self-esteem might be affected in a more subtle way. We do not see enjoying back rubs as worthy of praise or admiration because we do not find back rubs themselves intrinsically worthy (as I mentioned in 1.3, we can find something enjoyable without believing the object of our enjoyment has positive worth). By contrast, we may well think that enjoying ballet has positive worth, since it makes sense to think of ballet itself as possessing positive worth. Now in this latter type of experience lies an important source of inherent reasons for self-esteem. In order to analyse this experience, we have to expand our understanding of intrinsic worth.

In 1.6 the concept of intrinsic worth was introduced in the context of justifying a reason for self-esteem. A Reasonable Person asks himself whether he sincerely finds a self-ascription worthy of praise or admiration for what the relevant property is in itself. But it is not only properties of people (and thereby the people themselves) that we find worthy of praise or admiration, but the properties of other entities as well. Recognizing this fact, we can add the following dimension to our understanding of intrinsic worth.

When we find something praiseworthy or admirable on account of its intrinsically worthy properties, then we are disposed to *attend* to the entity with a distinctive pleasure. This attentive pleasure is partly constituted by aesthetic and moral feelings or dispositions. In particular, we are disposed to judge that it would be morally wrong, or at least morally regrettable, to destroy, damage, or harm the entity, even if the entity could be replaced by another entity which is equally praiseworthy or admirable. This aspect of intrinsic worth is to be contrasted with the attitude of seeing something as having purely *instrumental value* (I say "purely" because in some cases we value things as both intrinsically worthy and instrumentally valuable). In the case of instrumental valuing, we *see past* the entity, as it were, to some need or desire which the entity serves; moreover, replacing the entity with another of equal value does not cause moral regret. Think of the difference, for example, between looking at a quilt purely from the point of view of whether it will keep one warm versus attending to the quilt on account of its beauty and workmanship. If my sole interest is in being warm, then any given warm quilt will do; and it could be replaced, without regret on my part, by any other quilt with equivalent thermal properties. On the other hand, if I attend to the quilt on account of its beauty or workmanship, then I am disposed to judge it wrong or regrettable to destroy the quilt, even if it could be replaced by another of equal worth. In this sense, the quilt has for me an irreplaceable value. There are now several clarifications to make.

In the first place, when we attend to something as intrinsically worthy, I do not mean to imply that we necessarily believe it wrong, *all things considered*, to destroy, damage, or harm that thing, for other, weightier moral considerations may override. Indeed, we may attend to something as intrinsically worthy and yet judge that its moral value, all things considered, is relatively small. At the same time, when weightier considerations do override, we still feel that something of irreplaceable value has been lost; thus there is moral regret. Another aspect of this point is as follows. If something of intrinsic worth is destroyed and then replaced with something of equal worth, we still believe it would be better if the original entity were *also* in existence. In this sense, though we may be happy with the replacement, we do not regard the value *per se* of the original entity as ever replaced.

Note, secondly, that on my analysis, what has intrinsic worth is relative to an agent. It follows that if there were no agents to appreciate or attend to things, then so far as my analysis goes, there would be nothing that has intrinsic worth. It might be argued that in the final analysis, judgments of intrinsic worth, though relative in themselves, nevertheless presuppose some higher-level belief in impersonal or absolute values. I grant this possibility. However, I leave the question open, since nothing in my argument hinges on how the question is answered.

Finally, our judgments of intrinsic worth arise in response to a thing's characteristics. For example, it is (we may imagine) the ballet's *beautiful movement* and its *emotional subtlety* which elicit our judgments of intrinsic worth. It follows that when we say the ballet has intrinsic worth, we really mean that the ballet-insofar-as-it-displays-beautiful-movement, and so on, has intrinsic worth. This means that an entity's intrinsic worth, on my analysis, is contingent on the characteristics it exemplifies. At the same time, it not that we value the beautiful movement abstracted from the particular event which is the ballet. Attention to a *particular* entity or event is an ineliminable part of the experience of intrinsic worth.

Keeping these clarifications in mind, let us now see how the enjoyment or appreciation of what has intrinsic worth can give rise to inherent reasons for self-esteem. To find a ballet intrinsically worthy is to manifest interest in the ballet. A person who does so, therefore, has the self-ascription of attending to the ballet on account of its intrinsic worthiness. If now a person attributes positive worth to this self-ascription, he thereby has an inherent reason for self-esteem; that is, he *derives enhancement* through attributing positive worth to the self-ascription of attending to the ballet on account of its intrinsic worthiness.

Note that the enhancement which comes from having an inherent reason of this kind is generally experienced *unselfconsciously*, for this enhancement is part and parcel of an experience which consists mainly in a heightening and deepening of attention to the object of interest. On this point, we must make the following distinction in the phenomenology of self-esteem. There are, on the one hand, distinct feelings of enhancement or diminution which occur at specific moments in our lives, and which may become the focus of our attention. On the other hand, there is also a constant hum of feeling-tone in the background to what is occupying our attention from moment to moment.[8] This background tone varies in its hedonic quality and results from a mixture of feelings, some of which are purely somatic. An important element in this mixture, however, is constituted by the kind of self-esteem feelings I have been describing: the sense that what one is doing, enjoying, or appreciating has intrinsic worth. Moreover, the absence of this kind of feeling is felt as background displeasure and is connected to that form of unhappiness in which a person has no settled ideal self (see 1.9).

I have said that these self-esteem feelings are typically experienced in an unselfconscious way. It might be asked whether this characteristic is consistent with their being *self*-esteem feelings, since, on my analysis, such feelings have to be connected to a self-ascription, and a self-ascription presupposes at some level, it might be argued, direct attention to self. But the fact is, our consciousness has the kind of complexity which allows us both to be absorbed in something and to be aware of *our* being so absorbed (unless our absorption is so intense that we are in rapture). In general, when we are undergoing or doing something, we at the same time know that we are undergoing or doing this thing: if someone, for example, were to ask us what we are doing, we can generally stop and answer him. But to be self-aware in this fashion is to have a subconscious self-ascription which at the same time leaves our attention focused on something outside ourselves. This kind of self-ascription is most often the grounds for the enhancement which lies in the background of our attention. There is, therefore, no contradiction between undergoing an inherent reason for self-esteem and focusing on something of intrinsic worth outside ourselves.

This discussion helps us further understand the notion of a secondary self-esteem desire introduced in 1.8. I said there that self-esteem desires constitute part of the motivation underlying many of our actions, including actions which are properly regarded as other-concerned. It is easier now to see how such desires could enter into an act's motivation and at the same time not negate that act's being genuinely other-concerned, for self-esteem desires arise, as I explained in chapter 1, through the occurrence or anticipation of self-esteem feelings. Once we see, therefore, how such feelings, through their connection to inherent reasons, can lie beneath the surface of attention, we can better understand how the intention of an act may be other-concerned, even though part of the underlying motivation consists in self-esteem desires. I shall return to this topic in chapter 9. Let us now turn to the second species of inherent reason.

5.6 We feel enhanced when we believe we have significantly contributed, through our voluntary acts, to some valuable state of affairs. I shall call one such type of inherent reason *achievements*. Achievements are usefully contrasted with another type of enhancement connected to voluntary acts, namely, that enhancement which accompanies a person's belief that he has done what is morally right – the feeling of a good conscience. This latter reason typically occurs in the context of some choice in which we believe the possibility of doing wrong is also open to us. In the case of achievement, on the other hand, the relevant contrast is not between right and wrong, but between success and failure.

Take the example of Smith's sense that building her own house is an achievement. The concept of achievement, as I shall understand it, implies that the following two conditions hold: (1) Smith believes that the state of affairs she has helped to produce (in this case the house) has positive worth; and (2) she believes that the valued state of affairs is above some standard, a standard relative either to her own customary performance or above the standard for such performances generally.[9] Smith might believe, for example, that her house has an especially attractive design or that completing it on schedule required an extraordinary effort. Apart from these defining conditions, there is the following important fact about achievements. The ability or effort required for an achievement usually requires a series of voluntary acts stretching over a significant period of time. So, for example, if a house is to be built, plans must be made, materials bought, helpers hired, planks sawed, and so on. In this way, achievements bind together diverse acts in a person's life through forethought, memory, and a common goal.

An important type of enhancement, which we may call *feelings of desert*, is often supervenient upon the original enhancement of achievement. When we judge that a person gets something he deserves, we see a benefit or harm coming to that person which is fitting to something he is or has done. For example, we might say of Smith, who has worked hard to finish her house, that she deserves a rest or that she deserves to enjoy the house. The benefit here is the rest or the enjoyment, and we judge these to be deserved because we see them as fitting to Smith's achievement. Now if she herself sees these benefits as deserved, then she comes to have the self-ascription getting-what-I-deserve-for-building-my-house. This self-ascription may then enter into her inherent reason for self-esteem and thereby deepen the enhancement she experiences on account of her achievement.

There is one kind of benefit a person may see as deserved which requires special mention, namely, the benefit of recognition from informed others. Smith, say, is a good architect and derives enhancement from this fact. We may also imagine that her colleagues admire and respect her for being a good architect and thereby contribute to her reputation. Her good reputation is a benefit she may well believe she deserves. Given this, the enhancement related to her recognition must deepen Smith's inherent self-esteem regarding her architectural work. As well, we may assume that she herself respects and admires some of her colleagues, who respect and admire her. This fact must both further intensify her inherent reason for self-esteem (through what in chapter 2 I called mixed reflected self-evaluations) and at the same time engender a sense of fellowship with her colleagues. This complex mental state is one of the deepest and most satisfying a person can experience. In chapter 6, we shall see how the Reasonable Person has open to him sources of this inherent reason in virtue of his defining commitment.[10]

Before turning to the connection between inherent reasons and the trait related to such reasons, I shall mention a contrary way of conceiving inherent reasons and their relation to justifiable self-esteem. In the contrary view, what is inherent to an agent is *solely* his achievements, and reasons for self-esteem are justifiable only insofar as they can be linked to what a person directly produces through his voluntary acts. In proposing such a view, Robert J. Yanal, for example, writes that "a person [gains justified] self-esteem just when he pins his self-esteem on those of his qualities he has a large share in bringing about."[11] But what such a theory misses is precisely that species of inherent reason which derives from our appreciating what has intrinsic worth. We do not directly control our manifestations of interest. Nor do we usually have a major part in bringing about the worthy states of affairs to which we attend. Nevertheless, on my theory, self-ascriptions related to such inherent reasons issue from ourselves just as much as do achievements. We shall see the significance of this aspect of my theory when, in chapter 6, I describe how the RP can feel himself part of a worthy tradition.

5.7 A person with the trait of corporativeness has a self-image tied integrally to social groups. A person with *a sense of inherent worth*, on the contrary, has a self-image which deepens his sense that he is a distinct individual. In the following sections, I want to show, first, the connection between inherent reasons and the sense of inherent worth and, second, how the Reasonable Person, through being disposed to have inherent reasons, acquires a sense of inherent worth. Before turning to these arguments, we must first understand what is meant by a person's sense that he is a distinct individual.

However closely any two people resemble each other, it is an incontrovertible fact that they are numerically distinct (i.e., unique) individuals. Indeed, every entity is in this sense distinct from every other entity. In addition, each person possesses a distinct point of view and history (as do members of other animal species). Most of us believe that this history began at a specific time and will end with death. On a person's death, then, a unique point of view and history ceases to exist. The property of possessing a unique point of view and history, as it applies to humans, I shall call *person-distinctness*. (In later chapters, I shall also sometimes use the more emotively charged *person-singularity* to denote the same concept.)[12] Now to give moral (and thereby psychological) weight to this property as it applies to oneself is what I mean by possessing a sense of inherent worth. To clarify this latter notion, I must say more about person-distinctness.

The concept of person-distinctness is implicit in the way we exercise our capacity to make self-ascriptions. To ascribe a characteristic to oneself is to refer to oneself (which in English we do mainly with the word "I"), and to refer to oneself is *ipso facto* to distinguish oneself from all other entities in the world. Many of our self-ascriptions presuppose we have a history. This assumption is most evident when I ascribe to myself the characteristic of having done or felt something in the past. It is also evident when I ascribe to myself some personality trait, such as being quick-tempered, for such a self-ascription presupposes I have behaved in a quick-tempered way in the past.

Now it is one thing to apply the concept of person-distinctness to oneself and yet another to give moral weight to the self-ascription. In an analogous way, we can imagine that two people each know that the property of being a Canadian applies to himself, but that only one of them attaches weight to the fact. And just as we can ask what factors contribute to a person's giving weight to his being a Canadian, so we can ask what factors contribute to a person's sense of being a distinct person. Before discussing such factors, I must make the following clarification.

Few philosophers would deny that we are distinct individuals with a history and an inner life – subjects-of-a-life, to use Tom Regan's apt phrase.[13] Difficulties arise, however, when we try to say more clearly in what our identities through time, *qua* distinct individuals, consist. Does the concept of personal identity presuppose, for example, that there is some one unchanging thing which we uniquely are and which remains the same throughout our lives? In this case, the unity of our lives from birth to death would be ascribable to this underlying entity which binds the temporal stages of our lives together. If our ordinary concept of personal identity does presuppose this, does the ordinary concept, as some argue, rest on a false belief? Would it in fact be truer to say that our identity through time consists simply in the continuity and connectedness of our changing properties, without there necessarily being some one thing which remains the same? In this latter view, we would ultimately be a kind of association of changing life-stages. Now it is important to see that neither of these metaphysical interpretations denies that we are distinct individuals with a history and an inner life. In particular, my being an association of evolving properties does not mean I do not exist as a numerically distinct individual, just as a table's being composed of ever-changing molecules does not mean that it is not a table distinct from other tables. Perhaps, if we accept this "association" view, we might have a reason, as Derek Parfit argues, to think of our being distinct individuals as of less psychological and moral importance than we are ordinarily inclined to think.[14] But then, as Parfit himself says, this judgment of less importance is not a logical entailment of the association view. It follows that we might have reasons, independent of either view, to attribute importance to our person-distinctness.[15] In the following section, I shall argue that undergoing inherent reasons for self-esteem inclines us to deepen the weight we give our person-distinctness. Then later in the book I shall argue that, from the moral point of view, this can be a good thing. The gist of my argument in this paragraph has been that there is nothing in the metaphysical debate over personal identity which itself precludes the position I shall defend.

5.8 Our esteem for others, via attributions of intrinsic worth, contains a moral-cum-aesthetic response to these others. In a parallel way, when we esteem ourselves, there is implicit in our esteem this same attentive pleasure, though in our own case this pleasure often constitutes part of that background feeling-tone I described earlier. It is through this attentive aspect of self-esteem that we can partly understand how inherent reasons add positive weight to our sense of personal distinctness and thereby give us a sense of inherent worth.

When the corporative personality esteems himself, he sees himself with pleasure, but only through some relationship to a social group. By means of his role, his status, the praise he engenders, or the social conventions through which he expresses his inner life, the corporative personality values himself as part of a larger entity. Analogously, I might look with aesthetic pleasure at the hill outside my window, but only in so far as it is an integral part of the general landscape. For me, the hill has no properties in its own right which draw an aesthetic response. We should note that I am still aware of the hill as an object distinct from other objects. It is just that I do not attach *significance* to the hill as a distinct object. Similarly, the corporative personality, although he is aware of himself as a distinct individual, nevertheless values himself only as part of a larger whole.

On the other hand, take the case of Smith's achievement of building her own house. As I discussed earlier, she sees this achievement as issuing from her own self, and this view provides the grounds for an inherent reason for self-esteem. As well, in the broad sense of "responsible" which characterizes manifestations of interest, Smith feels responsible for this value which issues from her self. For these reasons, the moral-aesthetic pleasure connected to her inherent reason is directed to Smith herself, that is, to Smith as an entity distinct from others. Moreover, as we should gather from my earlier discussion, Smith's self-attentive pleasure causes her to feel that she possesses irreplaceable value; for if it were not for her, as distinct from others, there would be *that* much less intrinsic worth in the world. Smith's inherent reason, then, not only leads her to be aware of herself as a distinct individual, but also causes her to give positive weight to this fact. And insofar as this is true, her sense of inherent worth is deepened. A similar point applies to any other inherent reason. For example, when I derive self-esteem through appreciating what has intrinsic worth, such as in the case of the ballet, then my sense of myself as a distinct individual is deepened. For I implicitly feel myself responsible for my response, and I thereby experience the positive worth connected to the response as issuing from myself as an entity distinct from other entities.

Two other features of inherent reasons serve to deepen our sense of inherent worth. First, there is the fact that it is often through inherent self-ascriptions that we see ourselves as different from others. I see myself as different from those who do not enjoy ballet, different again from those have not built their own houses, and different yet again from those who do not love the people I love. None of these self-ascriptions are necessarily unique to me, and so it is not that they logically establish my personal distinctness.[16] But in entering into my self-image through being connected to inherent reasons, these self-ascriptions nevertheless give psychological weight to the way I differ from others and thereby enliven my sense of inherent worth: they are the colours and contours in terms of which I picture myself as distinct from others.[17]

A further way that inherent reasons deepen our sense of inherent worth lies in the manner in which achievements, personal attachments, and the enjoyment of what has intrinsic worth bind together past events in our lives with present and future concerns. We saw in 5.6 how this is true regarding achievements, such as Smith's building her own house. Similarly, John's love for Jane is likely to be steeped in memories of things they have done together, as well as in thoughts for the future which involve the two of them. In this way, his sense of himself as having a distinct history and inner life is deepened through attributing positive worth to his love for Jane.

As a corollary to our discussion, there is the following relevant consideration. We can imagine a person who is doing all he wants to do with his life (and so has maximum freedom in this sense), but nevertheless lacks a strong sense of inherent worth. One cause of such non-inherence, of course, might be that a person's self-esteem is dominated by reflected, competitive, or derived reasons. But a distinct cause is that he lacks either the interest or the capacity to attribute worth to the way he manifests interest as a focus of attention in its own right. For example, it may be that for such a person it is only his impact on the external world which matters, whereas his inner response to things matters very little (one could imagine such a person keeping an appointment book, but not a real diary). This kind of personality is sometimes found in men and women of action and also in some saints. From a quite different point of view, George Orwell in *1984* describes a society in which people lack a sense of inherent worth because they have been conditioned not to care, even implicitly, about their inner responses. In thinking about his mother, Winston has the following insight about the workings of the Party:

He would have liked to continue talking about his mother. He did not suppose, from what he could remember of her, that she had been an unusual woman, still less an intelligent one; and yet she had possessed a kind of nobility, a kind of purity … Her feelings were her own, and could not be altered from outside. It would not have occurred to her that action which is ineffectual thereby becomes meaningless. If you loved someone, you loved him, and when you had nothing else to give, you still gave him love. When the last of the chocolate was gone, his mother had clasped the child in her arms. It was no use, it changed nothing, it did not produce more chocolate, it did not avert the child's death or her own; but it seemed natural to her to do it … The terrible thing that the Party had done was to persuade you that mere impulses, mere feelings, were of no account, while at the same time robbing you of all power over the material world. When once you were in the grip of the Party, what you felt or did not feel, what you did or refrained from doing made literally no difference. And yet to the people of only two generations ago … [what] mattered were individual relationships, and a completely helpless gesture, an embrace, a tear, a word spoken to a dying man, could have value in itself.[18]

For the people in Orwell's dystopia, as for "practical" people who care only about results, a strong sense of inherent worth is absent, just as it is absent in the lives of people whose self-esteem focuses on reflected, competitive, or derived reasons.

In the context of the above discussion, it is important to emphasize a point analogous to one I made in the previous chapter. A sense of inherent worth is not at all incompatible with a view of oneself as embedded, to a significant degree, in social relationships. Smith, for example, might be deeply conscious of how her architectural skills have been shaped by traditions which go back generations, or of how her desire to design and build a house issues from obligations she feels toward her family. Nothing I have said implies that these social connections are incompatible with a sense of inherent worth. Philosophers who suggest such an incompatibility often fail to make subtle enough distinctions related to our self-esteem. With this point in mind, I now turn to the relationship of the Reasonable Person to the sense of inherent worth.

5.9 In the previous three chapters, we have seen that when the RP evaluates reflected, competitive or derived reasons, he is disposed to undercut these reasons. What I wish now to show is that this process contributes to his having a sense of inherent worth.

In the first place, we can see that when the RP undercuts a pure reflected self-evaluation in himself, he thereby generally acquires an inherent reason. Take as an example Smith's deriving enhancement through a pure reflected self-evaluation grounded in the fact that the Rotary Club has honoured her for the design of her new house. As an RP, Smith must decide about the appropriateness of the club's evaluation of her achievement. In considering its reasons for valuing her designs, she may come in her *own right* to accept these as good reasons. This outcome in turn allows her to see the honour bestowed on her as deserved. Smith now has two intermingled reasons for self-esteem: that related to her achievement and that which arises out of the club's recognition. Moreover, the primary reason, upon which the second reason supervenes, is an inherent one. Thus, in evaluating and undercutting her reflected reason, Smith's sense of inherent worth is strengthened.

There is the further point that, insofar as Smith is an RP, she sees herself as having the ability to determine her own reasons for self-esteem through making these reasons autonomous. Now people exercise their capacity for autonomy by means of voluntary acts. It is appropriate, then, for Smith to see her autonomous activity as issuing from herself. Here, therefore, is the basis for an additional, powerful inherent reason for self-esteem, a reason, moreover, which is grounded in her defining commitment *qua* RP.

The RP also comes to have inherent reasons when he evaluates competitive self-evaluations. Take a person, for example, whose self-esteem is focused on his being a better piano player than specific others. We saw in 3.3 that in undercutting this competitive reason, our pianist RP is led to focus on the quality of his own piano playing, and in particular to think of his piano playing in terms of a grading self-ascription rather than as a purely competitive self-ascription. This in turn opens up the possibility for the RP to attribute positive worth to his own piano-playing ability and thereby be provided with the basis for an inherent reason for self-esteem.

It is clear, as well, that the RP comes to have inherent reasons when he undercuts derived reasons in himself. To have derived reasons regarding a group is, we have seen, to be pliant regarding the group's norms. In chapter 4 I showed that, regarding any group norm, the RP sees himself as capable of evaluating the norm in accord with the critical guidelines. This means that he sees the authority for determining his beliefs as ultimately lying in his own capacity for reasoning, rather than in either the group itself or in some representative of the group. Since the RP exercises this capacity through voluntary acts, the reasons for self-esteem which arise from this exercise are inherent reasons; and so again his sense of inherent worth is strengthened. Another angle on this same point is as follows. To have an identification reason in relation to a group is to manifest interest in that group. Now the RP must determine, from the point of view of the guidelines, whether the way he manifests interest is reasonable.

In determining this, he is at the same time made aware, through the process of evaluation itself, that the way he manifests interest is *his* responsibility and does not follow automatically from his membership in the group. This awareness in turn makes the RP conscious of his distinctness from the very group in which he manifests interest. In considering this process, we see again the insight of Burckhardt's claim that the rise of individualism is tied historically to people's capacity to treat social groups "objectively."

We saw in the previous chapter that the RP is apt to experience ambivalence in his loyalty to groups. There was first the point that he is not disposed to exclusive altruism, which means that loyalty to his own group is never undivided when its interests conflict with the interests of people outside the group. Second, there was the fact that the RP recognizes that the attachment he feels toward his group is always in potential conflict with his commitment to reflect on the norms of the group, especially those norms which structure his own social roles. I said in 4.9 that the tension generated by this ambivalence may be productive of good. Now one effect of his the RP's ambivalence toward group membership is that he is made more intensely aware that it is he himself, and not the group, who must determine what his beliefs and loyalties are to be. This in turn strengthens his sense of inherent worth.

The Reasonable Person, as I have been describing him, starts from a strong commitment – his defining commitment – to apply critical guidelines 1–5. In this part of the book, we have seen how this defining commitment, when applied to his self-esteem, leads the RP to regard certain traits as consonant with his defining nature: these are the *consonant traits* of autonomy, non-competitive self-esteem, non-corporativeness, and an inherent sense of worth. His ideal self, with its motivational thrust, comes then to incorporate these consonant traits. This enlarged commitment is what I call the Reasonable Person's *core nature*. In previous chapters, we saw that there are powerful forces which pull the RP away from his defining commitment. What we must now see is whether his core nature supports a way of life which can counter these forces.

PART TWO

Elements in
a Way of Life

6 Finding Meaning in Reasonableness

In this chapter, I show how meaning is added to the Reasonable Person's life through her identifying with a worthy tradition. One aspect of this identification is that she comes to have self-respect *qua* Reasonable Person. Then in chapter 8 I argue that, in virtue of her core nature, the RP acquires *egalitarian self-respect*, that is, the attitude that she has equal moral status to any other person. These two kinds of self-respect are significant personal goods, and they help the RP sustain her defining commitment. My argument, then, requires that we have an understanding of self-respect. We shall see that both forms of self-respect relevant to the RP exemplify a common structure.

A: SELF-RESPECT

6.1 Although self-esteem and self-respect are sometimes used synonymously, there are forms of self-evaluation which the concept of self-respect brings into much sharper focus.[1] That the two concepts are usefully distinguished can be seen as follows. Consider the case of Jane, who fails to protest when her legal right not to be sexually harassed is violated by her boss, even though she could have protested without great sacrifice. We judge her to lack (egalitarian) self-respect if we assume that her failure to protest shows that she sees herself as having less moral status than her boss.[2] At the same time, we need not assume that Jane lacks self-esteem (or, in my terms, experiences diminution) on account of her failure to protest. She may simply find it natural to see her interests as counting for less than her boss's. In this situation, we might indeed think that Jane *ought* to experience a fall in self-esteem for showing lack of self-respect. This example clearly shows that the two concepts are usefully distinguished.[3]

Although philosophers usually concern themselves specifically with egalitarian self-respect, self-respect clearly has non-egalitarian applications. We talk in particular of people being or not being self-respecting Xs, where X stands for some social role, position, or status. We say, for example, "No self-respecting *carpenter* would make a table like that." Mrs Denner from *Felix Holt*, as we saw in chapter 4, thinks of herself as a self-respecting *servant*. It is this concept of self-respect which I analyse in a moment. I shall then apply this analysis to the case of the Reasonable Person in part B of the chapter. In addition, this analysis will clarify the relationship between self-respect and self-esteem. Moreover, as we shall see in chapter 8, egalitarian self-respect is properly seen as one specification of the generic concept where "human" or "person" have come, in the course of history, to be an available substitutions for the X: no self-respecting *person*, we say, would permit what Jane permitted. Important philosophical lessons emerge when we see egalitarian self-respect in this context. I begin, then, by stating five conditions which hold when we judge a person (including ourselves) to be or not to be a self-respecting X, where X stands for some social role, position, or status:

1 We judge the person genuinely to occupy the role or position in question. We would withdraw our accusation of John's not being a self-respecting carpenter, for example, if we discovered that he was not, and made no pretense of being, a carpenter, even though he did engage from time to time in carpentry activities. I shall call the role or position which grounds our self-respect judgments in this way the *status attribute*.

2 We accept that there are norms which count as fulfilling the relevant role or position properly, successfully, or adequately.

Then:

3 When we judge that a person *is* a self-respecting X, we judge that the person (a) meets the relevant norms and (b) meets these norms because she is strongly motivated to do so on account of evaluating herself positively *qua* X.

And:

4 When we judge that a person is *not* a self-respecting X, we judge that the person (a) does not meet the relevant norms and (b) fails

to meet these norms because, though she may value being an X, she does not value being an X strongly enough to be sufficiently motivated to meet the norms.

And:

5 When we judge a person to be a self-respecting X, we expect her to experience enhancement when she meets the relevant norms and diminution when she fails to meet them. Moreover, a self-respecting X expects others, or at least believes it appropriate that others, should respect or admire her when she meets the relevant norms.

It is important now to ask why conditions 3b and 4b are necessary to understand our self-respect judgments. Say John is a carpenter and meets the criteria for being a good carpenter. Suppose, however, that he is cynical about the profession of carpentry and sees it only as a way of making money: he finds no intrinsic worth in carpentry. We would not in this case judge John to be a self-respecting carpenter, even though he satisfies conditions 1, 2, and 3a. For he must meet the norms *because* he values in the appropriate manner his status attribute of being a carpenter. In a parallel way, we would not judge John not to be a self-respecting carpenter if we thought his failure to meet the relevant norms was due to circumstances beyond his control. Rather, the failure must be due to his lacking the motivation because he does not value in the appropriate manner his being a carpenter. How more specifically are we to understand this self-valuing by the agent of the status attribute when she is judged to be a self-respecting X?

It is clear that what is required is that the agent attribute *positive worth* to the relevant status attribute. Now to attribute positive worth to a self-ascription is to be disposed to feel enhanced self-esteem. There are then two distinct ways our self-esteem becomes engaged in our self-respect. There is the enhancement or diminution we feel when we meet or do not meet the relevant norms, as detailed in condition 5 above. And there is the disposition to experience enhancement when we ascribe to ourselves the relevant status attribute.

If John is a self-respecting carpenter, we are to imagine that he attributes positive worth to his being a carpenter. But then the question can be asked, On what basis does John make this attribution of worth? It cannot be that his justification rests mainly on the good results which occur when he himself meets the norms for being a good carpenter. For then the justification would run in too tight a circle, since John is motivated in the first place to meet the norms because he attributes positive worth to his being a carpenter. What is open to John, however, and what I believe fits such cases, is that he should see the worthiness of his being a carpenter as justified by what we can think of as the *tradition* of carpentry. He could justifiably believe that carpentry is a valuable tradition, both because of the subtle talents which it fosters and because of the beautiful and useful things carpenters, past and present, have built. For these reasons, John would find it natural to see being a carpenter as intrinsically worthy and thereby be motivated to meet the relevant norms for what counts as being a good carpenter; that is, be motivated to become a self-respecting carpenter. I am using "tradition" here in a very broad sense and mean by it simply a set of skills, practices, styles of thinking, which is passed on, subject to evolution, over a series of generations. This definition will suffice for the present, but in part B I shall expand on it. We may now generalize the point I have been making in this paragraph in terms of the following condition:

6 Whenever a person judges herself to be or not to be a self-respecting X, we may typically see these judgments as grounded in a reason for self-esteem which attributes positive worth to being part of the X tradition.

In concluding this analysis, we must note the connection between self-respect and the exercise of rights. Prior to equal human rights becoming widely institutionalized, rights attached to people mainly in virtue of their class, occupation, role, or social status. The social stratification of people was reflected in the legal stratification of rights. This meant that people found it natural to assimilate the norms which defined their rights to the norms which defined their class or occupation. These rights-related norms in turn became a component of the norms which defined how a self-respecting X was to behave (*per* condition 2 above). So, for example, if members of the carpenters' guild had the right to first bid on new lumber, then we may imagine that exercising this right became part of what counted as a self-respecting carpenter. Moreover, to see oneself as possessing a right is to see oneself, by definition, as having a claim on others to respect that right.[4] The self-respecting carpenter, then, would see it as her *proper due* that others respect her right to first bid on new lumber, and she would be disposed to protest if this right were violated. We can see as well that the self-respecting carpenter would regard the propriety of exercising her rights *qua* carpenter as resting on the prior value she attributes to the status attribute of being a carpenter (per condition 6 above). We shall see more of the significance of this connection between rights and self-respect when we come to egalitarian self-respect.

In light of the above analysis, I turn now to show that the RP can regard reasonableness as a tradition and thereby see being an RP as a status attribute upon which to ground her self-respect. This self-conception provides direction and meaning in her life, especially when she regards science as a sub-tradition within the broader tradition. I realize that it is not usual to regard reasonableness as a tradition: there is no self-identified tradition "out there" for the RP to adopt, as there is for someone who decides to become, say, a Roman Catholic. I shall argue, however, that the RP, from her own point of view, can construct the concept of such a tradition and thereby derive benefits analogous to those which people derive from more conventional traditions.

B: REASONABLENESS AS A TRADITION

6.2 I have defined a tradition as a set of skills, practices, styles of thinking, which is passed on, subject to evolution, over a series of generations. It is useful to begin by showing how reasonableness can be conceived as fitting this rather limited definition.

In the first place, we can see reasonableness as a *skill* which people possess to varying degrees. This skill consists in forming beliefs, both theoretical and action-guiding, in accord with standards such as I have outlined in the critical guidelines. That is, to be reasonable is to exercise the skill of forming beliefs which are in accord with the relevant evidence (guideline 2); which are consistent (guideline 3); which are weighted in accord with any relevant values (guidelines 1, 5, and 6); which are subsumed, when appropriate, by more fundamental beliefs (guideline 4); which are open to relevant criticism by others (guideline 2); and which are not influenced by biased or wishful thinking (guidelines 2 and 5). Recalling the analysis in chapter 1, my claim is not that these skills are self-consciously exercised when people make reasonable judgments. Nevertheless, a person who denied that the exercise of these skills is partly what constitutes holding a reasonable belief would be as mistaken as a person who denied that whales are mammals.

We exercise the skill of reasonableness when we make up our minds what to believe or what to do, and also when we debate, discuss, or argue with others. Such activities are the *practices* relevant to the tradition of reasonableness. These practices result in attitudes, arguments, theories, world-views, and books; these latter in turn influence the practices of later generations, and so the tradition evolves. The RP enters into these practices, moreover, with a distinctive spirit. For it is characteristic of her that she assigns priority in her scheme of values to exercising reasonableness, and this commitment must show itself in her behaviour. For example, we would expect the RP to strive to make her beliefs or actions reasonable, even at some personal cost. And we would expect her, in discussion with others, to focus on achieving reasonableness rather than allowing her mind to be influenced by irrelevantly emotional or egoistic considerations. Later in this chapter, I shall give an example of this spirit at work. But first I must expand our understanding of what a tradition is.

6.3 To feel herself part of a tradition, the RP must be able to look to the past and see that earlier expressions of the tradition have influenced her own way of being reasonable. She must also see that the relevant skills and practices have undergone evolution – that they have a history. Another requirement is that the RP encounter in this history admirable people whom she regards as fellow-spirits or exemplars. Now some writers claim that a tradition's history must necessarily be embedded in social groups whose members share customs, rituals, language, and a specific geographic locale. Alasdair MacIntyre, for example, writes, "Traditions are always and ineradically to some degree local, informed by particularities of language and social and natural environment, inhabited by Greeks or by citizens of Roman Africa or medieval Persia or by eighteenth-century Scots."[5] This view, however, is overstated. The Judaeo-Christian tradition, the tradition of Western art, and the tradition of democracy embrace many cultures, languages, and geographic locales, yet they are properly called traditions. What *is* true, however, is that these transcultural traditions typically encompass the localized traditions to which MacIntyre refers. The lesson we should draw is that if we want to conceive of reasonableness as a tradition, we need not be forced into thinking of it in terms of one specific geographic location, or in terms of one set of customs or rituals. At the same time, we should also expect to find socially and geographically particularized instances of the broader tradition. In examining how the RP may look to the past to construct a tradition of reasonableness, we shall find this lesson useful.

Another important fact about traditions is that many of them embody defining purposes with which their members identify.[6] For example, one of the defining purposes of the Catholic tradition is to transmit religious truth. Moreover, such traditions often see themselves as competing with other traditions with which they share a defining purpose, each viewing itself as the best means to achieve the purpose in question. So, for example, to understand the tradition of Catholicism, we must compare and contrast it to other religious traditions, such as Protestantism, with which it has competed historically. Now through the concept of a defining purpose, and also the contrastive way many traditions must be conceived, lies the path to understanding reasonableness as a tradition.

In the first place, I want to say that we should see the defining goal of reasonableness as that of achieving epistemologically worthy beliefs, both theoretical and practical. Another, equivalent way to describe this goal is to say that reasonableness aims to increase our understanding of the world and of the best way to act. A question now for the RP is whether she can see her way of exercising reasonableness as continuous with the way others, in different times and places, have formed their beliefs. I want to say, in answer to this question, that by looking at specific historical conflicts over epistemological issues, it is often possible to judge one of the adversaries to be carrying the standard of reasonableness, even though reasonableness in each situation does not mean exactly the same thing. Let us briefly consider two examples of such defining historical contrasts.

(1) If Aristotle were transported to the present, with his beliefs and method of doing science intact, he would hardly be regarded, by today's standards, as the great contributor to the tradition of reasonableness that he is. But what makes the RP see Aristotle as a watershed is twofold: (a) For the first time in history, the RP sees systematically enunciated some of the principles she now accepts as critical guidelines;[7] and (b) the RP sees a determination to apply these principles in explicit opposition to myth-making, prophecy, and divination; these latter practices being strong competing traditions against the epistemological standards Aristotle was developing.[8] In examining his writings in the context of these Greek debates, then, the RP recognizes Aristotle as a precursor.

(2) In seventeenth-century Europe, Galileo's writings led to conflict between defenders of the new science and various forms of philosophical and theological authority. Natural philosophers of the time, for example, objected to his view that objects in the heavens could undergo change in the same way as objects on earth. Against Galileo, the philosophers brought, often dogmatically, the authority of Aristotle.[9] Theologians objected to Galileo's view that the earth moves, and they relied, often dogmatically, on biblical authority.[10] Now as contemporary scholars have shown, intelligent and good-willed people of the period legitimately disagreed, in terms of the evidence then available, over some of Galileo's specific claims. Also, through all his difficulties, he never ceased to see himself as a loyal Catholic.[11] But what makes the Reasonable Person recognize in Galileo a precursor is disclosed through the contrast between him and those who dogmatically defended the authority of Aristotle or the

Church. Against their dogmatism, Galileo advocated understanding nature through empirical testing, mathematical reasoning, openness to falsification, and the separation of science from theological intervention.[12] It is through examining this conflict in its concrete historical setting that the RP comes to see Galileo as a precursor.

These two examples suggest how the RP can gain for herself a sense of belonging to a tradition, even given the diversity of beliefs and styles of thinking shown by contributors to the tradition.[13] Moreover, through this same contrastive approach, she can see the tradition of reasonableness evolving from the present into the future. The contemporary world presents many ideologies, theories, and religions which compete for people's epistemological allegiance. In bringing the guidelines to bear on these competing belief systems, the RP naturally distinguishes between those which are epistemologically worthy and those which are not. In making these distinctions, she is, with the help of others, clarifying for herself the nature of reasonableness, just as she does when she examines conflicts of the past. In this way, she helps to sustain the evolution of the tradition.

6.4 It may be hard to see how the tradition of reasonableness, which lacks shared social structures and rituals, could engender feelings of belonging. I shall partly address this issue later under the topic of *local communities*. However, there is an aspect of it to be considered here relating to the question of exemplars.

Even if the RP does not have available to her shared structures and rituals, she has books and her imagination to connect her to worthy precursors. And these can engender a sense of belonging. She can connect to people who, in part precisely because of their reasonableness, demonstrate integrity, egalitarian self-respect, courage, and fairness, and who further humanity's understanding of the world. Such people inspire in the RP a sense of the worthiness of the tradition, and motivate her to fulfil her core nature; that is, to herself become a more complete self-respecting Reasonable Person. I want now to consider an example of this type of worthy precursor.

Henry Sidgwick, the nineteenth-century English philosopher, was by all accounts an admirable man who did much good. His goodness, moreover, was inextricably connected to his reasonableness (as the goodness of most other good people is not).[14] For example, he showed courage, integrity, and independence of mind in dealing with the crisis of religious faith which dominated his early adulthood. Sidgwick thought that Christianity, which he had been brought up to believe in, contributed both to his own happiness and, at least in the short term, to the well-being of society. However, he came to doubt that the main Christian doctrines were true. He therefore, over a period of years, examined these doctrines with a view to determining whether they were worthy of belief, all the time hoping that they would be. His journals and letters show how scrupulous he was to make his beliefs consistent with the evidence, and also how much anxiety these investigations caused him. Finally, he decided that he could not continue to call himself a Christian. At that time, Cambridge University demanded that its fellows be adherents of the Church of England. Sidgwick therefore resigned his fellowship, even though it would have been easy for him to pretend belief, as had other fellows. This act threatened his means of livelihood (in the end, however, his example led the university to change its regulations). Sidgwick's journals indicate that, in this whole episode, his overriding concern was to believe what was true (or at least not believe what was false), to make his actions consistent with his beliefs, to be honest, and to set an example as someone who cared about having epistemologically worthy beliefs. He wrote, "I happen to care very little what men in general think of me individually: but I care very much about what they think of human nature. I dread doing anything to support the plausible suspicion that men in general, even those who profess lofty aspirations, are secretly swayed by material interests."[15]

Sidgwick took an active part in the political issues of his day, and in particular was a leader in the campaign for the right of women to attend university: he was a founder of the first woman's university college and gave much of his time and income to the cause. Moreover, it is clear from his own writings and from what others wrote of him that his political activities flowed, to a significant degree, from his reasonableness. An adversary remarked of Sidgwick, "There was in him an extraordinary belief in following reason – a belief and hopefulness which continued up to the last."[16] A similar point applies to Sidgwick's well-documented disposition for fairness in argument, as well as to his lack of envy and spite in circumstances when these emotions might be expected. Once again, it is impossible to separate his possession of these virtues, when one reads accounts of him, from the importance he attached to being reasonable.[17]

For some RPs, Sidgwick has the force of an exemplar; whereas for others, his temperament and academic routine would inhibit that degree of emulation (a commitment to reasonableness allows for very different forms of life within its basic framework).[18] Nevertheless, all RPs would recognize in Sidgwick an admirable person who shared their defining commitment. In making herself aware of such people, the RP deepens her sense of belonging to a worthy tradition.

6.5 Let us note now an important fact about the way the RP values reasonableness. As we have seen, reasonableness may be regarded, from one point of view, as the skill of following a set of epistemological guidelines. Looked at this way, the value of reasonableness would seem to lie mainly in its being a means to other ends, for it hardly makes sense to think of sticking to guidelines as having worth in its own right.[19] Some recent writers follow this line of thought and argue that the value of rationality must be understood wholly in instrumental terms (what these writers mean by "rationality" is close to my guidelines 1–6). For example, Harold I. Brown, in his book *Rationality*, writes that "rationality is a tool for attempting to understand the world we live in and for deciding how we ought to act."[20] Stephen Nathanson, in *The Ideal of Rationality*, carries this instrumental approach a step further. He first argues, like Brown, that rationality is valuable as an instrument to serve our interests. What, then, about the view that through rationality we come into contact with the truth? Here Nathanson doubly applies his instrumental approach. Rationality is the best instrument to get at the truth, but truth itself is valuable only because it serves our interests.[21]

Now my analysis paints a different picture as to the way reasonableness is valued by the RP. The instrumental picture is that of a person's intrinsic interests, on the one side, and of her judging that reasonableness is the best means to satisfy these interests, on the other side. But what is typical of the RP is that, from the start of her self-reflective life, she finds herself with the disposition to feel self-diminution when she does not abide by the guidelines. Moreover, this disposition is infused by contact with exemplars, whether directly or through reading. From the start therefore, however inchoately, there is in her mind a relationship between abiding by the guidelines and admirable character traits. Then, as this feature of her personality deepens, to-be-reasonable comes to have intrinsic worth for the RP. She may later, as we have been doing, raise the question whether, or how, reasonableness is congruent with her interest in certain admirable traits. But even this line of thought is, for her, different from wanting to know whether reasonableness is an effective instrument, as Brown and Nathanson conceive it, for satisfying other interests. For these other interests, in the case of the RP, are often not specifiable independently of her defining commitment. Consider an example.

A person may possess the good of autonomy without being an RP. However, when the Reasonable Person probes whether being an RP is congruent with *her* autonomy, what she discovers is that this trait, as she possesses it, is really *part* of being a Reasonable Person. The picture, then, of reasonableness as a neutral instrument for acquiring autonomy (a disposition not to envy, a sense of inherent worth, egalitarian self-respect, etc.) is misleading. The more accurate picture is that of the RP's deepening her understanding of her defining commitment and thereby realizing that autonomy (non-envy, etc.) is encompassed by this commitment. Analogously, a Christian may come to understand that forgiveness of one's enemies is part of what it means to be Christian, and then this recognition may in turn influence her to become, what she had not been before, a forgiving person. If this change occurs, then this person's forgivingness is not understandable apart from her commitment to Christianity.

Given the above discussion, we can now understand how the RP could regard reasonableness as a status attribute in which to ground her self-respect *qua* RP. Assuming that she lives up to her ideal of being reasonable, she then derives enhancement both through her sense of belonging to a worthy tradition and through her meeting the norms for being a self-respecting RP. To have these sources of self-esteem is a significant good, which in turn supports the RP's commitment to reasonableness.

C: SCIENCE AND MEANING

6.6 The gist of part B has been that the RP adds meaning to her life through identifying with, and helping to sustain, the tradition of reasonableness. But people can only sustain a tradition by involving themselves in specific aspects of the tradition, as when a person who loves music develops expertise in the violin. There are many aspects, indeed sub-traditions, to reasonableness and correspondingly many ways of sustaining the tradition. But one of the most important, I maintain, is science; in this regard, there is ample evidence that a certain kind of RP finds the thought that she contributes to science deeply meaningful. Let us examine, then, how science is congruent with the RP's nature and how contributing to science may thereby add meaning to her life (through identification reasons).

I have been concerned mainly with how the RP uses the critical guidelines to evaluate beliefs which enter into her self-esteem. But I have also made it clear that she is motivated to apply these guidelines wherever appropriate and that she is sympathetic to enterprises which support the application of the guidelines. Science, however, can be just one such enterprise. In her pursuit of knowledge, the scientist brings her beliefs against standards which are shared by other members of the scientific community. But these standards, in many instances, are expressions or variations of the critical guidelines.

The most important of these is that which prescribes that theories must be tested against the empirical evidence (a variation of my guideline 2) and that, accordingly, the scientist should be willing, as a general principle, to give up her beliefs if they are falsified by contrary evidence. This is not to say that scientists necessarily reject a theory when there appears to be evidence against it, since it is usually reasonable to hold on to a theory until there is a better one to take its place; nor is it to say that the primary motivation of all scientists is to bring their theories up against the relevant evidence, since amongst individual scientists, as with other people, there is mixed motivation. But it is to say that the scientific community holds as its governing ideal, an ideal which is made concrete by methodological checks and balances, the notion that hypotheses and theories are to be accepted or rejected on the basis of impartial evidence.

There are numerous ways that scientific methodology has changed, and some of these changes have been revolutionary. For example, there was the invention of the experimental method in the sixteenth and seventeenth centuries, which included Boyle's idea that it is as important to report failures as successes;[22] and there was the advent of statistical methods in the nineteenth century.[23] Moreover, methodological principles accepted by one generation of scientists have sometimes been rejected by later generations. For example, Galileo rejected Aristotle's notion that mathematics could not be of much use in describing natural phenomomena.[24] It is indeed a mistake to think that there is some one eternally valid scientific method. Even the famed hypothetico-deductive method cannot fit this bill, since it does not adequately explain why scientists accept a theory such as that of evolution.[25] Nevertheless, when we look at the way scientific methodology has evolved, we see that there are broad regulative guidelines lying in the background which have influenced this evolution. Examples of these guidelines are as follows: (a) a methodology is better to the extent it guarantees impartiality and rigour in data collecting and theory testing; (b) a theory is improved to the degree that its laws or empirical generalizations can be ordered in terms of a deductive hierarchy; (c) a theory is better to the degree it eliminates inconsistencies; and (d) a scientist is better for being non-dogmatic. These are not themselves concrete methodological principles. But we can see these regulative guidelines at work throughout the evolution of scientific methodology. Now it is evident that these same regulative ideas are encapsulated in the critical guidelines which define reasonableness. Therefore we can understand why the RP would naturally regard science as a sub-tradition within the tradition of reasonableness, and also why she is likely to look to science to form her beliefs about the natural world. Later in the chapter, we shall see that the consonant traits reinforce this point that science is congruent with her nature. But now, assuming that the RP (or at least one species of RP) is disposed to identify with the advance of science, let us examine how meaning can be added to her life. (What I say in the next sections has to be balanced with my comments about scientism at the end of the chapter. It will be clear that my interest is not to defend, on the RP's behalf, any kind of science worship.)

6.7 Given the above discussion, we may grant that the Reasonable Person wants to see science flourish and to prevent it from decaying. Now there are two dimensions to the way science may flourish. In the first place, it flourishes the more that new, interesting, and persuasive theories are produced by scientists themselves. Secondly, science flourishes the more that there are people who genuinely understand and take pleasure in scientific theories. As with artistic or athletic traditions, the tradition of science is sustained as much by *informed* appreciators as by its primary producers. (I emphasize "informed" here to distinguish this kind of appreciation from dilettantish appreciation, which in fact is detrimental to a tradition. I shall have more to say about this later.) The RP, therefore, may feel herself a genuine contributor to science either by being herself a scientist or by being a genuine appreciator of science.

The main reason the RP finds value in science is that she sees it as a way of increasing her own and others' understanding of the world. A person, however, may believe that she contributes to something of value and yet find that, subjectively, meaning is not added to her life. This occurs when the activity of contributing to what has value is not pleasurable, and in particular does not bring self-enhancement. Take, for example, the full-time housewife who believes that she is contributing to what is valuable (the welfare of her family), but finds her work overwhelmingly boring. She might say truthfully that her work has meaning, but it is unlikely she would say that this work adds meaning to *her* life.

Now those who value science do, as a matter of fact, derive pleasure, often very intense pleasure, in discovering or coming to understand scientific theories. Of special significance is that it is common to find appreciators of science describing a scientific theory in aesthetic terms. Indeed, it is virtually impossible to make judgments in science without bringing to bear quasi-aesthetic concepts such as coherence, comprehensiveness, and simplicity.[26] It is, moreover, a short, natural, and in some cases inevitable step from applying such concepts to making full-blown aesthetic judgments. Scientific theories, for example, are commonly said to be beautiful, to be subtle and deep, or to possess organic unity. However, what makes the pleasure derived from a scientific theory more than, or at least different from, purely aesthetic pleasure is the belief, which is intrinsic to the pleasure, that the theory explains some aspect of the world. From the point of view of the appreciator of science, if a scientific theory is subtle, it is subtle because it reflects or brings to light some subtle aspect of the natural world; if it is deep, it is so because it deepens our understanding of reality; and if it possesses organic unity, it has this attribute in virtue of the diverse aspects of the natural world it unifies in its laws and models.

The distinct kind of pleasure derived from discovering, coming to understand, or applying scientific theories has often been described. Here, for example, is Bertrand Russell talking about the growth of his interest in science during his youth: "It was ... above all the application of mathematics to the real world which I found exciting. Newton's Principia ... was in the shelves. I pulled it out and read his deduction of Kepler's laws from the law of gravitation. The beauty and clarity and force of the reasoning affected me in the same kind of way as the greatest music."[27] Russell's feelings are especially intense, but such experiences, even if not so intensely felt, are in fact common in the mental life of appreciators of science. It is important to see that Russell is not only reacting to the beauty of Newton's theories in aesthetic terms, though partly he is doing so. It is also that he believes that, through Newton's theories, his own mind comes into contact with the natural world. Moreover, in experiencing Newton's theories as beautiful, Russell is at the same time, he believes, experiencing the world as beautiful. It is important to pursue this theme further.

As I said in chapter 5, we may relate to things either in terms of their having intrinsic worth or in terms of their having instrumental value (or a combination of the two). When we relate to something as having intrinsic worth, I said that we attend to the entity, as opposed to seeing past it to the desires the entity may satisfy – recall my example of the two ways of relating to the quilt. Now there are traditions which, in very different ways, enhance one's capacity to attend to things: traditions such as painting, gardening, photography, and cooking. Science, I want to say, is also such a tradition. (In emphasizing the way science may increase our capacity to attend to things in the natural world, and in aligning science in this regard with painting, gardening, etc., I distance myself from Aristotle's and Spinoza's view that intellectual activity is necessarily the best, or even the only, adequate way to bring our minds into contact with the world.) As an amateur astronomer, for example, I can attest to how becoming skilled in astronomy engenders a deepening of pleasurable attention to the night sky. Partly it is question of learning to notice things one would otherwise not notice. This noticing is deepened through learning astronomical names embedded in theories relating to the distances and origins of sky objects. Moreover, these same theories, through suggesting questions and puzzles about sky objects, further deepen one's attentiveness.[28] Here is a typical example of the way that observation and theory interact to deepen a group of amateur astronomers' pleasurable attentiveness to the night sky. (In reference to amateur astronomers, the relevant contrast is amateur-professional, not amateur-expert, for amateur astronomers often possess enormous expertise, as is shown by the frequency with which they make discoveries. Expert amateurs are dependent on other experts for both theories and observation reports, but this is true of professionals as well.)

During August 1984, Bruce Waters, Kai Millyard, and I ... observed three bright flashes of light near the same spot in the sky. We cautiously contacted other meteor observers, believing that the mysterious flashes might have been "point meteors." What else could bright spots that high in the sky be, anyway, but meteors coincidentally heading straight toward us [the definition of "point meteor"].

On October 18th, however, I received a letter from Mark Zalcik, an expert meteor observer, who thought the flashes could not have been caused by point meteors. He suggested that some sort of star might be repeatedly but irregularly outbursting in a nova-like fashion. That same night Zalcik went out and looked at the suspected position in the sky and he, too, saw a flash.

Suddenly our little group of observers had a giant-sized mystery ... Ken Tapping of the Herzberg Institute for Astrophysics kindly talked to us about it and suggested an unusual possible answer: the flashes might be coming from a gamma-ray burster, an as-yet unexplained star that periodically throws off immense amounts of energy for a duration of several seconds. After hearing this, we nicknamed the object "the Ogre," which stands for Optical Gamma Ray Emitter, and decided that no matter how long it would take to find, we'd chase it.[29]

The article goes on to describe in great detail how to locate this flash, how to distinguish it from other sky events with which it might be confused, and how to take pictures of it. I have taken this example from astronomy because it is a field with which I have had personal experience. But this passage, in suggesting the way science enhances increased pleasurable attentiveness to the natural world, reflects an experience common in several fields of science.

The way that becoming deeply informed in some aspect of science increases one's attentiveness to the world helps to distinguish the genuine appreciator of science, as I am defining this person, from others who are only more or less interested in the subject. These others may be able to talk with some depth about an aspect of science, but what distinguishes them from the genuine appreciator is that their knowledge and interest do not go deep enough, or absorb them enough, so as to radically affect their way of pleasurably attending to the natural world.

When the appreciator of science is under the influence of experiences such as I have been describing, it is not uncommon for her to feel that there is a harmony between herself and that part of the world to which she is attentive. Recall as well the way unselfconscious feelings of enhancement generally occur when our minds are focused on that which we experience as having intrinsic worth (as in the discussion of the person who appreciates ballet in 5.4). It follows that when the appreciator of science experiences the world as beautiful, which is one way to experience something as having intrinsic worth, then she concurrently experiences enhancement. As we saw in the example of the bored housewife, such enhancement is necessary if a person is to feel that subjective meaning is added to her life. Moreover, mental states which give us a sense of harmony between ourselves and the world, and at the same time are self-enhancing, sometimes strengthen our capacity to cope with suffering or loneliness; and this is one of the main contexts in which we think of our lives as possessing meaning.[30] Here is a passage from a biography of the great geneticist Barbara McClintock which speaks to this last point, as well as to the other issues I have been raising regarding attentiveness and science:

In particular, before the effects of specific genetic crosses can be counted, distinct phenotypic and cytological traits need to be identified. Both of these processes of identification require kinds of experience not easily communicated to those who have not participated in the actual observations. They require an extensive training of the eye. And McClintock's eye was surpassingly well trained. "Seeing," in fact, was at the center of her scientific experience.

... Especially illustrative is the story she tells of how she came to see the *Neurospora* chromosomes. Unwilling to accept her failure to see these minute objects under the microscope – to pick them out as individuals with continuity – she retreated to sit, and meditate ... There she "worked on herself." When she felt she was ready, she returned to the microscope, and the chromosomes were now to be seen, not only by her, but, thereafter, by others as well.

... Through years of intense systematic observation and interpretation ... McClintock had built a theoretical vision, a highly articulated image of world within the cell. As she watched the corn plants grow, examined the patterns on the leaves and kernels, looked down the microscope at their chromosomal structure, she saw directly into the ordered world.

... This intimate knowledge, made possible by years of close association with the organism she studies, is a prerequisite for her extraordinary perspicacity. "I have learned so much about the corn plant that when I see things, I can interpret [them] right away" ... At the same time, [her scientific work] has sustained her through a lifetime of lonely endeavour, unrelieved by the solace of human intimacy or even by the embrace of her profession.[31]

Few scientists make breakthroughs as important as McClintock's. Nor amongst highly original scientists are many as isolated, and even scorned, by their peers as she was. Yet many less gifted scientists, as well as appreciators of science, relate experiences similar to those of McClintock regarding the value of science in their lives.

6.8 The above ways that science can add meaning to a person's life presuppose, of course, that scientific theories do tell us something about the world. Now in order to believe this about scientific theories, we need not hold that they are absolutely true. I have no doubt that current theories are not absolutely true, just as Newton's theories were not. At the same time, it would be absurd, in my view, to think that these theories tell us nothing about the natural world or that current theories do not explain more of the world's phenomena than the theories they have supplanted. Although the problem of how to see scientific truth and progress is very difficult, I do not believe I have to solve this problem in order to maintain reasonably that science allows its appreciator to experience the world with increased attentiveness. Whether we take a realist view of scientific theories, an empiricist view, or something in between, it would still be true that science brings our minds into contact with patterns in the natural world. Only an extreme scepticism about science, such as that of Paul Feyerabend, would undermine my way of attributing value to science. But his scepticism depends critically on the notion that scientific theories are incommensurable, which notion in turn supports a radical epistemological relativism.[32] There are powerful arguments, however, against this extreme form of scepticism, including the plausible view that the doctrine is self-contradictory and there-fore incoherent.[33]

Given the availability of these arguments, the RP has the right to be sceptical of Feyerabend's scepticism regarding the epistemological value of science. But there is another way for her to look at scepticism about the value of science, whether Feyerabendian or other sorts. The fact is, many healthy traditions incorporate arguments about the value or viability of their defining goals.[34] Think, for example, of religious, political, and artistic traditions, where debate about funda-mentals can be a sign of health. From this point of view, science and the broader tradition of reasonableness itself are no different from other traditions. This point is related to a further issue regarding the connection between science and meaningfulness.

I have been working with two concepts of meaning, namely, mean-ing in (what we can call) an external sense and meaning in a subjec-tive or psychological sense. In the external sense, the housewife thinks of her activities as meaningful because they contribute to her family. Nevertheless, from her own subjective point of view, meaning is not added to her life. Similarly, a religious person might believe that human life has meaning because it has been created for a specific purpose by God, and yet she might not *experience* her life as mean-ingful. To believe one's life has meaning in the external sense, then, is to see oneself as related to an entity (one's family, God, etc.) which has significant moral value. But implicit in the notion of external meaning is the possibility that what an agent *thinks* gives her life external meaning in reality does not (perhaps the housewife's family is not worth the sacrifice; perhaps there is no God, etc.)[35] Now this consideration puts extreme sceptical doubts about science in perspec-tive for the RP: she sees that the fact there is a (remote) possibility that science is not what she takes it to be does not place her in a worse position than any other person for whom external meaning matters. I turn now to some other ways that science can add subjec-tive meaning to the life of the Reasonable Person.

6.9 Meaning is added to people's lives when they contribute to something larger and more enduring than themselves. Now science extends hundreds of years into history, is spread over many parts of the earth, and will continue into the indefinite future. Moreover, the history of science tells a story (though not one imposed from above) of humankind's slowly improving its understanding of the natural world and thereby gaining a more realistic picture of its own place in the scheme of things (relevant here is the sense of forward direc-tion made possible by shared, impersonal guidelines). Of special significance in this regard are scientific theories which suggest a picture of our biological origins and of our place in the vastness of space and time. Whereas some people find such theories a cause for anxiety, the Reasonable Person of a certain temperament finds them deeply moving and liberating. Of added significance is that as science better explains natural events, it offers to humankind the possibility of controlling these events with awesome power for good (and also for evil). The RP sees science, when viewed in these ways, as a valuable part of human culture; she also sees herself working, along with others who share her values, toward goals which will carry on beyond her own life.

There is a further related sense in which the appreciator of science may have meaning added to her life. This has to do with the fact that the more our minds are attentive to the natural world, the less we focus on our own concerns. If, for example, I come to take pleasure in understanding the life cycle of the salmon, my mind is focused on this feature of the world, and to that degree, I am not thinking of my own narrow interests. We can even in a straightforward, non-mystical way bring our minds into contact with the universe as a whole. For example, if I come to understand, through the study of cosmology, why it is likely that the universe is expanding, then I am thinking about the universe as a whole – after all, "the universe" is the grammatical subject of the sentences I am considering. When these non-egocentric mental states also give rise to experiences of beauty, then a particularly powerful source of meaning is added to the life of the appreciator of science.

We should not ignore the fact, moreover, that the kind of experiences I have been describing can, at their most intense, lead people to experience what Stuart Hampshire has aptly called "occasions of transcendence."[36] A colleague of the great astronomer Edwin Hubble, in speaking of his mentor's achievements, said, "If you really had the discovery of the way [some aspect of] the universe is organized, that's such an ineffable thing that happiness is not the appropriate word."[37] Lest one think this kind of experience is reserved only for astronomers, or only for someone like Hubble who made great discoveries, here is a passage from a novel by C.P. Snow regarding a much more mundane discovery. Snow is describing the feeling of a young scientist who has just confirmed a hypothesis regarding the structure of a crystal (as Snow himself had done as a young scientist):

Then I was carried beyond pleasure. I have tried to show something of the high moments that science gave to me: the night my father talked about the stars ... Austin's opening lecture, and the success of my first research. But this was different from any of them, different in kind. It was further from myself. My own triumph and delight and success were there, but they seemed insignificant beside the tranquil ecstasy. It is as though I had looked for a truth outside myself, and finding it had become for a moment part of the truth I sought; as though all the world, the atoms and the stars, were wonderfully clear and close to me, and I to them, so that we were part of a lucidity more tremendous than any mystery.[38]

To say that such experiences are at all regular occurrences in the lives of those who value science would be a romantic distortion; but to deny that they sometimes occur, though most often in a less expansive form, would equally be a distortion. It is clear that a person who undergoes this kind of peak experience has meaning added to her life.[39]

6.10 An important fact about finding subjective meaning through science is that it can be a non-competitive good. If Jones appreciates some scientific theory, then this does not make that theory any less available to Smith. This good, then, differs from other goods, such as money, prestige, or prizes, in which someone's having more of them usually means that someone else must have less. The non-competiveness of appreciating science is an important advantage for the RP, since it is congruent with her rejection of competitive self-esteem. This congruence, moreover, contributes greatly to the RP's being able to participate successfully in *local communities of reasonableness*. As I define such groups, they are constituted by people who, interacting on a regular basis, have as their defining purpose the aim to sustain, in some specific form, the tradition of reasonableness (I do not mean that such groups think of their aim under this description). Local communities of reasonableness, then, include astronomy, geology, and philosophy associations or clubs.

Because the interests which define such groups are shareable goods, their members have the opportunity to develop non-competitive relationships with each other and to enjoy sharing the pleasures of reasonableness. This in turn creates an atmosphere in which mutual trust and friendships grow.[40] In these local communities, the RP finds opportunities to experience that sense of belonging which is the mark of feeling oneself part of a tradition.

An important feature of such local communities is that there is mutual sharing of expertise. The ideal is that all members become equally knowledgeable about all things within their sphere. But in most cases, especially those which involve science, this is an impossible ideal; for no single person can encompass more than a small part of any scientific sub-discipline. If one were to analyse a typical justificatory claim made by a scientist or appreciator of science, it would have the following form: "I believe p in part because fellow expert A believes q, which supports p; and fellow expert B believes r, which supports p; and fellow expert C believes s, which supports p; etc." And then A's, B's, and C's claims to know q, r, and s would in turn require analogous support by other experts.[41] What this means is that to enter into a scientific discipline is to acquire a strong sense of how one's own beliefs are interdependent with the beliefs of others who share one's interests and values. This aspect of local communities of reasonableness increases the RP's bond with her fellows, and so her sense of belonging. On the surface, such dependence on others' expertise may appear to conflict with the trait of autonomy, which is part of the RP's core commitment. Let us investigate this question.

In 2.2 we saw that the RP inhibits reflected reasons in herself in virtue of her defining commitment. I made it clear (see especially 2.7) that this argument works because she must ask herself whether she can sincerely attribute moral worth to the self-ascription component of her reason. If a person does not raise this question as part of her evaluation, then it is as if she assumes (usually falsely) that she lacks the capacity to determine for herself which self-ascriptions have worth. But now this line of thinking does not apply in the case of scientific beliefs, for we have seen that no person can make up her own mind regarding all the beliefs needed to support any given claim. However, although in one sense the RP is, so far as science is concerned, epistemologically dependent upon experts, it is important to see that the dependent-autonomous distinction is appropriately drawn from another point of view. For the RP has her own, autonomous reason for believing that scientific experts are in general reliable authorities. The reason lies in her understanding that, because of the checks and balances inherent in scientific methodology, the claims of scientific experts are likely to conform to the critical guidelines. This does not mean that every expert is to be taken at her word, for experts disagree and some are better than others. But the person who is not mystified by expertise knows that there are procedures by which the non-expert can make reasonable judgments between experts when they clash; she knows too that, if necessary, she can suspend judgment until there is consensus amongst the experts.

The RP's attitude to scientific experts contrasts with the blind dependency on experts characteristic of some people. In the latter case, there is acceptance of the experts' claims without any autonomously held reason for understanding why the claims should be regarded as trustworthy. Now it is the person with this attitude toward experts who is apt to have the other-dependent trait. It is this person, in other words, who is apt to regard scientific experts with mystique, to be overly pliant toward them, and to have a sense of inferiority when in their presence (see 2.6). The Reasonable Person, on the other hand, understands that the reliability of an expert's claims lies not in some mysterious quality of the expert herself, but in the capacity of the expert, as part of the scientific community, to abide by the critical guidelines. Therefore, the RP, who sees herself as possessing this same capacity, even if she does not fully exercise it on the same matters, is apt not to be other-dependent regarding scientific experts. There is now a related point to make regarding her attitude toward science.

I have talked of the RP as identifying with science and wanting science to flourish, and of science being spread over different parts of the earth. To speak of science in this way is to see it as an abstract entity. Social groups are also abstract entities, and some of the issues I raised in chapter 4 regarding attitudes toward social groups are relevant here. It is easy enough, for example, to find people expressing loyalty and other positive attitudes toward science. In the auto-biographical notes Darwin wrote for his children, we find sentences such as "What is far more important, my love of natural science has been steady and ardent."[42] Or from the person to whom Darwin entrusted some money for the advancement of biology and geology, we read: "I was much impressed by the earnestness, and indeed, deep emotion, with which [Darwin] spoke of his indebtedness to science, and his desire to promote its interests."[43] Given these ways of thinking, it is important to understand that the RP does not stand in a corporative relationship to science.

In order to stand in such a relationship, she would have to see science as having a higher moral status than herself. But here the distinction I drew in chapter 4 between two ways of valuing an abstract entity proves important. One can see such an entity as being valuable for its own sake, and as there to be served by people who have less value than it; or one can see an abstract entity as having value ultimately only because it contributes to the well-being of individual sentient beings. Viewed in the latter way, to value an abstract entity, even to the point of sacrificing one's own interests, would not entail that one believes the entity has a higher moral status than oneself. Now the Reasonable Person values science because it permits humans to gain an understanding of the world, because it is one way of allowing people to experience the world as beautiful, because it makes possible the control of nature for the benefit of sentient beings, and for other such reasons. Therefore the RP values science in the second way I described and so does not see it as having a higher moral status than herself; nor is she subject to corporativeness in her relationship to science.

There is the related point that the corporative trait implies a pliant attitude to the norms of the valued group. Now, as we have seen, the norms of science, at their most general level, are variations of the critical guidelines. It is important to keep in mind, then, that the RP is committed to these guidelines *independently* of her valuing science. It could not be, therefore, that she adopts these guidelines through being pliant to science or to scientists. In relation to science, as with other abstract entities, the RP maintains her capacity for imaginative disengagement and critical scrutiny.

6.11 To find science valuable in the ways I have been describing may seem an overly austere ideal to which not many people could possibly be attracted. The ideal of the Reasonable Person is not designed, to begin with, to have universal appeal. Nevertheless, finding meaning in science is not so rare as one might at first imagine, as the many serious amateur science clubs and magazines partly indicate. Moreover, one of the key ingredients of finding meaning in science – namely, attending to the natural world with a heightened sense of aesthetic pleasure – speaks to a strong interest (or even need) shared by many people, an interest which finds expression in diverse forms. For example, this interest partly accounts for hobbies such as bird-watching, which are a kind of proto-science and which seem to grow in leaps and bounds as people gain more leisure time. (There are now about 25 million serious bird-watchers in North America, triple the number in 1965.)[44] That the RP's way of valuing science resonates to this common chord shows, in this respect at least, that we are not dealing with an overly austere ideal.

There is a vein in modern intellectual life which is appalled by any attempt to value science in the ways I have been describing.[45] In some cases, such as that of Feyerabend, I believe these anti-science intellectuals are simply mistaken. Mistaken too, I believe, are those who identify science with a crude mechanism or reductionism, and who thereby see science as an inevitable source of callous and exploitative attitudes toward nature. When filtered through the minds of some people, science does, I agree, contribute to callous and exploitative attitudes. On the other hand, as has been implicit in my argument, it can engender just the opposite attitudes and actions.

Although I am on the opposite side of those thinkers who believe that science must be a force for moral impoverishment, I do not deny the great danger of scientism. By scientism I mean a misguided worship of science which precludes recognizing the significance of other values. Some typical manifestations of scientism are: (1) the view that science represents the only form of rational activity, implying that argument about moral, political, or aesthetic values is really a waste of time; (2) the view that science, or perhaps more generally reason, is the only important thing in life and that therefore personal relationships, especially those which involve passionate commitment, are at best an inferior element of a worthwhile life; (3) the view that there is nothing much to learn about human beings from literature, or that the arts in general are at best a source of relaxation or diversion; (4) an underestimation of the extent to which emotion plays a part in science itself; (5) a failure to recognize that science is situated within a larger cultural context, that history and philosophy are part of this wider context, and that scientific work can reflect the biases of the culture in which it is situated; (6) a too-easy dismissal of the significance of religious sentiments in human history and a belief that if only everyone gave up religion, all would be well; (7) the view that with the progress of science there is an *inevitable* growth of civilized feelings and behaviour; and (8) the view that the advancement of science necessarily outweighs other significant moral considerations, such as animal suffering as it occurs in scientific experimentation. Now nothing I have said in this chapter implies that the RP must adopt any of these scientistic views. In particular, to say that science is one thing she values is not to say that it is only thing she values, or that she must fail to recognize the complex and varied factors which go into making a civilized culture.

This chapter has shown that reasonableness can be a source of self-respect and meaning to the RP. Here therefore is a countervailing force to those forces, as described in part 1 of the book, which pull her away from her ideals.

7 Egalitarian Respect

Egalitarian respect, as I define it, is the disposition to treat any person, including oneself, as having equal moral status. There is no uncontested interpretation of "equal moral status," either in our common culture or amongst philosophers. I shall forge my own interpretation, therefore, borrowing from others as need be. This is the work of part A of the chapter. My analysis, as we shall see, makes "treating people as equals" a more demanding commitment than it is conventionally regarded. In part B, I argue that there is no justification for egalitarian respect which could have persuasive force for all rational and good-willed people, that is, a justification which could be, as I say, *impersonally groundable*. However, as we shall then see in chapters 8 and 9, the RP's core nature is especially congruent with egalitarian respect, in spite of the attitude's not being impersonally groundable. This is to his advantage and gives him further reason to sustain his defining commitment.

A: INTERPRETING EGALITARIAN RESPECT

7.1 I analyse egalitarian respect in terms of five criteria. To this end, it will be useful to speak of egalitarian respect as a trait and to say of someone who has the trait to a high degree that he is an *egalitarian agent*. In developing my five criteria, then, I will be asking how an egalitarian agent is disposed to act, think, and feel with reference to any other human being. Note that I do not see my five criteria as defining egalitarian respect in the strict sense of stating necessary and jointly sufficient conditions. People might meet some, but not all the criteria and thereby possess the trait to varying degrees (hence, I do not regard each criterion as a necessary condition); as well, I grant the list could be augmented – indeed, history shows that a given generation can deepen its notion of moral equality in ways unimaginable to previous generations (hence, I do not regard my five criteria as jointly sufficient). I should say too that I do not intend to beg the question whether, or in what sense, other animal species should be treated with egalitarian respect. But to raise the issue in this part of the chapter would divert my main argument; the topic is broached later in the chapter and in chapter 9.

We sometimes think of egalitarian respect in terms of treating *others* as having equal moral status to ourselves and sometimes in terms of treating *ourselves* as having equal moral status to others. These sub-traits of egalitarian respect I call *other-respect* and *egalitarian self-respect* respectively. It will be convenient to conduct my analysis in terms of other-respect and then explain egalitarian self-respect in terms of it. My five criteria for other-respect, then, are as follows:

1 *Non-Servility*   An agent, A, has the trait of other-respect to the degree that he would not enjoy or encourage servility, obsequiousness, or excessive deference to himself on the part of any other person.[1] On the contrary, in situations where he has power over B, such as when he is B's employer or teacher, A takes steps to discourage B from feeling or acting servilely, etc. As well, if B acts servilely toward A, then A is made uncomfortable and disesteems B for showing lack of egalitarian self-respect. On the other hand, if B does not act servilely toward A, even when there are social conventions which would make such behaviour appropriate or natural, then A is more at his ease. In general, A feels indignation at the thought of any other person being expected or made to act servilely, even when the relationship does not directly touch him. Finally, A is disposed to work toward altering social conditions which imply or encourage servility.

A's feelings and behaviour toward B, I want to say, *express* his belief that B has equal moral status to himself. At the same time, it is only because this belief *causes* A's feelings, and thereby motivates his actions, that his feelings and actions count as expressing egalitarian respect. He could have behaved as he did because he wanted B to like him or because he wanted something from B. In that case, he would not be, on my analysis, expressing egalitarian respect for B. (Analogously, an act of gift-giving does not express love unless the act is motivated by love.) This does not mean that the belief or judgment of equal moral status must be a separately occurring mental event. Indeed, in most cases the belief and the expression of the belief are one and the same, in the sense that the judgment of equal moral status is implicit in the feeling or the act (expressing an attitude in our actions is not so much like clothing our body, as it is like putting a thought into words). It might be asked how we could judge that a belief which is not phenomenologically distinct from its expression could at the same time be active in the feeling or act. The answer is that we make this kind of judgment all the time through paying attention to the context in which the feeling or act occurs and through asking the agent himself why he acted as he did.[2]

This point about motivation is central to the moral outlook I shall defend as congruent with the nature of the Reasonable Person. In this outlook, egalitarian respect is to be regarded as a morally worthy trait precisely because it *expresses* the attitude of regarding people (including oneself) as having equal moral status. The *expressive significance* of egalitarian respect, I argue in chapter 9, is a deep reason for valuing the attitude distinct from the reason that it affects people's interests for the better (though the latter is *also* a reason).

We can apply the non-servility criterion now to help us understand egalitarian self-respect. In the first place, to have egalitarian self-respect is to be disposed not to be servile, obsequious, or excessively deferential, especially when one stands in a relationship to someone of superior power, social status, or achievement. And it is to have this disposition because one regards oneself as of equal moral status to any other person. Secondly, to have egalitarian self-respect is to be disposed to feel resentment and to protest, if any other person expects or demands servile behaviour of one. Finally, the egalitarian agent is disposed to suffer in his self-esteem if he believes he has acted servilely. There is tension between this last disposition, taken as a property of egalitarian self-respect, and the first disposition. Clearly, if a person were to act servilely too often or too readily, he would not have egalitarian self-respect in the first place, even if he were to suffer in his self-esteem. So this last disposition speaks only of the exception in the behaviour of a self-respecting person.

What counts as servile behaviour varies depending on social context. In some contexts, a ritual bow indicates servility, whereas in other contexts it is a sign of non-servile respect. The expectation that a person will do the family laundry could be a sign of egalitarian disrespect; but it could also be part of a justly struck bargain over how to divide household chores. What makes an act servile is the notion that one participant in a relationship has less moral status than the other. The notions of non-servility and equal moral status (or egalitarian respect), then, are implied in each other. To recognize this relationship is important, but it hardly takes us very far in explicating either concept. To probe further, we must turn to the other criteria.

2 *Egalitarian Dialogue*   A significant proportion of our dialogue with others has the goal of determining what to believe. Let us call dialogue which has this goal *epistemic dialogue*. Now an agent has the trait of other-respect if he is disposed to make his epistemic dialogue with any other person as egalitarian as possible. *Egalitarian dialogue*, to begin with, is characterized by an attempt to weigh considerations impartially, regardless of the social or other inequalities that define the relationship between the agent and his interlocutor. In egalitarian dialogue, a person resists any desire to force his view on his interlocutor or to evade a consideration which counts against his view – however easy it would be to do so on account of some inequality in power, status, or achievement. This in turn means that the agent opens himself to changing his viewpoint if the interlocutor's considerations have greater weight. It follows that an egalitarian agent commits himself to understanding as thoroughly as possible his interlocutor's viewpoint: otherwise he would not be able to weigh impartially the other's considerations.

Note that the point about motivation raised in the previous criterion is essential as well to defining this criterion (as it is to the rest of the criteria). That is, people may consider the arguments of others impartially from a variety of motives, including purely self-interested ones. It is only, however, when the belief that the interlocutor has equal moral status to the agent enters into the agent's motivation that impartial discourse becomes egalitarian dialogue, and thereby an expression of egalitarian respect.

People sometimes discuss with each other an action or policy which is meant to affect their mutual interests. In this case, egalitarian dialogue implies that the agent gives the same *prima facie* weight to the self-identified good of his interlocutor as he gives to his own self-identified good.[3] (For the moment, think of "self-identified good" as meaning "interests as perceived by their possessor."[4] Later, however, I shall define the concept more precisely.) What I mean by "same *prima facie* weight" is explicated through the next three criteria.

3 *Fairness*   A person has the trait of other-respect if he is disposed to treat any other person with fairness. Now we need not detail the substance of a theory of fairness in order to use the concept to help define egalitarian respect. Let us define an *egalitarian* theory of fairness formally as one whose principles for distributing benefits and burdens are designed to express the belief that people have equal

moral status. There is disagreement amongst philosophers over exactly which principles best express this value. For example, Rawls, Nozick, and Dworkin each see their quite different principles as issuing from the assumption that people count equally, as do many utilitarians. But our formal definition allows us to bypass having to decide between these theories. It is enough to say that the concept of fairness used here is that as defined by some valid theory of egalitarian fairness (whatever that theory turns out to be).

Given this understanding, we may say that an agent, A, has the trait of other-respect if he does not demand or desire of any other person more than that person's fair (egalitarian) share in bearing the burden of a common enterprise; in this sense, A does not seek to use or manipulate any other person for his own gain. As well, he is disposed to support practices which guarantee to another that person's fair share of benefit from a common enterprise. More generally, fair treatment involves not overriding another's legitimate interests; or in the case of a clash between one's own and another's legitimate interests, then treating another with egalitarian respect means looking for a compromise, through egalitarian dialogue, in which each person's self-identified good is given equal weight. As well, fair treatment includes supporting practices in which people are not punished for a wrongdoing beyond what is a fair punishment, however "fair punishment" is properly defined from an egalitarian point of view.

4 *Equal Basic Rights*   One social benefit, open for fair distribution, is legally protected rights. In Western culture, all would agree that equal protection of *basic* rights is a necessary condition for treating people as equals. Such rights protect, to the same degree as others, a person's ability to pursue his self-identified good and to participate equally in decisions which affect his good (so long as this pursuit does not violate others' basic rights).

Now an egalitarian agent is strongly disposed not to violate the fundamental civil and political rights of others. He is further disposed to support or work to enhance another's rights, especially if that person (or group) lacks some basic right that others possess. Moreover, an egalitarian agent is disposed to feel indignation at the thought that any another person is deprived of equal basic rights, however distant that person is in time or space.

5 *Empathetic Politeness*   An agent has the trait of egalitarian respect if he is disposed to treat any other person with *empathetic politeness*. Empathetic politeness goes beyond respecting another person's

rights. In the first place, it implies not being contemptuous, disdainful, or condescending toward how another person pursues his self-identified good, even when such pursuits do not draw one's admiration or even interest. Here again, motivation matters. What lies behind the egalitarian agent's politeness is his recognition that any other person's self-identified good matters to that person as much as his own self-identified good matters to himself, and that for this reason, and in the light of the fact that people count equally, he ought to make an effort to see things from the other's viewpoint. A sincere effort at empathetic politeness generally precludes contempt, disdain, or condescension for the way another pursues his self-identified good (though, as I explain later, the moral principles implicit in other-respect may sometimes be properly overridden).[5]

Now there are times when the egalitarian agent recognizes that his commitment to empathetic politeness demands more than politeness. Some people, because of discrimination or other abuse, have severely damaged self-esteem. Such people are often driven, at the deepest levels of their personalities, to see themselves irrationally as possessing less moral status than others. For those who have not been subject to systematic abuse, a special effort of empathy and care may be required to grasp the psychological reality of those who have – to grasp, as Laurence Thomas has put it, their "profound sense of vulnerability."[6] An egalitarian agent is disposed, without being patronizing, to open himself to the narratives such people tell and to look for ways to rectify their situation.

With our five criteria of other-respect in mind, we can now briefly complete our definition of egalitarian *self*-respect. A person with this latter trait is disposed to engage any other person in egalitarian dialogue (in the appropriate circumstances of course), since he sees his own self-identified good as counting equally to any other person's. Moreover, he is disposed to feel resentment and to protest if any other person fails to engage him in egalitarian dialogue, or likewise fails to satisfy the fairness, equal-rights, or politeness criteria with reference to himself. On the other hand, in participating in relationships which satisfy the five criteria, the person with egalitarian self-respect derives enhancement through the thought that he is acting, and being treated by others, in accord with his proper status. I now make three important clarifications.

7.2   1 *Self-identified Good*   When we are being fair or polite to another person, what more specifically are we being fair or polite to? The answer, in very general terms, is that our behaviour is directed toward that which the other person *cares about*. From this perspective, then, egalitarian respect expresses the attitude that that which any one person cares about is as equally entitled to the benefits of egalitarian dialogue, fairness, protection through legally instituted rights, and empathetic politeness as that which any other person cares about. Now I intend the concept of self-identified good to designate the totality of what a person cares about, and so to help with this aspect of understanding egalitarian respect. More specifically, a person's self-identified good encompasses his voluntary acts, as these acts express his wants, interests, and goals. As well, a person's self-identified good encompasses his beliefs and feelings about what is good or bad, beautiful or ugly, and in general about what has value or disvalue.

2 *Moral Principles* Each of our five criteria can be converted into a corresponding moral principle, such as, "It is morally wrong not to engage any other person in egalitarian dialogue, when appropriate." A person who commits himself to egalitarian respect, then, commits himself to upholding the corresponding five moral principles. Now to adopt a moral principle is to allow that it ought to override non-moral considerations. It is also to have a sense of how important this principle is in relation to other moral principles. On my interpretation of egalitarian respect, the five moral principles have in one sense the highest priority; for the egalitarian agent regards them, in the manner of Rawls, as constraints on any of his other pursuits, including even those pursuits which aim to maximize what has intrinsic value. That the egalitarian agent commits himself to constraining his own ends in the light of these principles is precisely what gives substance to the notion that he counts others as having equal moral status to himself. I shall express this point by saying that egalitarian respect has *deontological force* for an egalitarian agent.

Note that even on this deontological view, one or more of the egalitarian principles may be properly overridden. This occurs, for example, when there is conflict, in some concrete situation, between the principles themselves – as when we inflict justifiable punishment on a wrongdoer through abrogating some of his rights, or when we withdraw empathetic politeness, and express contempt, when faced with an evil agent. In other cases, the sacrifice in overall intrinsic value might just be too great to reasonably uphold one of the five principles; for example, we might rightly decide to violate someone's basic rights in order to prevent great suffering. In this latter case, the egalitarian agent judges that one *prima facie* value, which in general takes precedence over another *prima facie* value, nevertheless must, in the extreme case, be overridden. To grant this is not to give up the idea that egalitarian respect generally has overriding value. But it is to accept that sometimes, unfortunately, intrinsic values have to be traded off against each other.[7] If I were presenting a complete theory of egalitarian respect, more would have to be said about this issue of prioritization. But it is enough for my purposes to have defined, in general terms, how egalitarian respect has central significance for the egalitarian agent.

3 *Self-Denial*   I want now to ask whether self-denial is likely to be required on the part of an egalitarian agent. I understand self-denial, with reference to egalitarian respect, as follows: a person is self-denying who is inclined to do X; but instead, because of his commitment to egalitarian respect, does not-X at some overall cost to himself. "Overall cost to himself" means the sacrifice of some interest of the agent without a net gain to himself. (This definition will suffice for the present, but later in the book I shall have to refine it.)

In discussing self-denial, I shall focus on an egalitarian agent for whom egalitarian respect coexists with other, more partial interests; I mean interests such as friendship, family, aesthetic enjoyment, and absorbing self-fulfilling projects. To possess such interests is the situation of anyone who has a meaningful life, including the Reasonable Person, whose interests, as we saw in the previous chapter, are shaped by his nature *qua* RP. Now it is evident that there must be situations in which the pursuit of such a person's own good would conflict with the principles of egalitarian respect; for example, it might sometimes be in an egalitarian agent's overall interests to violate another's rights or to not engage another in egalitarian dialogue. In such situations, the egalitarian agent must open himself to self-denial; for, as we have seen, egalitarian respect generally takes priority over, in the sense of constraining, his other pursuits.

It would be a mistake, moreover, to think that egalitarian respect demands only forbearance or non-interference. On the contrary, a consistent commitment to treating people as equals may sometimes require, as indeed we have already seen in the above, sustained positive action. To think otherwise is to fall fault to morally arbitrary distinctions. Consider, for example, the following two situations: (i) by doing X, A stands to gain unfairly from B; but because A is an egalitarian agent, he forbears from X and thereby undergoes self-denial; (ii) whatever A does he would gain unfairly from B, unless A were to take positive steps to change the status quo (perhaps by engaging in political action). Furthermore, although such positive steps would involve self-denial on A's part, there would be no more self-denial than that involved in (i). Now it is clear to me that if A forbears in (i) but fails to act in (ii), then he is not being consistent; for if his reason for forbearance in (i) is that B counts equally to himself, then surely precisely the same reason ought to govern his actions in (ii).[8] That the one case requires forbearance (which after all is a kind of intentional act), whereas the other case requires some positive act, hardly seems morally relevant. In thinking about situations such as these, we see the appropriateness of including the notion that the egalitarian agent works to change social conditions when these conditions result in people not being treated with other-respect.

In chapter 9, I argue that other-respect can be a desirable ingredient in the life of the RP. That other-respect opens a person to self-denial might seem to put in doubt its desirability, and in particular to risk engulfing his personal interests and relationships. But my argument will be that the self-denial connected to other-respect can be integrated, in a balanced way, into the pattern of the RP's life through being given a deeper meaning. Now a natural way to try to supply this deeper meaning would be to provide a moral theory which grounds egalitarian respect. Then, assuming morality is integral to a person's life, the self-denial connected to the egalitarian traits would be *pari passu* integrated. But what deeper moral reasons are there for acquiring or sustaining egalitarian respect? And granting that there are such reasons, how do they serve to integrate egalitarian respect into an individual's way of acting and feeling?

In the next part of this chapter, I consider several attempts to ground egalitarian respect in moral theories meant to appeal to *any* rational and goodwilled person. By a "rational and goodwilled person" I mean an individual who (a) can understand moral arguments and (b) is disposed to act on moral considerations. Clearly, these two (minimal) conditions are satisfied by people with widely different interests, ideals, and capacities. Indeed, most people (hence most non-RPS) satisfy these conditions. The moral theories discussed, then, are designed to be (as I say) impersonally groundable.

B: CAN WE GROUND EGALITARIAN RESPECT?

7.3 If my five criteria constitute at least one valid interpretation of "treating people as equals," then should there not be, in this egalitarian age, a plausible justification for the attitude ready to hand which could appeal to any rational and goodwilled person? But this thought rests on the assumption that egalitarianism grew, at least in part, because people accepted moral arguments which, in the end, rationally grounded the belief in the equal moral status of humans.

History, however, does not bear out this assumption. Consider, for example, the growth of egalitarianism regarding political rights.

The evolution of political egalitarianism from the 1600s to the present has been tied to the extension of basic civil and political rights from "in" groups to "out" groups.[9] In terms of reasoned debate, the key to these extensions has been arguments which pressed the moral arbitrariness of granting basic rights to one group but not to others. Thus, being propertyless, being Catholic (or Jewish or Muslim or atheist), being black, being non-British, and being female came in turn to be regarded as arbitrary ways of excluding these groups from the protection of basic rights, once these rights were granted to some one group. Note, however, that this dialectic is conditional in form. It says, "*Once* we include Xs, then in consistency we must include Ys." But this argument begs the question of what grounds there are for valuing all Xs in the first place – and valuing them, moreover, in a way which accommodates the intuition that, in consistency, basic rights ought to be extended to all humans. The fact is, most social groups simply have *taken it for granted* that "we" merit certain basic rights (or respect) which "they" do not. The consistency argument can be effective, given the right historical conditions, in extending these rights from "we" to "they"; but this does not mean that operative in these debates there has been some evidently correct deeper grounding for justifying a belief in equal moral status.

Many people in Western culture now take the belief in some form of equal moral status for granted, just as most people in previous times took extreme ethnocentric attitudes for granted. The statements "They're human too" and "I'm human too" have an unquestioned justificatory force in our culture. At the same time, many people who espouse a belief in equal moral status hardly come close to meeting the demands of a genuine other-respect. That this is so we can partly attribute to the fact that, for many people, the attitude hangs without a deeper motivating justification. A parallel point applies to egalitarian self-respect. Most people would say that they possess equal moral status to any other person, but their capacity to feel and act in accord with their belief is easily undermined. "I'm human too" does not seem to go deep enough either as a justification or as a source of motivation.

Staying for a moment with the case of egalitarian self-respect, we can see further the source of this justificatory-motivational gap. We observed in the previous chapter how being a self-respecting X rests on judgments about the *worthiness* of being an X (as in the case of the self-respecting carpenter). These judgments in turn engage a person's self-esteem, and therein lies a powerful source of motivation. A problem arises, however, if we try to treat being human as a status attribute such that it could support egalitarian self-respect in the way that being a carpenter supports the self-respecting behaviour of John. For humanity hardly counts as a tradition with clearly defined norms along the lines available for good carpentry.[10] Nor do people identify with the achievements of humanity *qua* humanity, such that being human could sufficiently engage their self-esteem. One may find ancient Chinese pottery beautiful, for example, but one hardly takes pride in such pottery on the grounds that the potters and oneself share the property of being human. A parallel point holds for other-respect. The attitude would seem to demand that all humans be equally worthy in some important sense, since other-respect is meant to apply equally to all humans. However, it is far from obvious in what sense it could be said that all humans are equally worthy. Certainly, attributes such as "equal inherent worth" or "equal dignity" do not serve as a solution, since they only beg the central question all over again.

Since the rise of egalitarianism, ethical theorists have attempted to fill the gap I have been describing. A key feature of these theories is that they try to provide an answer which is impersonally groundable, even granting the great differences in personalities and values amongst morally decent people. In seeing how these theories fail, important lessons will emerge.

7.4 If being human cannot itself ground egalitarian respect, then perhaps there is some worth-making property which subsumes being human and at the same time would strike any rational and good-willed person as intrinsically worthy. For some early modern thinkers, such an answer lay in the Judaeo-Christian view that all humans, in contrast to animals, are created equally in God's image. Here, it was argued, is a sufficiently ennobling characteristic in which to ground universal human rights and egalitarian respect. Such a religious backing, however, could never compel the consent of all rational and decent people; and as time has gone on, the religious argument has satisfied fewer and fewer people. This predicament has led some philosophers, most notably Kant, to theorize that the basis for equal moral status must lie in some property of humans whose appreciation is accessible to people independent of religious belief. The worth-making property Kant singled out was rational autonomy, the capacity people have to act in accord with self-discovered rational principles. Once we understand this capacity, he argued, we are moved to respect it as the basis for attributing equal moral status to any entity who possesses the capacity.[11] There are now several points I wish to draw from his argument.

Kant distinguished respect for rational autonomy from the respect which is similar to admiration or esteem, as when we talk of respecting someone's intelligence. He also distinguished it from the respect which is connected to fear, as when we talk about the need a canoeist has to respect the dangerous rapids.[12] By this distinctive form of respect, Kant meant in part a disposition to act in accord with principles not unlike some of those I have adduced to define egalitarian respect (it is through acting on such principles that the respect is expressed). But he meant more than an appropriate way of acting. He also meant a unique attitude, close to reverence or awe, which motivates the appropriate action. This attitude, Kant argued, is directed at rational autonomy *per se*; or, as he also put it, directed at our capacity to follow "the moral law."[13] Since humans possess the capacity for rational autonomy equally, he argued, the respect or reverence we hold for rational autonomy ought to be held toward all humans equally. Moreover, he saw this respect as objectively justifiable, since it issues, he said, from rational insight into the true value of autonomy, rather than resulting, as do other forms of respect, from subjective feelings. For Kant, then, the awe which motivates egalitarian respect at the same time rationally grounds the attitude. This is an important point to keep in mind for chapter 9, and it is therefore worth quoting Kant's words:

There might be brought against me here an objection that I take refuge behind the word "respect," in an obscure feeling, instead of giving a clear answer to the question by means of a concept of reason. But even though respect is a feeling, it is not one received through any outside influence but is, rather, one that is self-produced by means of a rational concept; hence it is specifically different from all feelings of the first kind, which can all be reduced to inclination or fear ... Respect is properly the representation of a worth that thwarts my self-love. Hence respect is something that is regarded as an object of neither inclination nor fear, although it has at the same time something analogous to both.[14]

We shall see that a notion analogous to Kantian "awe" plays a part in my theory, though with key modifications.

There is now a final lesson to be drawn from Kant's attempt to ground equal moral status. This is that his argument founders on the property he makes the basis for egalitarian respect. In the first place, all people do not possess the capacity for rational autonomy to an equal degree; some people indeed do not possess it all, even potentially. Moreover, to defend the idea that even most people possess rational autonomy to an equal degree, Kant had to argue that our capacity for rational action is unconditioned by empirical forces – that our will is radically free.[15] However, as he himself said, rational autonomy, interpreted in this way, is not accessible to human comprehension. This means therefore that his way of grounding equal moral status must be as little open to impersonal acceptance as the earlier religious doctrine; for the problem of freewill, especially as understood by Kant, seems to be as intractable as the question of God's existence.[16] A further crucial problem is that there are good-willed people, ranging from some secular philosophers to religious adherents, who do not see rational autonomy as itself worth-making at all, let alone as the singular value which could ground egalitarian respect.[17]

Kant's answer to the question of what grounds egalitarian respect is not alone in running into these difficulties. In fact, I would maintain that problems such as the above plague *all* other attempts to find an appropriate worth-making property (or set of properties) for equal moral status: either the proposed property, because transcendental, is not believable to all rational and goodwilled people; or the property is possessed by people in widely different degrees; or the worthiness of the property is something which goodwilled people can question.[18] (The second and third criticisms, for example, have been made against Rawls's attempt to ground egalitarian respect in the property of having a moral personality.)[19]

Although we have not canvassed all the possibilities, I believe we have done enough to show that anchoring[20] egalitarian self-respect in some deeper worth-making property, along the lines suggested by Kant, is not likely to succeed, so long at least as we are looking for a reason which is compelling to any rational and goodwilled person. What alternatives are there, then, for anchoring egalitarian respect in impersonal considerations? We learn something important if we now see why an approach which would seek to ground egalitarian respect in utilitarian considerations does not succeed.

7.5 The utilitarian, as I shall understand him, starts his moral thought, first, from a judgment as to what states of affairs have intrinsic value and, second, from a conviction that any rational and goodwilled person could be brought to share this judgment – perhaps by means of an appeal to clear-headed intuitions or by means of an argument from universalizability.[21] Starting from judgments regarding intrinsic value, the utilitarian then analyses his moral deliberations with the aim of producing the optimum amount of intrinsic value. Leading candidates for intrinsically valuable states of affairs include happiness and preference satisfaction. (I should note that some forms of utilitarianism *start* from a commitment to equal moral status. However, I need not consider these positions, since they must themselves face the question we are here trying to use utilitarianism to answer, i.e., how to ground a commitment to egalitarian respect).[22]

In terms of grounding egalitarian respect, then, the utilitarian strategy must be to demonstrate that possessing egalitarian respect helps to optimize what is intrinsically valuable. Now the desire to optimize utility, on the one hand, and the defining motive of egalitarian respect, on the other, are *as such* incommensurate mental states. A person who expresses egalitarian respect for someone constrains the pursuit of his own ends, even if so doing leads to less overall intrinsic value: optimizing intrinsic value, in other words, is not what is on the egalitarian agent's mind. If then the utilitarian is to ground egalitarian respect, he must follow an *indirect strategy*;[23] whereby he shows that to have the egalitarian traits optimizes utility, even though to optimize utility is not the actual motive of any given egalitarian act. This strategy, however, faces insurmountable difficulties. I shall mention the key one for my purposes.

In order to express egalitarian respect, a person must be moved by his belief that another person has equal moral status to himself (see 7.1). But just as a person cannot simply decide to believe that there are five people in a room or that a particular painting is beautiful, so he cannot simply decide to believe that others have equal moral status to himself. In all these cases, something in the external world has to strike a person in a certain way. At best, then, the utilitarian can decide to try to cultivate in himself the belief that any person has equal moral status to himself, just as people can try to cultivate in themselves the belief that peace will eventually reign on earth. But in order to do so, there must be some facts, relevant to his belief, which the agent can bring before his mind. Now in chapter 9 I shall describe the kind of facts which can give rise to the relevant motivating belief (at the same time we will have to give up the goal of impersonally grounding egalitarian respect). But even before making these arguments, we can see why it is highly problematic that the utilitarian's moral landscape has space for the relevant motivating belief.

To judge happiness or preference satisfaction (or the capacity to undergo these states) as intrinsically valuable is very different from making a judgment regarding equal *worthiness*. Happiness and preference satisfaction *per se* are what we may call "worthy-neutral." People derive pleasure, for example, from watching sports on television. When he views it as an innocent pleasure, the utilitarian will see this activity, taken by itself, as a valuable state of affairs. But it hardly makes sense to say that the activity is a worthy one or that the utilitarian could look on the agent, in virtue of his television watching, with that moral-cum-aesthetic pleasure which character-izes our judgments of intrinsic worth.

Of course, what the utilitarian does find intrinsically worthy are traits the possession of which result in the maximization of intrinsic value. In these terms, for example, he may admire and cultivate the traits of honesty, charitableness, and truthfulness. But being moved to find these traits intrinsically worthy could not ground a belief in *equal* moral status, for people possess these traits in radically different degrees; indeed, these are traits by which we differentiate one person from the other. (Note that this same problem would face an attempt to ground egalitarian respect in non-hedonistic or ideal utilitarianism, for it is evident that people do not possess equal capacities for such things as the acquisition of knowledge or the appreciation of beauty.) The problem, then, is that to ground other-respect, with its motivat-ing judgment, the utilitarian must cultivate in himself the disposition to be moved fundamentally by some fact shared equally by human beings. But neither his judgments about intrinsic value nor his judg-ments about intrinsic worth leave space for a response to that sort of fact.

There is, it is true, a sense in which the utilitarian sees people as equals, or rather treats them as equals. Since happiness or prefer-ence satisfaction is what has intrinsic value, then happiness is hap-piness and preferences are preferences, and *who* experiences the happiness or satisfies his preferences is in the end irrelevant. Given this framework, it follows, as a derivative principle, that my happi-ness or preferences do not count for more than any other person's. But this is very different from seeing people as possessing equal moral status to begin with, and for *that* reason holding certain ways of treating them to be right or wrong. This perception of equal moral status, I have been arguing, is simply not one of the fundamental dispositions the utilitarian brings to his moral choices; and neither hedonistic nor non-hedonistic valuing can be transmuted into this perception.

My analysis suggests that we should make the following distinc-tion regarding the utilitarian's attitude toward equality. On the one hand, most utilitarians do not regard equality between people, how-ever equality is interpreted, as an intrinsically valuable state of affairs. A distinct point (though clearly related to this first point) is the fact that such utilitarians do not take the *perception* of people as equals as fundamental to an inherently worthy motive. When they argue that equality is derivative (as they often do),[24] they are usually referring to the first point. My analysis, however, brings the second point to the fore.

It would be wrong to infer from the above that utilitarian considerations could play no role in the way a person values egalitarian respect. To recognize that the defining ground for egalitarian respect does not lie in utilitarian theory is nevertheless compatible with the following thoughts: (a) it is a very attractive feature of egalitarian respect that it does generally contribute to what is intrinsically valuable, such as people's happiness; (b) because this is so, one has an *additional* reason to cultivate egalitarian respect in oneself and to regard it as inherently worthy. We shall see later how these thoughts are taken up by the Reasonable Person.

7.6 Apart from its possible use to ground utilitarianism, universalizability, it might be argued, could be applied directly to ground other-respect. But in order for that to work, a person must first possess a grounding reason for his own egalitarian self-respect and then, under a commitment to universalize, apply this grounding reason to others. However, the problem of finding a worth-making property to ground one's own egalitarian self-respect, which could then be universalized to ground other-respect, is no different in the end from the original goal of finding a worth-making property to ground equal moral status. But that goal we have seen to be futile. Therefore, universalizability as a direct strategy to ground other-respect seems a dead end. There are two further problems with this strategy, however, which are worth mentioning for the purposes of the next chapters.

First, in order for this strategy to work, we must presuppose that the agent to whom the argument is put has an extremely strong commitment to universalizing his beliefs and attitudes. It is not only that he must be prepared to assert sincerely that if property X is worthy-making in himself, then it is also worth-making in others; but he must be prepared sometimes to let his own interests be overridden on account of this commitment to universalization (or he must see universalizability itself as generating the obligation).[25] It is hard to imagine, however, that someone would find the value of universalization in and of itself either a strong enough reason or a powerful enough motive to outweigh self-interest. At best, then, considerations of universalization have to be bolstered by other factors.

A second problem is related to the motive which grounds other-respect. Such a motive is undercut when a person attempts to ground other-respect primarily through a commitment to universalization. In effect, such a person would be reasoning: "I have property X and respect myself for that reason. I see others also have property X.

Because I am committed to universalize my beliefs, I must therefore respect these others." But a person who acts on the basis of this reasoning is not so much acting out of other-respect for others as out of a commitment to universalization. The situation here is analogous to that of the person who helps a friend mainly because he regards it as his duty to help friends. However useful such help might be, a person could hardly regard this help, insofar as it lacks direct concern for himself, as a genuine expression of friendship. Similarly, to be motivated by other-respect is to be directly moved, as I am understanding the attitude, by the belief that others count equally to oneself. But the person who grounds his behaviour in a commitment to universalization is not necessarily so moved. Such a person, it is true, has come to believe that others have equal moral status to himself; but it is not *this* belief which primarily moves him to act. I shall return to this issue in chapter 9, where we will see another angle on universalization.

7.7 I want now briefly to consider a strategy tangential to the previous one. Hegel and others have suggested the following line of reasoning.[26] To possess egalitarian self-respect, we need to believe that others recognize us as worthy of egalitarian respect. But to take seriously the recognition of others, we in turn have to see them as worthy of egalitarian respect. If we did not, then we could not take to heart their recognition of us. Then, given that we all want or need to have egalitarian self-respect, we are led rationally to express egalitarian respect for others. This is an intriguing argument; however, it can be questioned at every turn. For example, it is surely not true that in order to believe ourselves worthy of others' egalitarian respect, we have to believe that others (let alone *all* others) believe us worthy of such respect. The criticisms I want to focus on, however, recall some of our earlier discussion.

This Hegelian strategy for grounding other-respect rests on our believing that others' egalitarian respect for ourselves is integral to our own egalitarian self-respect. But then the question can be asked: What is the justification for this egalitarian respect that others bestow, or might bestow, on us? It cannot simply be that others recognize that in order to have egalitarian self-respect *themselves*, they have to other-respect us. This really would be a vicious circle, which would leave both attitudes hanging without a deeper reason. Perhaps then this circle of mutual egalitarian respect could be grounded in our own and others *need* for egalitarian self-respect? This line of reasoning would then go: each of us needs egalitarian self-respect, and since mutual egalitarian respect is integral to meeting this need, we are justified in believing that we and others have equal moral status. But now such a strategy would face a problem parallel to that faced by the utilitarian strategy, for having a need for X and being worthy of X are distinct facts or considerations. True, if egalitarian self-respect (and thereby other-respect) contributes to our well-being, then clearly we have reason to sustain the belief in equal moral status. But it is also clear that this consideration could not in itself give a deeper grounding for the belief. That this is so may be seen from the following simple consideration. It is perfectly consistent to think that the belief in equal moral status is in one's interest, but at the same time to hold that the belief is unjustified. Analogously, a person's recognizing that it would be in his interest if a painting of his were beautiful does not justify his believing that the painting *is* beautiful (i.e., possesses aesthetic worth).

7.8 We have been examining impersonally groundable strategies which might anchor the egalitarian traits in our personalities. These strategies have failed. In recognizing this situation, some philosophers have proposed that we treat the principle of equal moral status as a fundamental commitment which does not need a deeper grounding, apart from the fact that it coheres with our other beliefs and values. A *groundless commitment*, as I shall call it, is different from an attribution of intrinsic worth.[27] Finding that a property has intrinsic worth *is* grounds for believing that the property has worth. To adopt a groundless commitment, however, is to grant that there is no inherent reason for the belief in equal moral status. Kai Nielsen, for example, seems to defend such a view when he writes:

Most of us find egalitarianism a more attractive ideal than ... Nietzsche's ideals. I am not sure that we can justify such a fundamental ideal as the belief that all humankind has a right to an equality of concern and respect. And I am not confident that we even need to try, for it may very well be that there could be nothing more fundamental that we could appeal to make such a justification. Perhaps here we should say that justification comes to an end and that we just have make up our minds what kind of human beings we want to be.[28]

The pervasiveness of our human-based egalitarian ethos inclines most people to accept egalitarian respect in this groundless way. The statement "I'm human too," as I suggested earlier, has a justificatory force when people assert their rights or demand fair treatment, even though most people could not say why it should have this force. No doubt it is better for people to have such a groundless belief than to express no other-respect or self-respect at all.

Nevertheless, we must note just how curious such a commitment is, when advocated at the level of reflective thought. What, we may ask, is the difference between a conscious decision to adopt a ground-less commitment or belief, on the one hand, and a decision to act *as if* one held the belief, on the other? It is difficult to see that there is a difference. For to think that the best we can do is to "make up our minds" to hold a belief (perhaps because we think such a belief will have good consequences), while at the same time think there is absolutely no inherent reason for the belief hardly seems different from acting as if we held the belief without really holding it. (The same problem can be raised for the person who maintains that there is no evidence *at all* either for or against the existence of God, but claims nevertheless to have chosen belief in God because it helps him with his life. Does this person really believe in God or just act as if he does?) Insofar as a groundless egalitarian commitment excludes animals, it is not surprising that philosophers sympathetic to animal rights should see this commitment as sheer unsupported prejudice.[29] Given these considerations, we should be sceptical of "groundless commitment" as a way, at a reflective level, to justify egalitarian respect.

7.9 What now follows if we assume that an impersonally groundable justification for the egalitarian traits is not possible? Depending on favourable circumstances, a person may not be disadvantaged through not having a deeper grounding for these traits. (I am assuming, of course, that it is desirable to have the traits, a topic I discuss in the next chapters.) On the other hand, experience shows that egalitarian self-respect and other-respect are apt to wither when psychological or social circumstances turn unfavourable. Moreover, as I said earlier, people often do not fully live up to the commitments implied in other-respect. Now the Reasonable Person's egalitarian traits, just as much as any other person's, would have the support of an egalitarian ethos. But in the next two chapters, I want to demonstrate that the RP, in virtue of his core nature, is particularly suited to realizing these traits in his life. As a bridge to these chapters, I shall introduce the concept of a *personal grounding* for an attitude. By introducing the concept here, I can make a final clarification regarding the import of my argument in this chapter.

In contrast to an impersonal grounding, a personal grounding has justificatory force only for a particular agent (or agent type), where "particular agent" implies the possession of commitments and personality traits not necessarily shared by all rational and goodwilled people. Thus, for example, we do not expect all rational and goodwilled people to join astronomy clubs. In this sense, the pursuit of astronomy, if regarded as worthy, can have only a personal grounding, and we may therefore call such a pursuit a *personal ideal*. Now it is in this light that I want to regard egalitarian respect, in its fullest sense and its relationship to the RP. My argument in the next two chapters is that the RP, in virtue of his core nature, is in a particularly strong position to adopt egalitarian respect as a personal ideal.

It might be thought that the above view implies moral subjectivism. But subjectivism does not necessarily follow from my analysis. We should distinguish the following: (a) the belief that a trait can be only personally grounded; and (b) the belief that it is morally permissible or admirable for a person to have that trait. Note that even though the trait referred to in (a) is by hypothesis not impersonally groundable, it is still possible that the *beliefs* referred to in (a) and (b) *are* impersonally groundable. In arguing that the egalitarian traits are not impersonally groundable, therefore, I nevertheless leave open the question whether, at some other level, it may not be possible to give an impersonal grounding to the belief in their moral value. Recall, too, that egalitarian respect must express the motivating belief that others and oneself count equally. There are, however, other ways of treating people as equals which do not require such a grounding motive; and nothing I have said excludes the possibility that one of these ways may be impersonally groundable.

8 "I Do Not Count for Less ..."

8.1 We have been operating on the assumption that other-respect and egalitarian self-respect would receive a unitary grounding, say, of the following form. Humans equally have worth-making property X; therefore, they are equally worthy of egalitarian respect; since I am human, then I am justified in possessing egalitarian self-respect. (The other attempts at an impersonal grounding were equally unitary in form.) An alternative approach is that the two attitudes receive distinct groundings, and this is the strategy I shall now follow. Moreover, once we give up the idea of producing an impersonal grounding, then a dual grounding of the kind I am suggesting is more feasible. Given this perspective, we can then ask how the Reasonable Person, in particular, stands regarding egalitarian self-respect (the topic of this chapter), and then how she stands regarding other-respect (the topic of the following chapter). In each case I aim to show that the RP's core nature anchors the relevant trait in her personality, while at the same time contributing to her well-being.

The attitude expressed by the thought "I have equal moral status to others" can be bifurcated as follows: (a) "I do not have *less* moral status than any other person," which thought lies at the heart of egalitarian self-respect; and (b) "I do not have *more* moral status than any other person," which thought lies at the heart of egalitarian respect for others. Now we saw in the previous chapter that, when dealing with the egalitarian traits, the concept "self-identified good" can be appropriately substituted for reference to a person's self. Given this, we can say that the core to egalitarian self-respect is the thought "My self-identified good does not count for less than any other person's," where "count for less" is interpreted in terms of the five criteria. With this interpretation in mind, let us see how the Reasonable Person stands regarding egalitarian self-respect.

The RP's self-esteem is engaged by the way she applies the critical guidelines to her beliefs (and also by her acting in accord with the consonant traits). Imagine now that she examines some belief or attitude to the best of her ability and finds it worthy of acceptance in terms of the guidelines. Such an examination, we should recall, includes analysing the opinions of others as impartially as possible. What now would be the RP's attitude to this belief? It is evident that she would think it wrong of herself not to continue holding the belief (or at the very least wrong to hold a contrary belief). To think otherwise would contradict her own most fundamental commitment, *qua* Reasonable Person. More generally, the RP must adopt one of the following attitudes to *any* of her beliefs, even those which up until that point she has not subjected to the guidelines: (1) that the belief is, or will prove to be, justifiable after applying the critical guidelines; in which case she will believe it morally wrong not to continue holding the belief, or at least morally wrong to hold a contrary belief; (2) that the belief is, or will prove to be, unjustifiable; in which case she will believe it morally wrong to continue holding the belief; or (3) that the belief's justifiability is, or will prove to be, indeterminate; in which case she will believe it morally wrong not to suspend judgment, or at least morally wrong to hold a contrary belief.

Now implicit in the Reasonable Person's seeing her beliefs in terms of one of these three attitudes, I want to say, is the concept of her system of beliefs, or point of view, as *worthy of not being transgressed by any other point of view.* If another point of view imposes itself on her, then this must mean she is forced to accept a belief, or act as if she accepts a belief, to which she has not adopted one of these three attitudes; but that would be out of keeping with her defining commitment. (This principle applies even if the imposed belief is one she would accept in her own terms.) The RP holds, then, that no other conceivable point of view has the right to impose itself on her point of view. In this sense, she believes, we may now say, that no other conceivable point of view counts for more than hers. Let us see how this argument applies specifically to egalitarian self-respect.

As I defined a person's self-identified good (7.2), it encompasses her beliefs about what is valuable or disvaluable, as well as her voluntary actions. But voluntary actions themselves can be interpreted in terms of a person's beliefs about what is valuable or disvaluable. For example, if John chooses wood X rather than wood Y in order to build a house, he must have beliefs, integral to his choice, about why X is better than Y, and indeed, why it is desirable to build the house. Given this connection between voluntary actions and beliefs, we can now say that a person's system of beliefs, or point of view, encompasses her self-identified good *in toto* (i.e., including her voluntary actions).

Now since the Reasonable Person believes that no other conceivable point of view has the right to impose itself on her point of view, it follows that she has a concept of her self-identified good as worthy of not being transgressed by any other's self-identified good. In this key sense, implicit in her defining commitment, she has a concept of her self-identified good as not counting for less than any other's self-identifed good.

Given the above self-understanding, the RP must be strongly disposed to have egalitarian self-respect, or in other words, to judge it wrong for any other person to treat her with egalitarian disrespect. To see one's self-identified good in the above manner is tantamount to believing that others ought not to violate one's basic rights; that others ought to engage one in eqalitarian dialogue, especially when their actions might affect one's welfare; that others should not have a greater voice than oneself in deciding how common enterprises are to be run; and that others would be wrong to condescend to the way one expresses one's self-identified good. My point is not that the RP holds this set of conditions explicitly in mind. It is rather that, given the dispositions set in motion by her defining commitment, she judges it wrong if someone ever tries, in one of the ways mentioned, to treat her with egalitarian disrespect. Consider now a specific example.

Say that John is an RP. Given that he believes wood X is better than wood Y, he must be strongly disposed to protest and feel resentment if Jim tries to impose his view that Y is better than X. For if he accepts Jim's imposition without protest or resentment, then it would be as if he were saying that his own belief is not worthy of being held. But to think that would be contrary to his defining nature *qua* RP. It follows that, all things being equal, John must believe he has a right to pursue this aspect of his self-identified good; that in a common enterprise with Jim, his view regarding what wood to choose should have at least as much weight as Jim's; and that Jim has no good reason to be condescending toward John's choice. In these senses, John holds that his belief merits Jim's egalitarian respect. Now John, as an RP, must see that this same thought process applies to any constituent of his self-identified good and that, for this reason, his self-identified good *in toto* merits the other-respect of any other person. But for John to see himself in this light is to possess egalitarian self-respect.

There is a further way the RP's defining commitment supports egalitarian self-respect. The guidelines dictate that she must test her beliefs against the appropriate canons of inductive and deductive reasoning and push from her mind irrelevant considerations. But a person who refuses to engage the RP in egalitarian dialogue is, by the definition of the previous chapter (7.1), trying to influence her by just such irrelevant considerations (i.e., considerations of status, power, etc.). Hence, the RP will likely regard it as wrong if another refuses to engage her in egalitarian dialogue, and in this sense, she is disposed to express her egalitarian self-respect (see further 9.10). There are now three clarifications to make.

In the first place, we can now see more clearly how the RP's grounding for her egalitarian self-respect is importantly different from the impersonal strategies we earlier considered. It is not that she first forms a concept of her self-identified good as subsumed by some independently worth-making property and then concludes that her self-identified good does not count for less than others. It is rather that, given her defining commitment, the RP is disposed to judge it wrong when any other person treats her with egalitarian disrespect. She does not judge it wrong because "I am a Reasonable Person, and being a Reasonable Person has such-and-such a worth-making property"; but because "*this* belief or attitude is mine to make my own, and therefore *this* person has no right to impose her belief on me." At the same time, the RP can see, when she reflects, that *any possible* belief or attitude of hers would merit the egalitarian respect of others, given her commitment to being an RP. In this sense, she can formulate a concept of her self-identified good *in toto* as meriting egalitarian respect. This belief in turn can play a role in the way the RP thinks about herself or discusses moral and political issues with others. As well, we should recall that she has reasons, as discussed in chapter 6, for finding the tradition of being an RP admirable. These reasons do not directly ground her *egalitarian* self-respect (as they do her self-respect *qua* RP); but they do of course strengthen her commitment to being an RP, and this commitment, as we have now seen, supports her egalitarian self-respect.

Secondly, the RP's egalitarian self-respect grows out of her commitment to being an RP and not from an impersonal grounding. But this means, *so far as the argument has gone*, that she has no reason to believe that others, from *their* point of view, have any deeper reason to treat her with egalitarian respect.

It might be argued that the very fact the RP thinks in terms of "right" and "wrong" commits her to believing that there are objective moral reasons to treat her with egalitarian respect; that is, reasons which hold for any person, whether that person realizes it or not. But I do not see that an argument for objective reasons follows necessarily from our use of "right" and "wrong." For in the first place, and as a general point, ordinary concepts may rest on false presuppositions, and therefore we cannot validly move from "our ordinary concepts imply X" to "X is true."[1] Secondly, and more specifically, our concepts "right" and "wrong" allow us to formulate both objectivist and subjectivist theories of moral reasons – this much is proven by the history of Western philosophy. Given this fact, the question must be, not what our ordinary concepts of right and wrong presuppose, but rather what is the correct theory about moral reasons, after all the relevant considerations are in. We must conclude, therefore, that the RP's holding that it is right for others to treat her with egalitarian respect does not necessarily mean she must believe that these others have a reason, objective or not, to treat her with egalitarian respect.

There is a further point to make on this issue. Even if we assume that there are objective moral reasons for egalitarian respect, the question of what leads one person, but not another, to act on these reasons would remain. On the other hand, if there are no objective moral reasons, there would still be the question of what leads people to commit themselves to egalitarian respect. In this sense, the question of objective reasons can be bypassed if our main concern is to determine what actually motivates people to other-respect. As we shall see, this is the perspective I take in the next chapter. For now, we can return to the RP and egalitarian self-respect.

A third clarification is that my argument helps us understand the RP's attitude toward her capacity for autonomy. We see that it is her *commitment* to exercising her autonomy which counts for the RP, rather than mere possession of the capacity. Here we understand more deeply a point discussed in 2.7. I said there that what matters for the RP is *that* she can make her beliefs her own, and not how she compares to others in terms of autonomy (remember the analogy with finishing the marathon). We now see this same point taken to a deeper level. For it is the RP's commitment to exercise her autonomy sincerely, and not how she compares to others in terms of the capacity, which gives her the concept of her self-identified good as worthy of not being transgressed by any other person.

In two respects, my position on autonomy asks less of this capacity than does Kant. First, Kant wants to provide a rationale that *any* rational and goodwilled person would accept as grounds for treating all humans equally (a demand which we saw, in the previous chapter, autonomy cannot meet). My position, on the other hand, starts from the perspective of the Reasonable Person and so is not addressed to those who do not share her defining commitment. Second, and related to the previous point, my position differs from Kant's with regard to the issue of universalizing egalitarian respect from self to others. Since many people do not share the RP's commitment to autonomy, it follows that she cannot use universalizability, in this regard at least, as a way to ground a commitment to respect others. Kant, on other hand, specifically relies on this type of universalizability to ground respect for others (I do not say universalization *of this type* is his main argument for grounding universal respect, but only that it is one argument).[2] My use of autonomy, though more modest than Kant's, is also more realistic, for his position, I would maintain, overreaches itself. Why, after all, would a person who respects rational autonomy in herself feel obliged to extend her respect equally to another if that other does not care to exercise her rational autonomy? Why would a person who is moved to respect the moral law in herself be led, in consistency, to universalize this respect to someone who does not at all act in accord with the moral law? These are critical questions which arise naturally against Kant's view. We shall see more of this issue in the next chapter.

I have so far argued that the RP's defining commitment strongly disposes her to have egalitarian self-respect. I now turn to showing that her commitment to the consonant traits further reinforces her egalitarian self-respect.

8.2 The RP's ideal self is engaged by her attraction to certain traits and her rejection of others. As our discussion in the previous chapters has shown, she sees autonomy and the sense of inherent worth as congruent with her nature. At the same time, she rejects other-dependency, competitive self-esteem, and corporativeness. How now do these dispositions support egalitarian self-respect? In order to discuss this issue, we must first understand more about the self-evaluation implicit in egalitarian self-respect.

Egalitarian self-respect implies a self-evaluation which stands in contrast to our self-image as ordinarily projected by our self-esteem. Our self-esteem is often conditional on some achievement or subject to reflected and competitive self-evaluations. By contrast, egalitarian self-respect implies a positive self-evaluation which is unconditional and indefeasible by our shortcomings and comparative value. When we assert our basic rights, for example, we imply that others owe us egalitarian respect *whatever* our properties. Usually, of course, it is the ups and downs of our episodic self-esteem which preoccupy us. But the self-evaluation implicit in our egalitarian self-respect is also part of our mentality, and this self-evaluation may be weakened or strengthened, to good or bad effect, by social and psychological forces. In what follows, I describe four ways the consonant traits strengthen the RP's egalitarian self-respect. In each case, my strategy is to show how a consonant trait is congruent with an aspect of the unconditional self-evaluation implicit in egalitarian self-respect.

1 *Non-Competitive Self-Esteem*   To express egalitarian self-respect is implicitly to value one's self-identified good independently of how one's abilities, achievements, social status, or moral qualities compare to others. This is reflected, as I previously mentioned, in the way we think of human rights; but the same self-evaluation lies implicit in the other four criteria for egalitarian respect. Now in undercutting competitive self-esteem, the RP sees her reasons for self-esteem in non-competitive terms. She thereby forms an image of herself as esteem-worthy independently of how she directly compares to others. This self-image, as opposed to one grounded in competitive self-esteem, must reinforce the non-comparative aspect of egalitarian self-respect.

2 *Autonomous Self-Esteem*   To express egalitarian self-respect is implicitly to value one's self-identified good independently of others' attitudes toward oneself. One is not owed egalitarian respect, as we have the concept, because others find one instrumental to their ends, or because others esteem various of one's qualities. Now in undercutting reflected self-evaluations and thereby acquiring autonomous reasons, the RP sees herself as esteem-worthy independently of how others evaluate her. This self-image, as opposed to one grounded in purely reflected self-evaluations, must reinforce egalitarian self-respect. Recall, too, that the person with egalitarian self-respect protests and feels resentment when others treat her with egalitarian disrespect. But in order for a person to do so, she must be capable of not taking the egalitarian disrespect of others too much to heart; that is, she must possess a self-image which is not wholly susceptible to reflected self-evaluations.

3 *Non-Corporativeness and the Inherent Sense of Worth*   To express egalitarian self-respect is implicitly to see oneself as entitled to be treated as an equal, even apart from whether social conventions support the attitude. It is to see oneself, in Rawls's phrase, as "a self-

originating source of valid claims."[3] This contrasts with many other entitlements. It is only in virtue of social conventions, for example, that we can be entitled to a prize or to many of the rights defined by our jobs (the conventions in a sense create the prize or the rights). We think of egalitarian respect, however, in a different light. Even if, in some society, there were no social conventions which specified that people ought to be treated with egalitarian respect, it would still make sense to say that these people should be treated as equals. And we properly think that laws are instituted to protect our already existing moral right to egalitarian respect (rather than to create that right). Moreover, since we do not think of egalitarian respect as created by social conventions, we do not also think of it as expungible by social or institutional fiat.

Now in undercutting the corporative trait (role and status entrenchment, exclusive altruism, pliancy, pooled emotions, etc.), the RP sees herself as esteem-worthy apart from any integral relation to social conventions. This disposition is further strengthened by the way her commitment to the guidelines gives her a route to imaginative disengagement from her social roles and statuses (4.9). Moreover, the RP's manner of gaining episodic self-esteem leads her to regard esteem-worthy properties, such as achievements, as issuing from herself, as opposed to issuing from corporative facts. This view in turn deepens her sense of being a distinct individual with a unique history and point of view. These consonant traits, then, serve to reinforce that aspect of egalitarian self-respect which defines a person's worth independently of social conventions.

4 *Demystification*   To possess egalitarian self-respect is to believe that others have no right to expect one to be servile, that others owe one an effort at empathetic politeness, and that others ought not to condescend toward the way one pursues one's self-identified good. Now when people do *not* express this aspect of egalitarian self-respect (through protest and feelings of resentment), then mystification of others is often a significant cause: people are cowed or mesmerized into being servile, etc. But we have seen that the RP, through undercutting reflected, competitive, and corporative reasons for self-esteem, demystifies others. Therefore, her nature, in this regard as well, supports egalitarian self-respect.

In this part of the chapter, I have argued that the RP's core nature – her defining commitment, together with the consonant traits – disposes her to anchor egalitarian self-respect in her actions and feelings. I now turn to understanding why this fact contributes to a desirable life for the RP.

8.3 An obvious reason is that to be disposed to assert one's rights and to demand fairness for oneself must make one more effective in pursuing one's own good. As well, it is generally in people's interests to have an equal voice in decisions which affect them. Motivated by egalitarian self-respect, the RP demands such treatment as her due. Hence, she feels at home in democratic groups and is strongly disposed to sustain them.

The above considerations are good reasons for the RP to see her core nature as supporting a desirable life. However, we can carry our analysis to a deeper level. To do this, we must return for a moment to the general analysis of self-respect in 6.1.

We saw there that in judging ourselves to be a self-respecting X, we at the same time make self-esteem judgments of two distinct sorts: there is a positive judgment on account of our having met the norms for being a good X, and there is a positive judgment on account of our being part of the X tradition. Now these two self-esteem judgments are often combined in one experience, as when John judges himself to be meeting the relevant norms of good carpentry and thereby to be acting in accord with the worthiness of the tradition of carpentry. It is evident that self-respect, when connected to this doubled sense of enhancement, must be a great good for a person. When self-respect in this form is a settled part of a person's life, it brings with it self-confidence and a sense of wholeness. Bertrand Russell was referring to self-respect in this sense when, in a letter to a friend, he wrote, "What is absolutely vital to me is the self-respect I get from work – when (as often) I have done something for which I feel remorse, work restores me to a belief that it is better that I should exist than not exist."[4] Although Russell's feelings are extreme, he does not overstate the contribution self-respect can make to a person's well-being. Think, too, of the role that being a self-respecting carpenter might play in John's life, or being a self-respecting servant in Denner's. We can now extend this discussion to egalitarian self-respect.

In expressing egalitarian self-respect, an egalitarian agent satisfies one or more of the criteria analysed in 6.1 and thereby experiences enhancement. This disposition to derive self-esteem through expressing egalitarian self-respect, I shall call the *sense of dignity.* (Recall that enhancement connected to self-respect often remains in the background of our consciousness, and therefore we need not think of this mental state as egocentric.)

Like other forms of self-respect, a sense of dignity can contribute to our well-being. One way it does so is by helping us withstand onslaughts to our self-esteem from authority or the opinions of others. An extreme example occurs when a person finds herself living under conditions of degradation, in which even to protest is futile. In such conditions, an egalitarian agent may summon up as a source of strength the thought that, whatever else is inflicted upon her, *she* will not cease to respect herself. In deriving enhancement from this expression of egalitarian self-respect, a person's capacity to resist internalizing the judgment of her oppressors is strengthened. A sense of dignity is no doubt a slender foothold upon which to maintain one's sanity in situations of extreme degradation. But we know from reports of people who have been in such circumstances that the trait can play this role. For example, in describing his experiences in a concentration camp, Victor Frankl writes as follows about the apathy under which most of the inmates fell:

Besides these physical causes there were mental ones in the form of certain complexes. The majority of prisoners suffered from a kind of inferiority complex. We all had once been or fancied ourselves to be "somebody." Now we were treated like complete nonentities. (The consciousness of one's inner value is anchored in higher, more spiritual things, and cannot be shaken by camp life. But how many free men, let alone prisoners, possess it?). Without consciously thinking about it, the average prisoner felt himself utterly degraded ... Under the influence of a world which no longer recognized the value of human life and human dignity, which robbed man of his will and had made him an object to be exterminated ... the personal ego finally suffered a loss of values. If the man in the concentration camp did not struggle against this in a last effort to save his self-respect, he lost the feeling of being an individual ... a being with personal value. He thought of himself as only part of an enormous mass of people.[5]

A number of the concepts I have introduced are present in this description. In the first place, Frankl implies that being a self-respecting X, where X stands for some social role (being a "somebody"), is not enough to resist internalizing the evaluations of one's oppressors. Seeing oneself as a self-respecting X is usually inseparable from social conventions and the recognition of others, and as such, it is easily deflated when normal social conditions are overturned. To withstand making dependent self-evaluations, the inmate must maintain "consciousness of her inner value." That is, in my terms, she must continue to evaluate herself as worthy of egalitarian respect or, in other words, maintain her sense of dignity. We should note too that Frankl connects (what I am calling) the sense of dignity to the "feeling of being an individual." In my terms, he is relating the sense of dignity to having an inherent sense of worth, which in turn is connected to a person's disposition not to ground her self-esteem in corporative and reflected self-ascriptions (recall here our inclination to say of Jenny Rastall, mentioned at the beginning of chapter 5, that she lacks dignity). We can see, then, that there is mutual support between the RP's manner of gaining self-esteem and her disposition for egalitarian self-respect. Moreover, she has a further, related advantage.

We saw in the case of being a self-respecting X that one source of self-esteem focuses on the worthiness of being part of the X tradition. Recall now (7.3) that in the case of egalitarian self-respect, there is no analogous tradition upon which to focus a reason for self-esteem, so long at least as we are looking for an impersonal grounding. This fact partly accounts, I suggested, for why egalitarian self-respect is so weakly anchored for many people. But the situation of the RP is different, for she sees her egalitarian self-respect as growing directly out of her commitment to being an RP. Given, too, that she thinks of reasonableness as a worthy tradition, then her egalitarian self-respect would share in the motivating enhancement attached to being a self-respecting RP.

8.4 I have been describing ways the RP's core nature contributes to her well-being. In light of this emphasis, it is important to be clear about her motivation. Her defining commitment, the consonant traits, the tradition of reasonableness, and egalitarian self-respect are, for her, part and parcel of a worthy life. Now it is the RP's judgments of worth, not reasons of self-interest, which directly motivate her to express her nature. These judgments of worth, then, are powerful reference points which determine how she conducts her life. At the same time, we must imagine that she cares as much as any other person about her own well-being. The RP's well-being, then, also constitutes a significant reference point in her practical deliberations. Now clearly things go better for a person when her most significant values are in harmony (to use the terminology of critical guideline 6). When such values are not in harmony, there must be trade-offs (as when love and happiness sometimes diverge, or loyalty and truthfulness). Such trade-offs are always regrettable for the agent, and sometimes tragic. It is in this light that the RP regards the relationship between her core nature and her well-being: her core nature is not justified directly in terms of her well-being. But that the RP's core nature harmonizes with her well-being is clearly for the better, and therefore a further (and gratifying) reason for her to sustain her core nature.

9 "I Do Not Count for More..."

9.1 To contribute to the good of others is, for all normal people, part of a meaningful life. In this chapter I show that the Reasonable Person's core nature, through its connection to other-respect, is congruent with this ingredient of a desirable life. First, let us briefly see why, if a person has the trait of other-respect, he contributes to others' good.

Out of respect for others' basic rights (criterion 4) and out of fairness (criterion 3), an egalitarian agent constrains the pursuit of his own good, even when he could take advantage of others by violating their rights or treating them unfairly. Recall, too, that criterion 3 requires that when an egalitarian agent's good conflicts with another's, then he looks for ways of achieving a compromise: he is open to having his own interests weighed, by some fair egalitarian standard, against the interests of others. This aspect of criterion 3 is further strengthened through criterion 2, in which a person with the trait of other-respect commits himself to entering into egalitarian dialogue with those affected by his actions; with the possibility that his own point of view might change to their advantage. These aspects of other-respect must enhance the ability of others to pursue their own good, especially those others who, because of lack of power, status, or achievement, are vulnerable to the dictates and whims of the more powerful.

A second category of beneficence relates to the egalitarian agent's impact on other people's egalitarian self-respect. Motivated by his belief that others count equally to himself, he neither desires nor expects that others should be subservient; he is neither condescending nor disparaging to those whose interests are different from his own; and he enters into egalitarian dialogue with any other person, whatever that person's social status. Moreover, as criteria 3 and 4 detail, he supports those institutions through which society as a whole expresses the principle that each person counts equally. Clearly, a person, A, who is on the receiving end of these expressions of other-respect must have his egalitarian self-respect reinforced and thereby benefit in the ways described in 8.3. Note that A's reinforced self-respect depends on his believing that the egalitarian agent is actually *motivated* by the belief that A counts equally to himself. That is, A must believe that the egalitarian agent somehow *sees* A as an equal – rather than believe, for example, that the egalitarian agent is motivated by mere social convention or by self-interest. I shall later discuss this notion of seeing another as an equal. I turn now to the relationship between other-respect and the Reasonable Person's defining commitment.

9.2 We saw in the previous chapter that "I do not count for less than others" flows directly from the RP's defining commitment. In the case of "I do not count for more than others," however, there is no such direct connection. Nevertheless, my argument will be that the RP's core nature does in many respects *support* the trait of other-respect, once we assume that he has open to him, from sources outside his core nature, certain experiences. Before getting to this argument (in part C), it is important to see why other-respect does not flow directly from the RP's defining commitment.

I argued in the previous chapter that, since not all others share his defining commitment, consistency could not in itself require the RP to move from respecting himself to other-respecting all others. Following from this, we can see further that, barring some countervailing force, the RP must indeed be disposed to discount the interests of some others. There are people, for example, whose ideals are directly contrary to his defining ideal; those, that is, who regard competitive self-esteem, corporativism, and antipathy toward reasonableness as elements of a worthy life. If we imagine an RP whose attitude toward others is completely circumscribed by his defining commitment, then thinking of some others as counting for less than himself would follow naturally. Why, we could imagine such an RP asking himself, should I regard and treat with other-respect a person whose self-identified good stands against my deepest values?

We can see, furthermore, that there is nothing in the RP's reasoning to his own egalitarian self-respect which necessarily commits him to other-respect even other RPS. The reasoning which yields the attitude of egalitarian self-respect is relative, in the following sense, to the agent doing the reasoning. An RP's defining commitment yields the attitude "It would be morally wrong for any other person to transgress my point of view." But there is no automatic step from this thought to "It would be morally wrong for me to transgress the point of view of any other RP." At best, the RP understands that any other RP can also reason, from *his own* perspective, that it would be morally wrong for any other person to transgress his point of view. But recalling our discussion of objective reasons (8.2), this does not mean that the RPS in question have grounds, in virtue of their own reasoning, for mutual other-respect. What does follow from the RP's defining nature, specifically in terms of guideline 5, is a sincere willingness to esteem the trait of being reasonable in others. However, as I explained when analysing that guideline (1.7), the RP's commitment to consistency does not in itself entail a willingness to take into account, on an equal basis, the *interests* of others whom he esteems.

Nor should we think that the RP's commitment to weighing considerations impartially leads, *in itself*, to egalitarian dialogue. It is possible to imagine a person who, while committed to engaging the considerations of others impartially, is nevertheless imbued with an inegalitarian ethos. A citizen of ancient Athens, one imagines, could have given impartial consideration to the arguments of a slave; that is, he could have ignored the status difference between himself and the slave for the sake of the argument at issue (even if the argument were over the validity of slavery). Clearly, however, he would not have been engaging the slave in egalitarian dialogue. In the first place, the citizen's dialogue would not have been appropriately motivated; and secondly, in the case of conflict between the interests of the citizen and the slave, the former would not have sought, through discussion with the latter, a fair egalitarian compromise.

As I mentioned in chapter 7, even when people grow up in an egalitarian culture, they often do not possess the trait of other-respect in its fullest sense. Now for a person to do so, I believe he must be open to what I shall call *perspective-creating (or sustaining) experiences*. These experiences, if they are felt powerfully enough, cause a person to *see* any other person as having equal moral status to himself. Given this perspective, it then makes rational sense for an agent to commit himself to other-respect, assuming that the trait has, for that agent, what I call *expressive significance*. In part C, I show that the RP's nature is suited to his finding expressive significance in other-respect. But first we must understand more about these perspective-creating experiences.

B: PERSPECTIVE-CREATING EXPERIENCES

9.3 The impersonally groundable approach asks: "What reasons can we give any rational and goodwilled person for why he ought to adopt or cultivate other-respect?" The question I am now asking is: "What *experiences* might lead a person to see others as his equals, and so commit himself to other-respect?" This second question gives us a different angle on how other-respect could become grounded in a person's life.[1] In one way, this approach asks a lot from our understanding, for to be persuasive, it must realistically describe the experiences which can give rise to other-respect. In several ways, on the other hand, this strategy represents a more modest approach to our topic. In the first place, since we are starting from experiences, my approach makes no claim on someone who does not undergo the relevant experiences. In the second place, even when someone does undergo these experiences, he is not thereby given a logically coercive reason to adopt the moral principles expressive of other-respect. It might be suggested that these facts make this approach so modest as to render it uninteresting. However, after we analyse the experiences and understand their connection to other-respect, we shall see that this is not the case.

Before discussing the perspective-creating experiences, I make two important qualifications: (a) I gladly acknowledge that there are experiences other than the two I present capable of creating an egalitarian perspective;[2] and (b) although I sometimes present the experiences so as to suggest that a person's perspective changes all at once, nevertheless I do not mean to imply that this is the way such experiences always function. Often perspective-creating experiences work cumulatively and less dramatically, so as gradually to bring about a change in a person's way of seeing. Keeping these qualifications in mind, we can now proceed to the two experiences.

We (or at least some of us) can be powerfully struck by the thought that, behind all the differences between ourselves and others, we and they are (i) equally subject to death and (ii) equally subject to fortune. At such moments, the categories by which we distinguish ourselves from others can shrink to insignificance, and we can feel, to our core, a common bond even with utter strangers. From this perspective, the belief that we count for more than any other person appears deeply false; we *see* that any other person, whatever his status or achievement, counts equally to ourselves. Now how this perspective is expressed – if it is expressed – depends in part on the moral resources available in a person's culture. As I said earlier (7.1), egalitarianism is a historically evolving attitude, and so we find these perspective-creating experiences expressed in diverse ways and to different degrees. Indeed, as I shall discuss later, these experiences, because of countervailing dispositions, can easily stop short of yielding a belief in equal status. On the other hand, given the right personality in the right culture, they can sustain a commitment to egalitarian respect. For now, however, let us examine further the nature of these experiences.

That such experiences can move a person to see any other person as having equal moral status to himself is a claim about human psychology. Therefore, the evidence for this claim must lie in showing that some people are in fact so moved, and indeed there is ample evidence. In order to bring out points relevant to my argument, I shall consider several such accounts, relating first to our mortality and then to our subjection to fortune.

There have been cultures in which social divisions were so definitive of people's identities that there was no recognized deeper human solidarity. Such has been the case, for example, in some slave and caste societies. In the Middle Ages, on the other hand, even though social divisions were very rigid, there was an underlying sense of human equality. The idea that all humans are made in God's image was probably the ultimate underpinning for the attitude. However, one of the most common ways it found expression was through the theme that people, whatever their social position, are equally subject to death. "The thought of equality in the Middle Ages," writes historian John Huizinga, "was closely akin to a *memento mori*."[3] This sentiment was expressed in hymns, poems, and paintings. "Prince, remember, without disdaining the poor, that death holds the reins," says an exemplary ballad of the times.[4] That a culture such as that of hierarchical medieval Europe could express egalitarian sentiments testifies to the power that the experience of our common mortality has to sustain a form (in this case, a primitive form) of egalitarianism.

In her autobiography, Simone de Beauvoir recounts how one of her schoolteachers, a Monsieur Garric, had inspired in her a sense of egalitarianism. Garric recounted to his students how, facing the constant possibility of death during the First World War, he had "discovered in the trenches the joys of a comraderie that did away with social boundaries," and how he had come to see that "under all the differences, there is a common denominator between people."[5] Because of these experiences, he changed his life and politics, and de Beauvoir in turn was changed by him. She writes that Garric's words:

... struck an absolutely new sound to my ears. Certainly, around me there were many preaching self-sacrifice. But self-sacrifice was thought of in terms of the family. Outside of the family one did not regard others as fellow creatures. In particular, the workers appeared to be a species as dangerous as the Bosch or the Bolsheviks. Garric had swept away these barriers. There did not exist over the whole earth but one community, and all of its members were my brothers ... I must break through my class, my skin.[6]

When George Orwell was a police officer in Burma, he witnessed the hanging of a Hindu prisoner. As the condemned man was being led to the gallows, he "stepped slightly aside to avoid a puddle on the path":

It is curious, but till that moment I had never realized what it means to destroy a healthy, conscious man. When I saw the prisoner step aside to avoid the puddle, I saw the mystery, the unspeakable wrongness, of cutting a life short when it is in full tide. This man was not dying, he was alive just as we were alive. All the organs of his body were working – bowels digesting food, skin renewing itself, nails growing, tissues forming – all toiling away in solemn foolery. His nails would still be growing when he stood on the drop, when he was falling through the air with a tenth of a second to live. His eyes saw the yellow gravel and the grey walls, and his brain still remembered, foresaw, reasoned – reasoned even about puddles. He and we were a party of men walking together, seeing, hearing, feeling, understanding the same world; and in two minutes, with a sudden snap, one of us would be gone – one mind less, one world less.[7]

It is relevant to note that after Orwell quit the police force (which he had come to see as part of an exploitative colonial system), he lived among the poor for a number of years and wrote movingly of their lives.

In a moment I shall discuss the above passages. But first I turn to our second set of perspective-creating experiences. The idea that people, whatever their social position, achievements, or moral desert, are equally subject to fortune has struck human beings with great force throughout history. Although there are different ways the thought can be experienced, its essence is the sense that what ultimately governs people's lives is morally arbitrary. (Perhaps this puts the thought in a paradoxically active manner, since the experience is precisely that there is *nothing*, which makes moral sense, that ultimately governs what happens to people.) When we feel the force of this thought, it is irrelevant to be reminded that people sometimes do, through hard work and in other ways, get what they deserve, for this fact itself appears morally arbitrary from the perspective I am describing. How else, one asks from this perspective, do we explain that people so often do *not* get what they deserve? (Why should X be the one that gets what he deserves, whereas Y does not?) If humans were somehow to arrange life so that good and bad fortune were always proportionate to people's moral qualities, then this fact too would seem morally arbitrary. For it must seem morally arbitrary, from the perspective I am describing, that people living in this future age should be the beneficiaries of the new arrangement, whereas people in previous ages were not. (Why should X be the one to be born into this morally meritocratic utopia, whereas Y was not?)

A religious world-view might seem to preclude a sense of our equal subjection to fortune. Since the world is governed by an all-good and all-powerful god, it might be said, everything that happens has a morally relevant reason for why it happens. However, religious people are far from immune to the experience of moral arbitrariness. This is why the "appearance" of moral arbitrariness is seen as demanding an answer. The most usual answer is in terms of an afterlife where what appears to have been morally arbitrary in this life is shown in reality not to have been. But even people who hold this belief, or one which serves the same function, are often subject to the experience of moral arbitrariness (against their better judgment perhaps, but to their credit, I believe). Indeed, one of the most powerful descriptions of such an experience is the biblical story of Job; and Job was a religious man. That this experience breaks through deeply held religious beliefs shows the power of the "data" which evoke the experience.

I want now to mention one significant way the sense of our equal subjection to fortune can be experienced. This is the feeling that at the very moment some good or bad thing is happening to another person (or to oneself), a contrary experience is happening to oneself (or to another person). I call this the experience of *synchronic incongruity*. Such experiences have implicit in them the sense that there is no morally relevant reason why the other person is *there* undergoing his experience while I am *here* undergoing mine. Hence we are struck by how the two of us are equally subject to fortune, whether it is that our lives are going well or badly. Here are two descriptions of synchronic incongruity, the first from an essay by George Steiner and the second from a novel by C.P. Snow:

Precisely at the same hour in which Mehring or Langner were being done to death [through being tortured in a concentration camp], the overwhelming plurality of human beings [from the context it is clear that Steiner means above all to include himself in this plurality], two miles away on the Polish farms, five thousand miles away in New York, were sleeping or eating or going to a film or making love or worrying about the dentist. This is where my imagination balks. The two orders of simultaneous experience are so different, so irreconcilable to any common norm of human values ...[8]

It had been the same with the boy's death. While he was beginning to suffer fright and worse than fright, people had been living as healthily as these men around us in the bar, talking and making love or maybe being preoccupied with what seemed a serious worry of our own.[9]

9.4 My claim is that experiences such as these have the power, if the circumstances are right, to create or sustain a commitment to other-respect. I am indeed disposed to make a much stronger claim, namely, that other-respect, in its fullest sense, is impossible without such experiences. However, before we get to the connection between these experiences and other-respect, I want, through a relatively simple case, to analyse the way a perspective-creating experience may affect our behaviour toward others.[10]

Imagine that Smith has an intense dislike of Jones, and uses words such as "dishonest" and "power-hungry" when thinking of him. Because of these feelings, she is disposed to be ruthless when dealing with Jones (he is beneath consideration in her eyes). But then one day she chances to see him playing with his child. Suddenly he appears to Smith in a different light, a perspective from which ruthlessness seems utterly wrong. Now here, I want to say, it is not that Smith has discovered some characteristic of Jones to which she attributes positive worth, and which then provides a counterbalance to her attributions of negative worth. It is not, in other words, that she could rationalize her mental state as: "Anyone who plays with his or her child should not be treated as beneath consideration. Jones plays with his child; therefore, he should not be treated as beneath consideration." Rather, it is that Smith comes to see Jones as a fellow human being (and so as no longer beneath consideration), and this changes her whole view of him, while leaving her previous negative judgments intact (i.e., she still sees him as dishonest and power-hungry).

The key words in understanding Smith's change of perspective are "comes to see Jones as a fellow human being." Note it is through these words that she herself thinks of her change-of-perspective (as

Wittgenstein noted, change-of-perspective experiences often seem "half visual experience, half thought").[11] Now it is not that previous to this experience, Smith did not know that Jones was human, or even that he had a child. It is rather that these same facts come together for her in a novel way and *cause her* to see him in a different light.

Is "see" in this context mainly metaphorical, as it clearly is in other contexts?[12] To think so would be a mistake. Although it may be easiest to understand the change-of-perspective experience by means of value-neutral examples (such as the duck-rabbit diagram), nevertheless our experiences do not cease to be visual when coloured by aesthetic or moral judgments. Thus I may not have noticed the cruelty inherent in A's face until after seeing its similarity to another person's face.[13] This experience, which embodies a moral judgment, is as much a visual experience as my suddenly seeing a duck where before I had only seen a rabbit. What in part makes these two experiences different is not that one is visual and the other is not, but that the cruel face arouses emotions, and perhaps desires, whereas the duck-rabbit does not. There is clearly a continuum regarding the amount of moral or aesthetic judgment we bring to our perception. But "seeing" is no less visual for being infused by value judgments. Now I should not want to say that "fellow human being" is a visual quality like "cruel face"; I would want to say, however, that a person who sees another as a fellow human being has a different visual experience than he would, in the precisely the same circumstances, if he saw the person as beneath consideration. Support for this claim comes from studies of painting, photography, the mass media, and travel diaries; especially as these arts and letters deal with cultures foreign to that of the artist or writer.[14] Through these media, people often try to represent objectively the *visual* impression others make on them. When, however, we analyse these representations, we can often determine whether the artist, photographer, or writer saw those he was depiciting as his moral equals. Consider, too, cultures in which moral standing is strongly correlated with social standing. In such societies, there are always explicit visual indicators of social differences, such as clothing and deportment. In these societies, to see others as an equal or unequal must be a strongly visual experience. That we can literally *look upon* another person as an equal is a point to which I shall return.

What now is the significance of "as" in "seeing Jones *as* a fellow human being." Smith, by contrast, would not say she sees him *as* playing with his child, or *as* heavy set. The word "as" clearly signals that the agent, in his own mind, is seeing an entity from a particular perspective. I want briefly to spell out what "seeing from a particular perspective" means in this context.

First, let us say that a perspective is a *living option*[15] when there are some people in the agent's reference group who hold the perspective (it is, in other words, a perspective which the agent recognizes can in practice be held). Now when an agent, A, says to himself or to some other person that he is seeing an entity, E, from a perspective X, then the following conditions are implicit in his mental state: (a) A believes that though he is seeing E from perspective X, nevertheless E admits to being seen in terms of another perspective, Y; (b) A believes Y is a living option; and (c) A recognizes that X and Y are incompatible, in the sense that to see E in terms of X is *ipso facto* not to see E, at the same time, in terms of Y. That Smith does not say she sees Jones as playing with his child, then, implies that she is not thinking as she has this experience that there is some other, incompatible perspective, which is a living option, from which to view this state of affairs. Note that "incompatible" here may have logical import, but it need not. Thus it may be that an agent believes X is actually inconsistent with Y; such that if X is justified, then to see A in terms of Y is unjustified. On the other hand, it may be, as in the case of the duck-rabbit, that the incompatibility between X and Y is purely psychological; such that even though a person could not hold X and Y in his mind at the same time, he may nevertheless recognize that X and Y are not inconsistent ways of seeing E.

With the above analysis in mind, we can distinguish the following elements in Smith's change of perspective: (1) her seeing Jones as beneath consideration; (2) her ruthlessness toward Jones in the light of this perspective; (3) the event which triggers her change of perspective, that is, her seeing Jones with his child; (4) her new perspective of seeing Jones as a fellow human being; and (5) her actions regarding Jones in the light of her new perspective. How now are we to understand the connection between Smith's actions and her change of perspective?

Our seeing a person as kindly disposes us to act differently toward that person than if we were to see him as cruel. For example, we are disposed to put our trust in a kindly person but avoid a cruel person. Now it is not that these dispositions arise because we have first adopted a principle such as "One should trust people who are kindly"; rather, the dispositions are set in motion directly by our way of seeing the person. Similarly, Smith's change of perspective, I want to say, directly disposes her not to be ruthless toward Jones, even granting his nasty moral qualities. (Analogously, when we see something as dangerous, we are directly disposed to take cautionary action.) But now a disposition to act is not the act itself: Smith's seeing Jones as a fellow human being, and the dispositions which arise from that perspective, can be outweighed by other dispositions or considerations. Moreover, the potency of the original perspective-creating experience must inevitably dissipate, and so too the dispositions which arose in its wake. But if Smith's experience has made a significant impression on her, and at the same time this impression coheres with other beliefs to which she attaches importance, then it would be natural that she *commit herself* to act in accord with a principle such as "It is wrong that I treat Jones with ruthlessness; I must now, and in the future, treat him as a fellow human being." Smith's commitment to this principle, I want to say, gives expression to her new perspective. This *expressive commitment*, then, must be added as a sixth element to the five I earlier mentioned as constituting the perspective-creating experience. Let us now see how the above analysis can be extended to other-respect.

9.5 We want to understand how the recognition of our common mortality and common subjection to fortune could trigger, deepen, or sustain a commitment to other-respect. As will be clear from the above, we are not looking for reasons which would rationally coerce a person to adopt other-respect, but something more in the order of psychological congruencies between the perspective-creating experiences and other-respect. I shall focus on two such congruencies.

1 *Congruence with the Universal Scope of Other-Respect*   We have seen that when someone undergoes an experience like that of Garric, de Beauvoir, or Orwell, then social status, achievement, moral desert, and emotional closeness, which ordinarily shape the way we feel and behave toward others, become for a time irrelevant. The agent sees himself as sharing with others, whoever they are, a common fate and condition. Consider first the passage from Orwell. He did not know anything about the achievements or moral qualities of the prisoner; and the man's religion, nationality, social standing, and predicament were as different from his own as possible. In this sense, the man could be *any* person. But his impending death led Orwell to feel a bond with him and a sense of the finiteness, not only of the prisoner's life, but of his own. The phrases he uses are indicative of this sense of common fate: "he was alive *just as we* were alive"; "*He and we* were a party of men walking together, seeing, hearing, understanding the same world; and in two minutes ... one of us would be gone." Similarly, Garric and de Beauvoir talk of the social barriers between

themselves and others (most of whom they did not know personally) being swept away.

Synchronic incongruity, too, is often felt with reference to complete strangers, as when a person feels how morally absurd it is that he should be enjoying a hearty meal while at the same time another person, through the bad fortune of having been born in an arid country, is starving to death (I am not here talking about pity or guilt). Such experiences cause us to discount, for a time, the categories by which we judge or feel that one person has more importance than another.

As I have defined other-respect, the attitude is held impartially toward all human beings. Now it is reasonable to see a perspective triggered by the above experiences as congruent with this aspect of other-respect.

2 *Congruence with the Precedence Given Other-Respect in Our Actions*
In committing ourselves to other-respect, we constrain the pursuit of our own self-identified good out of respect for the self-identified good of others (7.2). The question then is how a perspective-creating experience could support this aspect of other-respect. My answer falls into two parts. First, I argue that the experience of our common mortality can lead us to see any human life, including that of an utter stranger, as awe-inspiring. This experience supports the precedence a person might give other-respect over his own self-interest, and even over maximizing what has intrinsic value; that is, it supports what I called in 7.2 other-respect's deontological force. (This is especially true, it should be said, when the experience of awe is conjoined with the sense of our common subjection to fortune.) The second part of my answer has to do with how the self-denial connected to other-respect can be integrated into a person's point of view. However, I do not take up this second issue till part C, where I discuss the specific situation of the RP. I turn then to the first part of the answer.

It is not only that Orwell feels the prisoner's mortality along with his own (which would be merely depressing), but that he is moved by this fact to sense, as he says, "the mystery, the unspeakable wrongness, of cutting a life short when it is in full tide"; and that with this stranger's death there would be "one mind less, one world less." In other words, Orwell's experience causes him to have a certain attitude to human life in general. What is this attitude, and what is its object?

In chapter 5, I introduced the concept of person-distinctness, or singularity. This is the idea that however similar two people are, each embodies a unique point of view and history. I said further that it is one thing to possess this concept, but another to give it moral (and thereby psychological) weight. I argued that one way weight accrues to our own singularity is through our having inherent reasons for self-esteem. I want now to say that the recognition of our common mortality can cause us to give weight, not only to our own singularity, but to that of any other person.

When a person we know dies, we are moved to think of his life as a single narrative. Even if the person underwent radical changes in circumstance or personality, we still think of his life, once it is over, as a unity: our interest lies in how the changes affected this single narrative. If the dead person was close to us, then we absolutely dwell on the details of his life. But in any case, whether the person was a friend, acquaintance, or stranger, we can, I want to say, find any human life awe-inspiring when we juxtapose that unique narrative with the thought that the life has ceased, or will cease, forever.

What we find awe-inspiring has to do with a life's uniqueness and unrepeatability. But it cannot just be these qualities which move us with awe, for any entity, including a grain of sand, is unique and unrepeatable. Yet, although standing in awe of a grain of sand may be possible (Blake talked of "seeing heaven in a grain of sand"), the awe we feel toward a human life is different. It has to do, I believe, with the juxtaposition of what I have called manifesting interest on the one hand and death on the other hand. For example, what sparks Orwell's thought about human life is his seeing the stranger move to avoid a puddle. The inference he draws is that the man *disliked* the idea of getting his feet wet. This dislike is a manifestation of interest, which we understand as issuing from the prisoner himself (remembering my analysis in 5.3 of "issuing from oneself"). The grain of sand, on the other hand, does not manifest interest. When we think of a person's life, we see it largely in terms of a history of these manifestations of interest, or as I also put it (5.7), in terms of the person being the subject-of-a-life.

As I am understanding it, then, to stand in awe of a human life is to be moved by the uniqueness of an entity which manifests interest, but which will cease to exist. It is this complex emotion which points to the mystery Orwell feels when he says that "in two minutes, with a sudden snap, one of us would be gone – one mind less, one world less." It is also, I believe, this emotion which is roused when we look at the body of a person who has recently died, even that of someone we never knew: the dead body calls up to our minds, and so becomes juxtaposed with, the image of a living person.[16] (Here is the place to the make the point, which unfortunately I cannot develop, that my position allows for an extension of some form of other-respect to other species of animals; for other species manifest interest, and we are capable of undergoing the kind of perspective-creating experiences I have been describing with reference to them.)[17]

Awe, as I am using the concept, is very different from an attribution of positive worth. With positive worth, our attention is focused pleasurably. As well, that to which we attribute positive worth must be intelligible to us; or at any rate, the degree to which it is not intelligible, then to that degree our attribution of worth is muted. With awe, on the other hand, we feel ourselves in the presence of something of deep significance which at the same time baffles our emotions. To feel awe is often to be transfixed and at the same time repelled or made anxious – as when, in the case at hand, we feel wonder at the singularity of a human life and at the same time understand that this life must end (it is through recognizing the inevitability of death that our two perspective-creating experiences are often conjoined, so as to yield a sense of our common humanity). The words "praiseworthy" and "admirable" do not capture this experience at all. It is not, for example, that Orwell found the prisoner praiseworthy or admirable in virtue of the man's humanity and mortality. Further light is shed on the role awe plays in my analysis if we compare it to Kant's concept of respect.

We saw in 7.4 that Kant sought to justify the belief in equal moral status in part through the notion of our feeling respect or reverence for rational autonomy. He believed that this attitude issues from objective insight into the nature of rational autonomy. We saw that one difficulty with this notion, even apart from understanding what Kant meant by objective insight, is that there are rational and good-willed people who do not in the least stand in awe of rational autonomy. A second difficulty is that people vary greatly in the degree to which they exercise, or even have the capacity to exercise, rational autonomy. Now the role that awe plays in my argument does not face these difficulties. In the first place, I do not claim that the experiences I have been describing are ones which any rational and goodwilled person must feel. Secondly, to be struck with awe by the singularity and mortality of a human life is something one can feel appropriately toward any human being, since the facts which give rise to the feeling hold true equally of any human being (including, as we have seen, complete strangers). Let us now see how our discussion connects to other-respect.

9.6 When we undergo an emotion to which we attach great significance, we naturally want to give expression to the emotion, and we can do this by engaging in actions which represent or stand for what we feel.[18] Thus, for example, by giving B a present, A can express his love for B. Now the act of present-giving, I want to say, expresses A's love because he sees it as representing or standing for his feelings. Clearly, in order for this to be true, his act must be motivated by his love, and he must recognize that this is so. Then, given that these conditions are met, A must see his act as a way of stating or communicating his love. When an act meets these conditions, then I say that it has *expressive significance* for the agent.

Seeing others as equals, I have tried to show, can be rooted in powerful emotions. It would be natural that a person who has such a perception would want to give it expression. If now this person is part of an egalitarian culture, then he would find practices ready to hand that could *represent* what he feels regarding the equality of moral status between others and himself. He could, that is, determine never to expect any other person to act servilely, and he could resist being condescending to the way others, with different interests or abilities, pursue their self-identified goods; he could seek to treat people with fairness, even when to do so demands self-denial; and so on. By committing himself to these practices, such a person states, both to himself and to others, that any other person counts equally to himself. Given now that an agent is motivated to these practices by his perception of equality, he is what I have defined as an egalitarian agent.

Recalling my discussion of Smith's change of perspective regarding Jones, it is not that the egalitarian agent has found some admirable or praiseworthy property that all humans possess equally. For example, he does not reason, "All humans are equally subject to death; hence all humans are equally worthy of egalitarian respect; therefore I ought to commit myself to treat all humans as equals." Nor does he employ an argument from universalizability such as, "I have egalitarian respect for myself on account of my mortality; others are also mortal; therefore I ought also to have egalitarian respect for them." It is rather, as we have seen, that the egalitarian agent makes a commitment to treat any other person as an equal because he wants to give expression to his perception that others and he count equally. A universalization-like thought process, it is true, could be a psychological vehicle for bringing about this egalitarian perception. A person, for example, might be moved from thinking about his own mortality, or the mortality of those he loves, to thinking about the mortality of any other person, and then, as a result of this thought process, be brought to see or judge that any other person counts equally to himself. But in this case, universalization acts as a *cause* to create a perception, and not as a logical principle to deduce a conclusion, as in the impersonal strategy.

It might be said that my position is no different from the strategy, which I earlier criticized, of the "groundless commitment" (7.9). But contrary to a groundless commitment, the egalitarian agent *does* have an inherent reason for his commitment to other-respect; that is, it is not just (recalling my discussion in 7.9) that the egalitarian agent justifies his belief in terms of its good consequences or its coherence with his other beliefs, for his other-respect is grounded in his way of seeing others. And just as seeing a painting as beautiful (even if others do not share one's perception) can be a compelling and justifiable reason for an agent to buy that painting, so seeing others as equals can be a compelling and justifiable reason for an agent to treat people as equals.

Seeing others as equals is not, to be sure, like seeing that the sun is yellow. Nor, however, is the experience best thought of as a mere feeling, without cognitive force, like Hume's sympathy or fellow-feeling.[19] Hume's analysis of our moral judgments, especially our judgments of moral equality, leaves hanging the following crucial question: "If subjective feelings are the sole source of our judgments of moral equality, then what reason do we have for giving precedence to these feelings in our actions, especially if these actions require self-denial?" In the final analysis, Hume's answer to this question is that our ultimate reason for treating others as equals lies in our own self-interest – in recognizing that it is in our own interest to have a system of moral rules which everyone will be disposed to obey.[20] It seems questionable that self-interest could ever be a sufficient reason for abiding by rules which might demand self-sacrifice, however fair the rules. But even apart from this point, a moral system which gives central place to our common bond with others, but in the end has to rely on self-interest as a final justification, is surely at cross-purposes with itself.

Now my way of conceptualizing our bond with others is not, in this respect, at cross-purposes with itself. The egalitarian agent's commitment to other-respect is justified, in his mind, by the way he sees other people and by his desire to express this perception in his life. Just as "I see that the sun is yellow" can in itself be a good reason (though not an incorrigible one) for a person to believe that the sun is yellow, so analogously "I see him as my equal" can in itself provide an agent with a good reason to treat another person as an equal.

As I have described the process of justification, egalitarian respect is adopted by an agent as a personal ideal. We should note, however, that there is an important sense in which to have this kind of personal grounding for an attitude is what we can call *impersonally understandable*. Any rational and goodwilled person can understand that, *if* a person sees a painting as beautiful or sees others as equals, then it makes rational sense, all things being equal, for that person to buy the painting or commit himself to other-respect. I shall develop this point in the next section.

9.7 Perspective-creating experiences are not impersonally groundable, and even when a person has been subject to them, they do not give that person a rationally coercive reason to adopt other-respect. What then, it might be asked, is the significance of such apparently limited moral phenomena? I want briefly to argue that their significance is great. First, I show that perspective-creating experiences play a pivotal role in the evolution of egalitarianism. Second, I discuss their significance for the individual agent within an egalitarian culture.

We saw in 7.3 that egalitarianism grew in part through appeals to consistency, whereby equal consideration was extended from "in" groups to "out" groups. But such appeals can never in themselves, I maintain, succeed in leading an "in" group to extend equal respect to an "out" group. Let us imagine two groups, the "Elites" and the "Ordinaries," which between them constitute the population of some society. The Elites, I shall assume, pride themselves on being open to rational debate and on taking moral considerations seriously. Now they have basic rights which, as they see it, are justifiably denied the Ordinaries. Moreover, they feel no disposition to accord the Ordinaries empathetic politeness or engage them in egalitarian dialogue. In justifying their inegalitarian society, the Elites cite their *superior culture*, as compared to that of the Ordinaries. (We do not have to suppose this is a hereditary elite; we can, if we wish, imagine that sometimes especially talented Ordinaries are admitted into the Elite ranks, while some unworthy Elites are demoted to the Ordinaries.) Now the question I want to ask is, how could a reformer get the Elites to extend other-respect to the Ordinaries?

The reformer could argue that the Ordinaries are no less capable of experiencing pain and enjoyment than the Elites, and that therefore their interests (in avoiding pain and attaining enjoyment) should have just as much moral weight as the interests of the Elites. This is a form of appeal to consistency. But this appeal could always be rebutted by the Elites through their arguing that *of course* the interests of those with superior culture should count for more than those without this property. To the Elites, it is the reformer who is being inconsistent by not taking into account a highly relevant difference. Nor, psychologically, are the Elites likely to be sympathetically affected by the pain or pleasure of an Ordinary to the same degree as they are affected by the feelings of an Elite (and, to the extent an Elite is so affected, he will dismiss his feelings as mere sentimentality). As for appeals by the reformer that the Elites should imagine themselves in the place of the Ordinaries, the Elites could reply that, thank goodness, they are not without superior culture, but that if they were, then it would be right to treat them accordingly.

The moral to draw from the above is that appeals to consistency can only move an "in" group to extend other-respect to an "out" group *after* the former have undergone some perspective-creating experience. Such an experience must cause those in the "in" group to discount what had previously been, in their eyes, relevant differences between their group and the "out" group, and then to see themselves and the "out" group as holding some deeply significant fact in common. But this shift in perception never follows logically from the mere recognition that the fact in question is held in common (just as Smith's change in the way she saw Jones did not follow logically from her recognition that Jones has a child). The new perspective, I maintain, is created, not by the power of some impersonal reason, but by the power of experiences such as those I have described. If this is true, then perspective-creating experiences have played, and must continue to play, a pivotal role in the evolution of egalitarianism – at least amongst those who lead the way to reform or who come to accept the justice of the reformers' arguments. I turn now to a second reason that perspective- creating experiences, even though they can provide only personal groundings for other-respect, nevertheless should be seen as having a wider significance.

As I said before, my argument is not that the majority of people living in an egalitarian culture necessarily have undergone such perspective-creating experiences, or if they have, that they make much of them in their lives. Many people, as I said in chapter 7, abide by the moral principles associated with egalitarian respect simply because they have absorbed them through being part of an egalitarian culture. These people are not full egalitarian agents, as I have defined the concept, since they do not generally act out of the motive that others count equally, nor do they open themselves to significant self-denial. But now even though the egalitarian agent's perspective is not necessarily widely shared, we need not think of him as an isolated eccentric whose reasons for acting are closed to others' understanding. For the perspective-creating experiences I have described are, in different guises and with diverse applications, part of humanity's general, if wavering sensibility. The egalitarian agent, therefore, can express in his actions a way of seeing which, even if not shared by the majority in his culture, may at least be understood by them.

I make the above point because in the end I want to show that being an egalitarian agent is part of a desirable life, especially when adapted to the Reasonable Person's core nature. That the egalitarian agent's grounding perspective speaks to deep, widely understood experiences must help the egalitarian to sustain his ideal. Note, too, that he would regard his commitment as issuing from himself in the manner of an inherent reason for self-esteem. This aspect of the egalitarian's ideal is further emphasized (see 9.4) through his recognizing that his way of seeing others is one perspective amongst other living options (for anti-egalitarianism is a perspective present in all cultures, even egalitarian ones).[21] There is also the point that the egalitarian agent experiences his egalitarian respect as having expressive significance. All of these factors, as we shall see in more detail later, can help make his commitment part of a desirable life. At the same time, as I emphasized in chapter 7, other-respect may sometimes require sustained self-denial. We must understand, then, what resources an egalitarian agent has for dealing with this self-denial. I shall discuss this issue in the context of examining the RP's relation to other-respect.

C: THE RP'S CORE NATURE AND OTHER-RESPECT

9.8 Our common mortality and common subjection to fortune are not esoteric facts. Given this, we can ask why, in an egalitarian culture, some people but not others respond to such facts in a manner which deepens their egalitarian perceptions and commitments. Clearly, this is a complex psychological question to which indeed there can be no universally applicable or complete answers. Light can be shed on this issue, however, if we concentrate on the specific case of the Reasonable Person. In this section, I discuss two ways the RP's core nature dismantles forces which often inhibit egalitarian perceptions and commitments. Then in the following sections, I turn to more direct ways that being an RP is congruent with other-respect.

In the first place, the corporative personality is strongly subject to exclusive altruism, mystification, pooled emotions, and group entrenchment. Such a person must find it especially difficult to discount the categories which divide him from people outside his social group. If Orwell, for example, had been a corporative personality, then it would have been impossible, I believe, for him to have been so deeply moved by the hanging of the Hindu prisoner. Now in chapter 4 I showed that derived reasons for self-esteem are an integral part of the corporative personality. When therefore the RP undercuts such reasons in himself, he at the same time dismantles a significant and common obstacle to deepening an egalitarian perspective. This argument can be seen from another angle.

Laurence Thomas has an insightful analysis of how parental love is an important condition for developing the trait of impartial respect for others.[22] His argument is that a person learns, through being the beneficiary of parental love, to value others independently of their achievements and other meritorious qualities. Now this analysis makes sense to me, but it is clear that we have to add a further important step, for love, parental or not, can easily develop a vein of exclusive altruism. When this happens, as I explained in 4.9, our capacity to act altruistically on behalf those outside the hallowed relationship is inhibited. As I further explained, derived reasons are often an integral part of exclusive altruism. Therefore, if parental love is going to do its work in developing a capacity for impartial altruism (of which other-respect is a species), then derived reasons must not be the focus of a person's self-esteem. This condition (albeit a negative one) is met by the Reasonable Person.

Secondly, in 3.7 we saw that envy (as well as begrudgingness) is rooted in competitive reasons for self-esteem. An envious disposition, by its very nature, inhibits a person's capacity to sustain an egalitarian perspective; for an envious person feels ill will at the thought of others as his equals. It is doubtful, moreover, that the basic structure of any society could do much to mitigate envy. A person with an envious disposition, I believe, finds things to envy or begrudge whatever his position relative to others, and however wealth and status are distributed.[23] The moral I draw from this is that in order to counter competitive reasons for self-esteem, a person must be attracted to some countervailing personal ideal. But now the RP's way of life is just such an ideal. Moreover, as I discussed in chapter 6, the RP finds a home in local communities of reasonableness, and this fellowship lends itself to non-competitive satisfactions. In undercutting competitive reasons, therefore, the RP removes a significant barrier to sustaining an egalitarian perspective.

9.9 Being other-respecting does not follow automatically from the RP's core nature. But given the arguments in the above section, we now have reason to believe that the RP, if he has been raised in an egalitarian culture, is at least open to acquiring egalitarian perceptions. Assuming our RP has acquired an egalitarian perspective, we can then ask: "Does this perspective reside as a distinct or even alien force in the RP's personality? Or are there positive factors in his core nature which could integrate his egalitarianism and thereby make possible a full commitment to other-respect?"

In answering these questions, my argument in outline is as follows: (a) it makes sense for the RP to recognize that a high degree of attention to self, via our need for self-esteem, is an inescapable part of being human; (b) at the same time, as we are imagining him, the RP is deeply struck by the fact that he does not count for more than others; (c) given point (b) and given his commitment to the critical guidelines, he will want to give expression to his egalitarian perspective; (d) but given point (a), the RP recognizes that any attempt to express an egalitarian perspective by negating his own self-esteem would be counter-productive; (e) the RP finds that to abide by the moral principles expressive of other-respect allows him to give proper weight to an egalitarian perspective, and at the same time gain self-esteem through expressing his core nature. In this way, other-respect becomes integrated into the RP's personality. I shall now deal with these points more fully, starting in this section with the inescapability of attention to self.

In 1.8 and 1.9, I analysed how self-esteem desires give rise to the ideal self and then how the ideal self provides forward thrust to our lives. I said further that although having an ideal self brings with it mental conflict, it is not that we are ever better off without a strong ideal self; for that would bring even worse forms of unhappiness. As well, there is the fact that our self-esteem desires arise from our capacities to make self-ascriptions and to attribute worth to these self-ascriptions. It is obvious that we could not cease to exercise these capacities without ceasing to be human, and in this sense the ups and downs of our self-esteem are an ineliminable part our lives.

Moreover, it is not difficult to imagine that natural selection would favour entities with strong dispositions to experience the self-esteem feelings. Recall, for example, the point I made in chapter 2 regarding our disposition to make reflected self-evaluations. We saw that it is likely natural selection would favour organisms (or genes) with this disposition, since the dispositon is a powerful mechanism by which groups mould their members. An analogous point can be made regarding identification reasons; the disposition to have such reasons contributes to group cohesiveness, and especially given our primitive pasts, group cohesiveness has (or had) survival value. Let us now consider a second way that the disposition to experience self-esteem feelings could become so deeply rooted in our nature.

In discussing the various forms of unhappiness associated with self-esteem, we saw that it is not only feelings of diminution which cause mental pain but also the *absence* of enhancement. This fact, together with some recent scientific work, leads to the reasonable speculation that feelings of self-enhancement are related, in part, to a biologically rooted need for positive stimulation. Let me explain.

We can begin by distinguishing two kinds of unpleasant sensations from which organisms seek relief. On the one hand, there are unpleasant sensations, such as hunger, the relief of which results in temporary quiescence. On the other hand, there are unpleasant sensations which are abated only through positive stimulation and activity. The clearest example of this latter form of displeasure is boredom.

The need for positive stimulation seems as much part of animal motivation as is the need for food or sex. Experiments show, for example, that curiosity is a powerful motive for many animals and that they sometimes even choose to explore novel situations rather than eat.[24] As well, there is much human behaviour which would be inexplicable apart from people's need for positive stimulation. There is, for example, our pursuit of risky activities such as hang-gliding, big-stake gambling, and car racing, as well as the stimulation spectators receive watching such activities. Significant too is the fact that there is a precise location in the brain which responds to positive stimuli of the kind I have been describing and which seems to account for the deep displeasure that results when this form of stimulus is lacking.[25] It is not difficult to understand why stimulus seeking behaviour would have survival value and so be rooted in our biology. For by being curious and active, even when the needs for food and sex are satiated, an organism's capacities to learn and to adapt are facilitated. Now feelings of enhancement are distinct from the kinds of sensations I have been discussing. Nevertheless, what I wish to suggest is that feelings of self-enhancement be seen as a specific case, at least in part, of this general biological need for positive stimulation – often supervening and hence reinforcing other forms of positive stimulation.[26]

If self-esteem feelings are as deeply rooted as I have been suggesting, then it makes sense to think of self-esteem as a *human need*; that is, just as people need proper food to live productively, so they need self-esteem. (I realize that this claim can sound trite. However, I believe that "need for self-esteem" can be made into a scientifically respectable notion, with import for non-trivial empirical studies.)[27] Seeing self-esteem in this light, we are led to accept the impracticality of reducing significantly the partiality and self-attention connected to our self-esteem (recall here my discussion of this partiality in 1.7 with reference to Smith's attitude to her own paintings).

The above consideration explains why moral ideals which run too strongly against our need for self-esteem are likely to be counter-productive. One good example is the way excessive humility and self-abnegation, when adopted as virtues, so often turn into their opposites. As a second example, consider an argument of Derek Parfit's.[28] In support of his reductionist view of personal identity, Parfit argues that whenever we use the concept "I," we could redescribe the same fact in impersonal terms without reference to "I." As a rebuttal to one type of anti-reductionist argument, he makes a good point. But he then goes on to suggest that to the degree we can live and think within this impersonal framework, we will have less self-concern and more impartial concern for others – "liberation from self." But now feelings of self-enhancement are impossible without an I-thought at some level of the mind. Hence, a person who tried to think from an impersonal perspective would indirectly be trying to eliminate feelings of self-enhancement and would thereby be straining against a human need. But just as people who deprive themselves of food become obsessed with food and for this reason as well as others, render themselves ineffectual, so a person who sought to transcend his need for self-esteem would probably make himself less capable of doing good rather than more, and more self-occupied rather than less.

9.10 The RP, as much as anyone, is driven forward by his need for self-esteem; he also, unless he an RP-saint, feels in himself disposi-tions to make dependent, competitive, and derived self-evaluations. At the same time, however, his core nature leads him to inhibit such self-evaluations and to acquire a different view of his self. This reac-tion in turn makes the RP, if he has been raised in an egalitarian culture, all the more open to deepening and sustaining egalitarian perceptions. But now his defining commitment, I want to argue, must motivate him to want to give *expression* to his egalitarian perspective. Why is this?

There is first of all critical guideline 1, which stipulates that to be reasonable is to give appropriate weight to one's reasons for self-esteem. Now once the RP has the view that he does not count for more than others, the attention he pays to his own self must seem, from within this egalitarian perspective, disproportionate (and even, in certain moods, absurd). Given this, the RP will want to find a way to give equal weight to the good of others, while recognizing that "liberation from self" is not the way to achieve this goal. Moreover, this desire must be further deepened through his commitment to guideline 2. This guideline stipulates that to be reasonable is to make one's beliefs as true and adequate to reality as possible. But an important and deep truth about reality, as the egalitarian RP sees it, is that he does not count for more than others.

Now the trait of other-respect precisely does give expression to the view that others count equally to oneself. Therefore, by committing himself to other-respect, the RP integrates, via guidelines 1 and 2, his egalitarian perceptions into his core nature, and other-respect thereby acquires expressive significance for him. Then given this integration, the RP experiences enhancement when he acts out of other-respect (recalling my discussion in 1.8, this enhancement must generally occur in the form of satisfying secondary self-esteem desires). Following from this principal way of integrating other-respect into his personality, the RP finds that other integrating forces come into play. I shall briefly mention two of these.

There is first the point, mentioned earlier in the chapter, that the egalitarian RP recognizes that his way of seeing people is one perspective amongst other living options. In this sense, other-respect is a response to the world which deepens his sense of inherent worth, a trait which is congruent with his core nature.

Secondly, the RP's defining commitment, especially guideline 2, leads him to consider the arguments and beliefs of others impartially. Moreover, there is the point (2.5) that it is only in dialogue with others that an RP can achieve the external viewpoint needed to test both the adequacy and fixity of his own beliefs, and thereby become autonomous. The RP can even regard the guidelines themselves, at least if considered individually, as beliefs to be tested for adequacy through dialogue with others. All of this means that he is especially motivated, on account of his defining commitment, to enter into impartial dialogue with others. Now I made the point in 7.1 that impartial dialogue does not *per se* mean egalitarian dialogue. It is clear, however, that when an egalitarian agent engages another person in impartial dialogue, he sees and treats his interlocutor as an equal (or he would not be an egalitarian agent). Given that impartial dialogue plays such a large part in the life of the RP *qua* RP, then the RP who is *also* an egalitarian agent must find other-respect, as expressed through egalitarian dialogue, especially harmonious with his nature. For through egalitarian dialogue, the egalitarian RP expresses at one and the same time both his egalitarian perceptions and his commitment to the guidelines.

The above discussion allows us now to understand how the self-denial associated with other-respect (7.3) can be integrated into the RP's personality. Let us distinguish between *alienated* and *integrated* self-denial. In the alienated case, even when a person does what he believes is right, the self-denial does not connect to anything deeper in his self-esteem. Into this category, for example, fall the actions of a person who sacrifices for a cause only because it is "his duty"; as soon as his duty is done, he puts the cause out of his mind. On the other hand, and as an example of integrated self-denial, there is the person who sacrifices for a cause about which he cares deeply. The self-denial, in this case, often has expressive significance for the agent, for it represents to him the depth of his commitment. In this way, integrated self-denial can add subjective meaning to a person's life. Now as we are imagining our RP, he regards a commitment to other-respect as a way to express a deeply felt egalitarian perspective. Given this, he will be disposed to experience the self-denial connected to his other-respecting behaviour as integrated, rather than alienated. That his self-denial is integrated in this way must in turn make it easier for the RP to be more fully other-respecting.

It would be a mistake, we should note, to see integrated self-denial as part of an agent's strategy for indirectly maximizing his long-term self-interest. As I defined it in 7.3, self-denying activity is, by definition, undertaken at a net cost to the agent; that is, an action X is self-denying at a time t only if there was some other action, Y, available at t which, had the agent done Y, he would have been better off. At the same time, we can see that, *once* self-denying activity is engaged upon, an agent is better off to the degree his self-denial is integrated, rather than alienated.

In conclusion, I mention one further way the egalitarian RP can see his core nature as beneficent. The person who grounds his self-esteem in reflected, competitive, or derived reasons is always looking over his shoulder to find out how he stands, and his self-esteem is thereby easily shaken. Now when a person's self-esteem is frequently shaken, there is a tendency to hurt others in turn. As well, such a person is invariably stingy with genuine praise and admiration of others. In these ways, a spiral of mutual hurt feelings is set in motion. This syndrome is one of the deepest sources of human misery, including the hatred which leads to war. But now the Reasonable Person, to the degree he can fulfil his nature, has a relatively self-sufficient self-esteem. Hence he is less vulnerable to having his self-esteem undermined, and thereby less likely to feed the syndrome of mutual hurt self-esteem. Moreover, there is an opposite spiral – that of mutual goodwill – which results when a person, because he is secure in his own self-esteem, is generous and non-envious in his judgments of others. The egalitarian RP's nature disposes him to contribute to such relationships of reciprocal goodwill.

I started this chapter with the statement that contributing to the good of others is, for all normal people, part of a meaningful life. We have now seen that the RP's core nature, when conjoined with egalitarian sentiments, can be congruent with this element of a good life. In striving to fulfil his nature, the egalitarian Reasonable Person contributes to the good of others; and in contributing to the good others, he expresses both his nature and his view of the world.

Notes

1 Hume, *An Enquiry Concerning the Principles of Morals*, 100.
2 Similar generic concepts, though with different labels, were used by William James, Spinoza, and Hume. See James's use of "self-satisfaction" and "self-abasement" in his *Principles of Psychology*, 1: 306–7; also Spinoza's use of *acquiescentia in se ipso*, variously translated as "self-satisfaction" or "self-contentment," in *Ethics*, part 3, propositions 53–5; and Hume's especially relevant discussion in the section of the *Enquiry* from which the passage at the head of this chapter is taken, in particular his use of "self-satisfaction" (100) and his discussion of the French *amour-propre* in the footnote on that page.

In recent philosophical literature, the concept of self-esteem is most often used to refer to a trait. Rawls has the trait in mind when, for example, he defines self-esteem in terms of a person's conviction that he can fulfil a worthy plan of life (Rawls, *A Theory of Justice*, 440). In this book, he uses self-esteem and self-respect synonymously, but in his later work he distinguishes between the two concepts. I discuss self-respect as a distinct concept in chapter 6. Laurence Thomas is also thinking of self-esteem as a trait when he defines the attitude as "tied to the conviction that our endeavors – the things we attempt to accomplish and the kind of life we attempt to lead – are worthwhile" (Thomas, *Living Morally*, 233). See also Moody-Adams's "Race, Class, and the Social Construction of Self-Respect," 254, for a further example of self-esteem defined as a trait, and for an interesting application of the distinction between self-esteem and self-respect.

In using the concept of self-esteem to focus on specific experiences, my emphasis is different from those who use self-esteem to refer to a trait. But clearly the two uses of the concept are complementary, since the trait must to a significant degree consist in the disposition to undergo the specific experiences.

3 For some purposes, it is no doubt useful to distinguish self-esteem from other attitudes of self-evaluation. For example, Stephen Darwall distinguishes, to useful effect, self-esteem from pride in *Impartial Reason*, 154; and John Deigh makes an interesting argument that shame is importantly different from loss of self-esteem in his article "Shame and Self-Esteem." As many have noted, there are significant differences between shame and guilt; see, for example, G. Taylor, *Pride, Shame, and Guilt*. Still, it is also sometimes important to have the broad categories.

4 To think of the cognitive element in emotions as beliefs is sometimes criticized. The concept of belief, it is true, involves the notion of assenting to a proposition, which does perhaps over-intellectualize our experience of emotions (and certainly does so in the case of irrational emotions). Nevertheless, in the standard case of an emotion, it is generally true that we *would* assent to a set of relevant propositions either during or immediately after the emotional experience. For this reason, I do not think it a distortion to talk, at least at this stage of my discussion, in terms of beliefs. Later in the book, however, I will have reason to make a distinction relevant to this issue.

That belief involves an attitude of assent or affirmation was clearly put by Price in "Some Considerations about Belief." The over-intellectualization of emotions is partly what is at issue in Annette Baier's criticism of Donald Davidson's "Humean" theory of pride (Baier, "Hume's Analysis of Pride"). Davidson's article is "Hume's Cognitive Theory of Pride." Also relevant is Roberts, "What an Emotion Is: A Sketch."

5 This concept of "rationalize" I take from Davidson, "Actions, Reasons, and Causes." Because of its psychoanalytic associations, "rationalize" is not an ideal word in this context, but I could not think of a better one.

Davidson wishes to see the beliefs which rationalize an action or an emotion as also the causes of these actions or emotions. Others deny that these reasons are best thought of as causes. This issue is not relevant to my argument, and so I bypass it here.

6 For a general theory of rationality which has the features I have been describing, see Brown, *Rationality*.

7 For a pioneering paper on the concept of reasonableness, see Sibley, "The Rational and the Reasonable." Following Sibley, Rawls attaches importance to the distinction between the rational and the reasonable as a way of delineating the reasonable. For his latest thoughts on the issue, see Rawls, *Political Liberalism*, chapter 1. For a parallel discussion of the rational and the reasonable, set in a context wider than academic philosophy, see Frye, "Literature as the Critique of Pure Reason," 176–8.

8 Erikson, *Childhood and Society*, chapters 3 and 4. For another interesting account of the way social environment influences attributions of worth, see Donald Broadbent's account of the differences between women in Cambridge, England, and women in Kalamazoo, Michigan (Broadbent, *In Defence of Empirical Psychology*, 185).

9 I am not claiming that an impartial attribution of worth ("Good painting is admirable whoever the painter is," etc.) is implicit in the *experience* of episodic self-esteem. On the contrary, as we have seen in the case of Smith, it is most often the thought of *my* having characteristic X which best articulates the experience of self-esteem. What I am claiming is that the impartial attribution is a commitment the RP adopts in *reflecting* on her experience. This explains why the criticism made of Donald Davidson's analysis of "Humean" pride, namely, that it mistakenly sees a universal value judgment implicit in the experience of pride, could not be made of my analysis of self-esteem. For the relevant criticisms of Davidson, see Baier, "Hume's Analysis of Pride"; and G. Taylor, *Pride, Shame, and Guilt*, 6 and 42.

10 Hare, *Moral Thinking*.

11 For further discussion of this issue see Mackie, *Ethics: Inventing Right and Wrong*, chapter 4; and Campbell, *Self-Love and Self-Respect*, chapter 4; also Williams, "Egoism and Altruism"; and Williams, *Ethics and the Limits of Philosophy*, chapter 4.

12 See here Robert Nozick's use of the "experience machine" to make the same point (Nozick, *Anarchy, State and Utopia*, 42–5).

13 An excellent summary of the psychological and sociological literature on self-esteem and its connection to motivation is found in Rosenberg, *Conceiving the Self*.

14 My thought here has been influenced by Frankfurt, "Freedom of the Will and the Concept of the Person"; and C. Taylor, "Responsibility for Self."

15 The novels of Chaim Potok, such as *The Chosen* and the Asher Lev stories, depict this form of mental conflict with great power.

16 Clearly, the psychological processes which explain why we internalize one set of norms rather than another are enormously complex and, in my

view, not well understood. Different theories are surveyed by Mussen and Distler in "Identification." It is a fallacy, I believe, to think of the agent in these processes as the passive product of socialization. In childhood and adolescence, we "reach out" to identify with ideal patterns of behaviour and feeling, just as much as we reach out for love. Moreover, as Richard Wollheim has emphasized, the process of identification requires a complex exercise of imagination whereby we picture to ourselves another's inner life (Wollheim, "Identification and Imagination").

17 This is a common diagnosis of the psychological problems experienced by many Canadian Indians. The following comments, for example, were made in an article summarizing the extremely high suicide rate among young people on an Indian reservation:

> Young Indians on this reserve, as on many others, are finding that without [self-] respect they can't function in a white man's world. Worse, they can no longer function in their own. After years of watching their language deteriorate and their parents chasing the white man's dreams, the young are looking for ways to go back. "What they see in the white man's world, they don't value," says Alex Fox, "but it's not enough just to say 'I'm Indian.' The culture must be imbedded in us. Otherwise we will be disoriented." And he might have added, the suicides will continue to devastate in Kaboni reservation. (Ferrante, "The Condemned of Kaboni")

CHAPTER TWO

1 Tolstoy, *Anna Karenin*, 158.

2 Woolf, *A Writer's Diary*, 265 and 267.

3 Hume, *An Enquiry Concerning the Principles of Morals*, 77. This passage from Hume first came to my attention through Lovejoy, *Reflections on Human Nature*, 147. Lovejoy's discussion of this chapter's topic is interesting (96ff).

4 The notion of taking-for-granted I derive from Price, "Some Considerations about Belief," 47.

5 The argument I outline has its ancestry in Plato's *Euthyphro* and in Kant's moral philosophy.

6 Gergen, *The Concept of Self*, 69.

7 On the way our faculties seem disposed to mislead as to what is rational, see Tversky and Kahneman, "The Framing of Decisions and the Psychology of Choice"; and McKean, "Decisions, Decisions."

8 What I touch on here is well defended in Singer, *The Expanding Circle*.

9 For a discussion of how our characters are partly shaped by the way we anticipate how others might react to us, see Thomas, *Living Morally*, chapter 6.

10 I say "own standards of reasonableness," since it would be absurd to think that someone could be persuaded to change her beliefs according to someone else's standards of reasonableness. But see the second clarification below in the text.

11 This notion of unalterable belief is analogous to Jonathan Glover's concept of unalterable intention; see Glover, *Responsibility*, 97–101. He makes the point that we do not count a person's act free if we think his intention, before he acted, was unalterable by the presentation of good reasons. Corresponding to the idea of an unalterable intention regarding our acts, we have the idea of an unalterable belief regarding our reasons; the one excludes freedom (or autonomous action), the other autonomous belief. For an analysis along the same lines as Glover, see Neely, "Freedom and Desire," 48.

The contemporary debate over how to analyse autonomy mostly focuses on autonomous desire or action, rather than on autonomous *belief* (for a survey of recent work on autonomy, see Christman, "Constructing the Inner Citadel"). We should not assume that analyses of autonomous desire are necessarily applicable in every respect to autonomous belief (see here John Christman's remark in footnote 8 of "Autonomy and Personal History," 4). Nevertheless, the use of subjunctive conditionals to capture a key aspect of autonomy is, I believe, as necessary to defining autonomous belief as it is to defining autonomous desire.

Some writers (for example, Young, "Autonomy and the 'Inner Self,'" 37) object to the use of subjunctive conditionals on general logical or epistemological grounds. There are, it is true, well-known problems about how to translate subjunctive conditionals into the canonical notation of symbolic logic. But this is surely more a problem for symbolic logic (and for theories of language which want to build on this logic) than it is for the conditionals themselves. No one would seriously suggest that subjunctive conditionals are meaningless, or that we should stop using them, on the grounds that their logical structure is unclear.

Testing the truth or falsehood of a subjunctive conditional can be problematic. But here again, it would be absurd to suggest that subjunctive conditionals are worthless for the purposes of definition because they are sometimes difficult to confirm. Morever, although the evidence which can be adduced to verify subjunctive conditionals must of necessity be indirect, nevertheless such conditionals are often easy enough to confirm or refute with a high degree of probability. For example, we may judge the statement "Jones would have been upset if he'd lost his money in the stock market yesterday" as very likely true on the evidence of what we know about human nature in general and about Jones in analogous situations. There is a good discussion of these issues in Haak, *Philosophy of Logics*, chapter 3.

12 My thought in this paragraph owes much to Hardwig, "The Achievement of Moral Rationality."

13 Relevant to what follows is Dworkin, "Moral Autonomy."

14 See, for example, Young, *Personal Autonomy*, 16–19; and Young, "Autonomy and Socialization," 567.

15 A primary source for this argument, with a description of the Jehovah's Witnesses' behaviour, is Bettelheim, *The Informed Heart*.

16 An interesting account of such indoctrination is Shaffir, "Chassidic Communities in Montreal," 280–5. Shaffir describes how all contact with the outside world is screened to prevent students from facing views inconsistent with orthodox Judaism. They are taught that it is evil even to entertain such views. The aim is to make children impregnable for life to opposing considerations.

17 My thought here has been influenced by J. Benson, "Who Is Autonomous Man?" See also Christman, "Constructing the Inner Citadel," 109. Christman cites Joel Feinberg's *Harm to Self* as an important source for the claim that "autonomy" has no "single, coherent meaning" (109).

18 John Christman has put forward an analysis of autonomous desire which also has the intent of de-emphasizing the intellectualistic aspect of autonomy. He wants to say, in part, that a person's desire counts as autonomous if that person would not have resisted the development of the desire had she attended to the desire in a rational manner. This analysis, then, leaves open the possibility that a person's desire or action counts as autonomous, even though she has not sustained the desire through active reflection (Christman, "Autonomy and Personal History"; and Christman, "Defending Historical Autonomy"). As I mentioned earlier, we need not think that the proper analysis of autonomy of desire is going to match in every respect that of autonomy of belief. Nevertheless, it is worth noting that Christman's autonomy speaks to a distinct sense of autonomy from that captured by my analysis, and that the one sense need not displace the other. He is especially concerned with the way our desires can be manipulated by outer or inner coercive forces. My analysis, though it includes Christman's concern, adds the notion of actively influencing our own beliefs through testing them against the guidelines. There is little advantage to saying that *the* true sense of "autonomy" is captured by one analysis rather than the other. Better simply to be aware that both senses capture an aspect of our experience which can properly be described in terms of the concept of autonomy.

19 I owe this clarification to an anonymous reviewer from the Humanities Research Council of Canada.

20 Useful discussions of the distinction between socialization and indoctrination are Moody-Adams, "Culture, Responsibility, and Affected Ignorance"; and Young, "Autonomy and Socialization."

21 Bartky, "Narcissism, Femininity and Alienation"; Friedman, "Autonomy and the Split-Level Self"; Christman, "Autonomy"; P. Benson, "Autonomy and Oppressive Socialization"; Thomas, "Moral Deference"; Dillon, "Toward a Feminist Conception of Self-Respect"; Moody-Adams, "Race, Class, and the Social Construction of Self-Respect."

CHAPTER THREE

1 Malinowski, *Magic, Science, and Religion*, 45.

2 Russell, *The Conquest of Happiness*, 68.

3 For similar considerations about rarity, see Gunn, "Why Should We Care about Rare Species."

4 See, for example, Rawls, *A Theory of Justice*, 530–41; Nozick, *Anarchy, State and Utopia*, 239–46; Cooper, "Equality and Envy"; Luper-Foy, "Competing for the Good Life"; Young, "Egalitarianism and Envy"; Ben-Ze'ev, "Envy and Jealousy"; Roberts, "What Is Wrong with Wicked Feelings?"

5 My envy might be of a more general type in which I envy unspecific others for their attractiveness. This is best understood as involving a proportionate comparison; which, as I have made clear, is also grounded in competitive self-esteem. The point that malicious envy does not have to bring in comparison with specific others is made by Ben Ze'ev, "Envy and Jealousy," 494.

6 Rawls's and Nozick's discussions have helped with my definition here.

7 Nozick, *Anarchy, State and Utopia*, 239–46. In an enigmatic footnote, Nozick hedges on this claim (244). I stick to analysing his main claim, from which, through seeing how it goes wrong, we can learn a lot.

8 An argument of this type is made in Luper-Foy, "Competing for the Good Life."

9 It should be clear from the previous note that I do not mean to suggest here that there are eternally set criteria for what counts as excellence in painting, good health, etc. My mainly negative argument is compatible with a number of theories about the way criteria come to be established; it is not even incompatible with theories which see these criteria as culturally relative.

10 For a similar example, see Rawls, *A Theory of Justice*, 524.

11 I worked out some of the ideas in this chapter in two papers delivered at conferences. "What Is Wrong with Envy?" was delivered at the Atlantic Philosophical Association meeting in 1978, and "Comparisons

to Others" at the Canadian Philosophical Association meeting in 1984. I would like to thank the discussants at these meetings, especially Peter Miller for his written comments at the latter meeting. I also had helpful written comments on that paper from Richmond Campbell.

CHAPTER FOUR

1 Burckhardt, *The Civilization of the Renaissance in Italy*, 121.
2 My interest here, needless to say, is not in the historical accuracy of Burckhardt's claim, about which there has been much controversy. See, for example, Greenblat, "Fiction and Friction," 35; and Cantor, *Civilization of the Middle Ages*, 331.
3 Eliot, *Felix Holt, the Radical*, 35.
4 Here I follow Singer, *Practical Ethics*, chapter 2.
5 For a similar distinction, see Rawls, *A Theory of Justice*, 522.
6 Under different guises and applied to different ends, this concept of two levels of thinking is found in many places; I have already made use of the distinction in 1.7.
7 According to recent expositors, Hegel's political theory is intended to combine democratic rights with the view that the state and its institutions have intrinsic, and even overriding, value. See C. Taylor, *Hegel and Modern Society*, 86; and Wood, *Hegel's Ethical Theory*, 258–9.
8 Rocco, "The Political Doctrine of Fascism," 342–3.
9 Fallaci, *Interviews with History*, 217.
10 Prescott, *History of the Conquest of Peru*, 59.
11 I take the phrase "pooled emotions" from Lovejoy, *Reflections on Human Nature*, 118.
12 Barber, "The Swarm," 42.
13 An element of the looseness in the way we rationalize identification reasons lies in our asymmetrical treatment of positive and negative reasons. We tend to focus on the positive characteristics of the groups to which we belong and downplay, so far as our self-esteem is concerned, any parallel negative characteristics (the same holds for our individual qualities). For the most part, this attitude is good for people and, apart from the qualifications discussed in the body of the book, seems justifiable from the point of view of the harmonization guideline. It would be a cold rationalism which argued, for example, that Canadians should not feel enhanced when their hockey teams win world championships unless they were prepared to feel equally diminished when their teams lose. There is a good discussion of this point in Isenberg, "Natural Pride and Natural Shame," 372–4. There is much insight in Isenberg's essay on other topics related to the self-esteem feelings.

14 I have argued for this conclusion in a paper, "The Self and Social Groups," delivered at the Canadian Philosophical Association, May 1990. I am grateful to Professor Wes Cooper for his helpful written comments.
15 Galston, "Pluralism and Social Unity," 722.

CHAPTER FIVE

1 Snow, *In Their Wisdom*, 258.
2 Awe and curiosity may legitimately be regarded as modes of manifesting interest. It is possible, however, to be awestruck or curious and yet be neither favourably nor unfavourably disposed toward the object of awe or curiosity. When this is so, it is generally because the person in question is baffled by the phenomenon in which he is manifesting interest. These exceptions, though they are to be noted, do not affect the main line of my argument.

It might be said that surprise should be classified with curiosity and awe as exceptions to the rule that to manifest interest in an object is to be either favourably or unfavourably disposed toward it. I am inclined, however, to think that surprise is best not so classified. When we are surprised, in the sense of being shocked by something (such as when we are surprised by someone approaching us from behind when we are lost in concentration), then it seems incorrect to say we manifest interest in the cause of our surprise. On the other hand, when we are surprised by some happy or sad turn of events, then it follows we are favourably or unfavourably disposed toward that turn of event. In one case, there is no interest. In the other case, there is interest, but interest which follows the rule.

It might be said that to adopt a neutral attitude regarding two partisan interests is to manifest interest in a situation without being either favourably or unfavourably disposed. Such a conclusion, however, is incorrect. For when we adopt a neutral stance, we do so for a reason, even if our reason is that we do not want to get involved. But to do something for a reason is to want to achieve some end. And to want to achieve some end is to be favourably disposed toward that end.
3 Strawson, *Analysis and Metaphysics*, chapter 10.
4 James, *Principles of Psychology*, 1: 301.
5 Ibid., 296–305.
6 Ibid., 305.
7 For a similar application of the concept of responsibility, see C. Taylor, "Responsibility for Self."
8 William James makes use of this idea in his analysis of the self, though he applies the idea to a different end (James, *Principles of Psychology*, 1: 333 and 376).

9 This point is made by G. Taylor, *Pride, Shame, and Guilt*, 42.

10 I only touch here on a complex issue. It is a mistake, for example, to assimilate recognition to being the object of praise or admiration, even of the non-reflected type. At its deepest level, recognition involves the sharing and validation of our values by others. For example, it matters to us that others acknowledge, through sympathetic words and behaviour, our grief when someone close to us has died. This is a form of recognition, but there is no praise or admiration involved. For a subtle analysis of the different aspects of recognition, see Glover, *I: The Philosophy and Psychology of Personal Identity*, chapter 16.

11 Yanal, "Self-Esteem," 366.

12 I owe this use of "singularity" to Hampshire, *Innocence and Experience*, 118. For a similar use of the word, see Burckhardt, *The Civilization of the Renaissance in Italy*, 122.

13 Regan, *In Defence of Animal Rights*, chapter 1.

14 Parfit, *Reasons and Persons*, part 2.

15 This theme is developed in Glover, *I: The Philosophy and Psychology of Personal Identity*. In this book, Glover combines what I have called the association view of personal identity with a deep sense of our unity through time.

16 In tracing the history of individualism as a moral and political ideal, Steven Lukes shows how the distinct concepts of numerical and qualitative "uniqueness" both played important roles. The latter notion was especially important in the Romantic concept of self-development (Lukes, *Individualism*, 67).

17 Erving Goffman has an interesting discussion regarding the way people in "total institutions," such as prisons and mental hospitals, use manifestations of interest to preserve their sense of personal distinctness (Goffman, *Asylums*, 271–80). In applying his argument more generally, he concludes by saying, "Our status is backed by the solid buildings of the world, while our sense of personal identity often resides in the cracks" (280). The "cracks" are the infinitely many ways people can manifest interest in the world. I owe this reference to Jonathan Glover.

18 Orwell, *1984*, 145–6. Of related interest is Lukes's discussion of privacy as a key ingredient of individualism (Lukes, *Individualism*, chapter 9).

CHAPTER SIX

1 In *A Theory of Justice* (section 67), for example, John Rawls treats the two concepts synonymously. However, in his later work he has accepted the importance of distinguishing the two concepts. See, for example, Rawls, "Justice as Fairness: Political not Metaphysical," 251.

2 The connections between self-respect, rights, and protest were some of the earliest issues explored in contemporary discussions of self-respect. See Hill Jr, "Servility and Self-Respect"; Boxill, "Self-Respect and Protest"; and Held, "Reasonable Progess and Self-Respect."

3 This point was first clearly made by Sachs, "How to Distinguish Self-Respect and Self-Esteem." Other important papers relating to this issue are: Thomas, "Morality and Our Self Concept"; and Darwall, "Two Kinds of Respect."

Conceptual distinctions, of course, can be made using different linguistic labels. As I see it, this is what is at issue in Stephen Massey's denial that there is a significant distinction between self-esteem and self-respect. Massey wants to distinguish between the concepts of subjective and objective self-respect, but what he means by "subjective self-respect" is close to the notion of self-esteem as I am using it. Therefore, linguistic appearances to the contrary, the conceptual distinction I and others mark by the words "self-esteem" and "self-respect" is also found within Massey's framework. See Massey, "Is Self-Respect a Moral or a Psychological Concept?"

4 For an analysis of rights as embodying claims on others, see Feinberg, *Social Philosophy*, chapter 4; and Feinberg, "The Nature and Value of Rights."

5 MacIntyre, *Whose Justice? Which Rationality?* 361. For a similar claim regarding the particularness of moral traditions, see Kekes, "Moral Tradition," 238. My thoughts about traditions have been greatly influenced, even where I have disagreed, by MacIntyre's discussion in *After Virtue*, chapters 14 and 15.

6 Following Michael Oakeshott, John Kekes draws a distinction between traditions which are guided by a specific goal, such as musical appreciation or helping the poor, and traditions which establish the conditions for the flourishing of goal-oriented traditions. Into the latter category, according to Kekes, fall many moral, legal, managerial, and law-enforcement traditions. These latter traditions he calls "enabling traditions." See Kekes, "Moral Tradition," 237. I believe there is a useful distinction here. However, as the very word "enabling" implies, it seems appropriate to see these latter traditions as goal-oriented as well. So the distinction has to be recast in terms of two types of goal-oriented traditions.

7 See, for example, Lloyd, *The Revolution in Wisdom*, 144, 187, 154, 158, and 355.

8 Ibid., 172.

9 Drake, *Galileo*, 38 and 44.

10 Ibid., chapter 4.

11 Ibid., introduction.

12 Galileo, "Letter to the Grand Duchess Christina."

13 It would be easy to add to this list of historical precursors through the contrastive approach I have described. One might analyse, for example, the debates Spinoza and Kant instigated, in their respective communities, over biblical interpretation and its relation to morality. See Yovel, *Spinoza and Other Heretics*, volume 2, chapter 1: "Spinoza and Kant: Critique of Religion and Biblical Hermeneutics."

14 My account of Sidgwick comes from Blanshard, *Four Reasonable Men*, 179–243. See also Schneewind, *Sidgwick's Ethics and Victorian Moral Philosophy*.

15 Blanchard, *Four Reasonable Men*, 190.

16 Ibid., 199.

17 Ibid., 201 and 227–33.

18 See, for example, the range of temperaments and ways of life described by Blanchard in *Four Reasonable Men*.

19 This attitude, I believe, accounts for the strangeness we feel regarding Kant's position of treating practical reason as awe-inspiring apart from any good consequences. This issue is interestingly analysed in Warnock, "The Primacy of Practical Reason."

20 Brown, *Rationality*, 228.

21 Nathanson, *The Ideal of Rationality*, chapters 5 and 6.

22 Putnam, *Reason, Truth, and History*, 195.

23 Hacking, *The Emergence of Probability*; and Hacking, *The Taming of Chance*.

24 Brown, *Rationality*, 215; and Hacking, *Representing and Intervening*, chapters 10 and 11.

25 See, for example, Putnam, *Reason, Truth, and History*, 188–200.

26 This point is made by Putnam, *Reason, Truth, and History*, 130–5.

27 Russell, *Fact and Fiction*, 45. Russell's aesthetic enjoyment focuses particularly on theoretical beauty, as opposed to the enjoyment which comes from attending to natural phenomena. These two enjoyments are interconnected for the appreciator of science, but some people are pulled more strongly to one than the other. Though I quote Russell at the beginning of my discussion, it will be clear that my main emphasis is on the way science can deepen our attentiveness to natural phenomena. For a discussion of this topic which emphasizes theoretical beauty, see Wolpert, *The Unnatural Nature of Science*, 57.

28 The point I am making here is independent of the commonly made point in the philosophy of science that all observation is necessarily theory-laden. For a recent defence of the opposite view, namely, that much observation in science takes place apart from evolving theory, see Hacking, *Representing and Intervening*, chapter 10.

29 Katz, "Chasing the Ogre."

30 This point is made by Dahl, "Morality and the Meaning of Life," 3–4.

31 Keller, *Feeling for the Organism*, 148–9 and 198.

32 Feyerabend, *Against Method*.

33 For critiques which use the argument of self-contradictoriness against Feyerabend, see Newton-Smith, *The Rationality of Science*, chapter 6; Brown, *Rationality*, chapter 3; Hacking, *Representing and Intervening*, 91; Putnam, *Reason, Truth, and History*, 114; Quine, "On Empirically Equivalent Systems of the World," 327; Siegel, "Farewell to Feyerabend," 343–69.

34 This is a point made by MacIntyre in *After Virtue*, chapter 15, and in *Whose Justice? Which Rationality?*, chapter 18.

35 Here my thought has been influenced by Dahl, "Morality and the Meaning of Life."

36 Hampshire, *Two Theories of Morality*, 95.

37 Moffat, "What Hubble the Man Saw."

38 Snow, *The Search*, 103–4.

39 Another "occasion for transcendence" expressed by some scientists has to do with the sense that the complexities of the natural world can never be exhausted by human understanding. For example, E.O. Wilson writes, "The honeybee is like a magic well; the more you draw from it, the more there is to draw ... Every species is a magic well ... The naturalist's journey has only begun and for all intents and purposes will go on forever ... It is possible to spend a lifetime in a magellanic voyage around the trunk of a single tree." I owe this point and the Wilson references to Godlovitch, "Ontology, Epistemic Access, and the Sublime," 69. The passages from Wilson are found on pages 17, 19, and 22 of his book *Biophilia*.

40 Relevant here is Steven Luper-Foy's description of "associational units" (Luper-Foy, "Competing For the Good Life," 174).

41 My thought here has been influenced by Hardwig, "Epistemic Dependence."

42 Darwin, *Autobiography*, 55.

43 Ibid., 344.

44 Hossie, "Birders No Longer a Rare Species."

45 The difference between the pro-science and anti-science camps in modern intellectual life is well captured by Rorty in his essay "Philosophy in America Today," 228–9.

CHAPTER SEVEN

1 The connection between the belief in equal moral status and non-servility is clearly drawn in the following articles: Hill Jr, "Servility and Self-Respect"; Boxill, "Self-Respect and Protest"; Held, "Reasonable Progress and Self-Respect."

2 Davidson, "Actions, Reasons, and Causes," has influenced my thought here.

3 In some cases, this may mean agreeing to be part of a bargaining process in which each participant starts from a position of equal power and then, in accord with rules mutually agreed upon, pursues his own self-interest. So, for example, I would not want to exclude labour negotiations, in which labour and management have equal bargaining power, as a possible form of egalitarian dialogue. For dialogue to count as egalitarian, however, the motive which establishes the rules in the first place must issue from a belief in the equal moral status of the participants. Contrariwise, a bargaining process instigated at the outset from pure self-interest would not count as egalitarian dialogue, however equal in power were the participants and however fair the procedural rules.

4 My notion of "self-identified good" has been influenced by Richmond Campbell's "self-identifying desire." At the same time, there are important differences between our two notions. Campbell's, for one thing, excludes desires of the agent which bring unwanted grantification or are in other ways "irrational." My notion, on the contrary, includes any desire the agent sees as part of his good, whether the desire is irrational or not. See Campbell, *Self-Love and Self-Respect*, chapter 6.

5 The phrase "effort at identification," as well as the central point regarding empathetic identification, I owe to Williams, "The Idea of Equality."

6 Thomas, "Moral Deference," 240. I owe this reference to an anonymous referee from the Humanities Research Council of Canada.

7 On this issue, see W.D. Ross's account of moral thought as involving independent intrinsic values and *prima facie* duties, which may sometimes clash (Ross, *The Right and the Good*). For a discussion of prioritizing intrinsic values, see Rawls, *A Theory of Justice*, section 7.

8 The ultimate moral vacuousness of the distinction between doing and refraining is relevant here. On this topic see, for example, Morillo, "Doing, Refraining, and the Strenuousness of Morality."

9 See Benn, "Equality, Moral and Social."

10 It is plausible to see Kant as suggesting that the norms of morality, *in toto*, constitute the criteria for a self-respecting person. So, on this interpretation of Kant, *any* breaking of a moral rule would demonstrate lack of self-respect. See here Massey, "Kant on Self-Respect." But this interpretation just serves to emphasize the difference between seeing, say, carpentry as a tradition and seeing humanity as a tradition. The norms regarding what constitutes good or bad carpentry are rich, concrete, and generally accepted. But moral norms, where rich and concrete, are not generally accepted, and where generally accepted, are not rich and concrete.

11 Kant, *Grounding for the Metaphysics of Morals*, 41.
12 Relevant here is Hudson, "The Nature of Respect."
13 Kant, *Grounding for the Metaphysics of Morals*, 14.
14 Ibid., 14.
15 ibid., 54–62.
16 This criticism has been pressed by Williams, "The Idea of Equality," 158.
17 For arguments which question the intrinsic worth of rational autonomy, see Cranor, "Limitations on Respect-for-Persons Theories," and Landesmann, "Against Respect for Persons."
18 For a criticism of two significant recent attempts to ground equal moral status in rationality, see Aaron Ben-Zeev's criticisms of Alan Donagan's and Alan Gewirth's ethical theories in "Who Is a Rational Agent?" Donagan and Gewirth reply to Ben-Zeev following the article. Ben-Zeev's essential argument seems to me valid. As he says, if we consider rationality to be a status attribute, such that all humans *qua* species possess the attribute, then it is difficult to see why we should say that the attribute is respect-worthy in itself. But if we regard rationality as an attainment attribute, then we must admit that people possess rationality in greatly different degrees; so we cannot adopt the attribute as the grounds for egalitarian respect.
19 Rawls, *A Theory of Justice*, section 77. For the criticism, see, for example, Singer, *Practical Ethics*, 16.
20 For this use of "anchored," I am indebted to Thomas, *Living Morally*, 17.
21 See, for example, Sidgwick, *Methods of Ethics*, where appeals both to clear-headed intuition and to universalizability are utilized to bring the reader around to utilitarianism. Hare is also a thinker who believes that any rational, goodwilled person can be brought around to utilitarianism by means of an appeal to universalizability. See Hare, *Moral Thinking*, chapter 6.
22 For a way of interpreting utilitarianism which treats equality as fundamental, see Kymlicka, "Rawls on Teleology and Deontology."
23 This terminology originated with Williams in Williams and Smart, *Utilitarianism: For and Against*, 118–35. See also Railton, "Alienation, Consequentialism, Morality." I do not claim to be using these terms with the exact same sense given to them by these other philosophers. For a further relevant discussion, see Adams "Motive Utilitarianism."
24 Most utilitarians would readily agree that equality is to be treated as a derivative, rather than fundamental, principle. So for example, Derek Parfit, speaking as a utilitarian, writes, "Utilitarians treat equality as a mere means, not a separate aim" (Parfit, *Reasons and Persons*, 331). For similar sentiments, see Smart, "Distributive Justice and Equality."

25 I am assuming here, for the sake of argument, that universalizability is a unitary notion. But a further problem with this strategy is that there are weaker and stronger forms of universalizability. To give the argument I have been considering a chance, a person would have to be committed to one of the stronger forms of universalizability. However, it is far from clear that these forms are a requirement of rationality *per se*. To the degree they are not such a requirement, these stronger forms of universalizability would then cease to be impersonally accessible. On the issue of weaker and stronger forms of universalizability, see Mackie, *Ethics: Inventing Right and Wrong*, chapter 4; and Williams, *Ethics and the Limits of Philosophy*, chapter 4.

26 Wood, *Hegel's Ethical Thought*, chapter 4; and Campbell, *Self-Love and Self-Respect*, chapter 7.

27 The phrase "groundless commitment" was suggested to me by Feinberg's phrase "groundless belief," also applied to the belief in equal moral status (Feinberg, *Social Philosophy*, 93). I have not used Feinberg's phrase because the meaning I want to capture is rather different from his. I shall have more to say about this in the next chapter.

28 Nielsen, "Justifying Egalitarianism," 264.

29 Singer, *Practical Ethics*, chapters 3 and 5.

CHAPTER EIGHT

1 Mackie, *Ethics: Inventing Right and Wrong*, chapter 1.

2 Kant, *Grounding for the Metaphysics of Morals*, 41.

3 Rawls, "Kantian Constructivism in Moral Theory," 54.

4 Russell, *Autobiography*, 1: 183.

5 Frankl, *Man's Search for Meaning*, 78–9.

CHAPTER NINE

1 My approach has been influenced by Feinberg, *Social Philosophy*, 93–4; and Williams, "The Idea of Equality."

2 For example, there is compassion for the suffering of others. Yet this experience is often closely tied to that of moral arbitrariness, which is one of the two experiences I do discuss. On compassion as a perspective-creating experience, see Blum, "Compassion"; also Coles, "Psychoanalysis and Moral Development," 56–61.

3 Huizinga, *The Waning of the Middle Ages*, 62.

4 Ibid., 63.

5 de Beauvoir, *Mémoires d'une jeune fille rangée*, 173 (my translation).

6 Ibid., 173.

7 Orwell, "A Hanging," 68. See further Glover, *Causing Death and Saving Lives*, 228.

8 Steiner, *Language and Silence*, 159.

9 Snow, *The Sleep of Reason*, 275.

10 In so doing, I am drawing on Wittgenstein's analysis of change-of-aspect experiences: Wittgenstein, *Philosophical Investigations*, part 2, section 11.

11 Ibid., 197.

12 Owen Flanagan treats perspectival "seeing" purely as a metaphor in his analysis of Carol Gilligan's use of the gestalt-switch notion in her theory of moral development. He asks how good a metaphor perspectival seeing is for conceptualizing the way people occupy either a justice or a care orientation. His answer is that the metaphor obscures more than it enlightens (Flanagan, *Varieties of Moral Psychology*, 212–17).

13 This is suggested by an example of Wittgenstein, *Philosophical Investigations*, 193.

14 See, for example, Gidley, *Representing Others*; and Said, *Covering Islam*.

15 This concept derives from William James, "The Will to Believe," which is reprinted in many places.

16 In an interview with Bill Moyers, Leon Kass describes such feelings regarding the human corpse, with reference both to an experience of his own and to that of medical students (Moyers, *A World of Ideas*, 362).

17 Such experiences are often felt, and described, as the experience of barriers breaking down between oneself and a member of another species. Such perspective-creating experiences are not limited to our relations with the higher animals, but here is one description specifically to do with chimpanzees. It is an account by Jane Goodall, which occurs at the end of her book *In the Shadow of Man*, 240–1:

> In those early days I spent many days alone with David. Hour after hour I followed him through the forests, sitting and watching him whilst he fed or rested, struggling to keep up when he moved through a tangle of vines. Sometimes, I am sure, he waited for me just as he would wait for Goliath or William. For when I emerged, panting and torn from a mass of thorny undergrowth, I often found him sitting, looking back in my direction. When I had emerged, then he got up and plodded on again.
>
> One day, as I sat near him at the bank of a tiny trickle of crystal-clear water, I saw a ripe red palm nut lying on the ground. I picked it up and held it out to him on my open palm. He turned his head away. But when I moved my hand a little closer he looked at it, and then at me, and then he took the fruit and, at the same time, he held my hand firmly and gently with his own. As I sat, motionless, he

released my hand, looked down at the nut, and dropped it to the ground. At that moment there was no need of any scientific knowledge to understand his communication of reassurance. The soft pressure of his fingers spoke to me not through my intellect but through a more primitive emotional channel: the barrier of untold centuries which has grown up during the separate evolution of man and chimpanzee was, for those few seconds, broken down.

18 For the idea that behaviour can represent or stand for feelings or emotions, see Langer, *Philosophy in a New Key.* I interpret Rawls's constructivist program as giving central place to what I am calling expressive significance; but I would not want to claim that he would see things in exactly that light. For what I am calling expressive significance in *A Theory of Justice*, see 253–5. My thoughts on expressive significance have been influenced by Charles Taylor's writings. See, for example, *Hegel and Modern Society,* chapter 1, and *Sources of the Self,* chapter 21.

19 Hume, *An Enquiry Concerning the Principles of Morals,* section 9, part 1; especially 74–5.

20 Ibid., section 9, part 2; especially, 79–89. The fact that we have to speak a common language is also given as a reason for why our moral judgments reflect a form of moral egalitarianism (48–9). But in the end it is the self-interest argument which Hume relies on.

21 Nor should we think that anti-egalitarianism is a view supported only by racists or other enemies of civilization. As recent discussions have shown, it may be advocated from within a democratic and humane perspective. See, for example, Sher, *Desert,* 132–44; and Kekes, *Facing Evil,* chapter 6.

22 Thomas, *Living Morally,* chapters 2 and 3.

23 A somewhat contrary view is proposed by Rawls, who argues that his version of a just society would significantly reduce at least one form of envy, what he calls excusable envy (Rawls, *A Theory of Justice,* sections 80 and 81).

But his arguments are not persuasive even regarding excusable envy. Accepting that envy arises from diminished self-esteem, he maintains that a society which follows the difference principle would be more protective of people's self-esteem than a society in which people were rewarded according to natural desert. One of the background principles Rawls uses to justify the difference principle is the notion that our abilities, including our ability to make an effort, are properly regarded as matters of luck. It is not at all clear, however, that we would be less disposed to make invidious comparisons if we thought that others' superior situation were due to luck rather than natural desert; but that at least those with a superior position contribute to the general well-being. Nor is it clear, as Rawls maintains, that the protection of basic equal rights could reach deep enough into people's psyches to diminish hurt self-esteem and envy.

For further criticisms of the view that an egalitarian society would necessarily reduce envy, see Nozick, *Anarchy, State, and Utopia*, 239–46; Shoeck, *Envy*; and Cooper, "Equality and Envy."

24 An important source for these ideas is Scitovsky, *The Joyless Economy.* See also his "The Desire for Excitement in Modern Society." On the question of the brain and an organism's need for positive stimulation, there is a good discussion in Restak, *The Brain*, chapter 2.

25 Restak, *The Brain*, chapter 2.

26 This idea, with special reference to self-esteem, was propounded in an influential article by R.H. White called "Motivation Reconsidered: The Concept of Competence." Published over thirty years ago, the article argues against models of motivation, such as behaviourism, which were then current. With the support of a wealth of data, White suggests that humans have a particular need for positive stimulation, which he calls feelings of efficacy. Such feelings fall within my category of feelings of enhancement and are related in particular to reasons for self-esteem connected to achievement. Of these feelings, White writes: "Under primitive conditions, survival must depend quite heavily on achieved competence. We should expect to find things arranged so as to favour and maximize this [sense of] achievement, particularly in the case of man where so little is provided innately" (330).

27 I have made this argument in a paper, "Self-Esteem as a Natural Need," delivered in 1986 to a faculty-student colloquium at Dalhousie University.

28 Parfit, *Reasons and Persons*, 251ff.

Bibliography

Achebe, Chinua. *Things Fall Apart*. Heinemann, 1961.

Adams, R.M. "Motive Utilitarianism." In J. Glover, ed., *Utilitarianism and Its Critics*, 236–49. MacMillan, 1990.

Baier, Annette. "Hume's Analysis of Pride." *Journal of Philosophy* 75 (1978): 27–40.

Barber, John. "The Swarm." *Toronto Life* 40, no.5 (August 1989): 16–19, 31, 42.

Bartky, Sandra Lee. "Narcissism, Femininity and Alienation." *Social Theory and Practice* 8, no.2 (1982): 127–43.

Benn, Stanley. "Equality, Moral and Social." *Encyclopedia of Philosophy*, ed. Paul Edwards, 1967.

Benson, John. "Who Is Autonomous Man?" *Philosophy* 58 (1983): 5–17.

Benson, Paul. "Autonomy and Oppressive Socialization." *Social Theory and Practice* 17, no.3 (1991): 385–408.

Ben-Ze'ev, Aaron. "Envy and Jealousy." *Canadian Journal of Philosophy* 20, no.3 (1990): 487–516.

– "Who Is a Rational Agent?" *Canadian Journal of Philosophy* 12, no.4 (1983): 647–61.

Bettleheim, Bruno. *The Informed Heart: Autonomy in a Mass Age*. Free Press, 1970.

Blanshard, Brand. *Four Reasonable Men*. Wesleyan University Press, 1984.

Blum, Lawrence. "Compassion." In Amélie O. Rorty, ed., *Explaining Emotions*, 507–17. University of California Press, 1980.

Boxill, Bernard. "Self-Respect and Protest." *Philosophy and Public Affairs* 6 (1976): 58–69.

Broadbent, Donald. *In Defence of Empirical Psychology*. Harper and Row, 1973.

Brown, Harold I. *Rationality.* Routledge, 1988.

Buchanan, Allen. "Revisability and Rational Choice." *Canadian Journal of Philosophy* 5, no.3 (1975): 395–407.

Burckhardt, Jacob. *The Civilization of the Renaissance in Italy.* Mentor, 1960.

Campbell, Richmond. *Self-Love and Self-Respect.* Canadian Philosophical Library, 1979.

Cantor, Norman F. *Civilization of the Middle Ages.* Harper Perennial, 1994.

Christman, John. "Autonomy: A Defense of the Split-Level Self." *Southern Journal of Philosophy* 25, no.3: 281–93.

– "Autonomy and Personal History." *Canadian Journal of Philosophy* 21, no.1 (1991): 1–24.

– "Constructing the Inner Citadel: Recent Work on the Concept of Autonomy." *Ethics* 99 (1988): 109–24.

– "Defending Historical Autonomy: A Reply to Professor Mele." *Canadian Journal of Philosophy* 23, no.2 (1993): 281–90.

Coles, Robert. "Psychoanalysis and Moral Development." In Arthur Dobrin, ed., *Being Good and Doing Right*, 55–83. University Press of America, 1993.

Cooper, David E. "Equality and Envy." *Journal of Philosophy of Education* 16, no.1 (1982): 35–47.

Cranor, Carl F. "Limitations to Respect-for-Persons Theories." In O.H. Green, ed., *Respect for Persons*, 45–59. Tulane University Press, 1982.

Dahl, Norman. "Morality and the Meaning of Life: Some First Thoughts." *Canadian Journal of Philosophy* 17, no.1 (1987): 3–14.

Darwall, Stephen. *Impartial Reason.* Cornell University Press, 1983.

– "Two Kinds of Respect." *Ethics* 88 (1977): 36–49.

Darwin, Charles. *The Autobiography of Charles Darwin.* J.M. Dent, 1959.

Davidson, Donald. "Actions, Reasons, and Causes." *Journal of Philosophy* 73 (1963): 685–700.

– "Hume's Cognitive Theory of Pride." *Journal of Philosophy* 73 (1976): 754–7.

de Beauvoir, Simone. *Mémoires d'une jeune fille rangée.* Gallimard, 1958.

Deigh, John. "Shame and Self-Esteem." *Ethics* 93 (1983): 225–45.

Dillon, Robin, S. "Toward a Feminist Conception of Self-Respect." *Hypatia* 7, no.1 (1992): 52–69.

Drake, Stillman. *Galileo.* Oxford University Press, 1980.

Dworkin, Gerald. "Moral Autonomy." In H.G. Engelhardt Jr and D. Callahan, eds., *Morals, Science and Sociality*, 156–71. Hastings-on-Hudson, 1978.

Eliot, George. *Felix Holt, the Radical.* Panther Books, 1970.

Erikson, Erik. *Childhood and Society.* Penguin, 1965.

Fallaci, Oriana. *Interviews with History.* Houghton Mifflin, 1976.

Feinberg, Joel. *Harm to Self.* Oxford University Press, 1986.

– "The Nature and Value of Rights." *Journal of Value Inquiry* 4, no.4 (1970): 243–57.

- *Social Philosophy.* Prentice-Hall, 1973.
Ferrante, Angela. "The Condemned of Kaboni." *Maclean's,* 12 January 1976, 17.
Feyerabend, Paul. *Against Method.* New Left Books, 1975.
Flanagan, Owen. *Varieties of Moral Psychology.* Harvard University Press, 1991.
Frankfurt, Harry. "Freedom of the Will and the Concept of the Person." *Journal of Philosophy* 68 (1971): 5–20.
Frankl, Victor. *Man's Search for Meaning.* Vintage, 1967.
Friedman, Marilyn A. "Autonomy and the Split-Level Self." *Southern Journal of Philosophy* 24, no.1: 19–35.
Frye, Northrop. "Literature as Critique of Pure Reason." In R.D. Denham, ed., *Northrop Frye: Myth and Metaphor, Selected Essays 1974–1988,* 168–82. University Press of Virginia, 1990.
Galileo. *Dialogue Concerning the Two Chief World Systems.* University of California Press, 1967.
- "Letter to the Grand Duchess Christina." In S. Drake, ed., *Discoveries and Opinions of Galileo.* Doubleday, 1957.
Galston, William. "Pluralism and Social Unity." *Ethics* 99 (1989): 711–26.
Gergen, K.J. *The Concept of Self.* Holt, Rinehart and Winston, 1971.
Gidley, Mick, ed. *Representing Others: White Views of Indigenous People.* University of Exeter Press, 1992.
Glover, Jonathan. *Causing Death and Saving Lives.* Penguin, 1977.
- *I: The Philosophy and Psychology of Personal Identity.* Allen Lane, 1988.
- *Responsibility.* Routledge and Kegan Paul, 1970.
Godlovitch, Shlomo I. "Ontology, Epistemic Access, and the Sublime." *Iyyun* 44 (1995): 55–71.
Goffman, Erving. *Asylums.* Penguin, 1961.
Goodall, Jane. *In the Shadow of Man.* Collins, 1971.
Greenblat, Stephen. "Fiction and Friction." In T.C. Heller, M. Sosna, and D.E. Wellbery, eds., *Reconstructing Individualism,* 30–52. Stanford University Press, 1986.
Gunn, Alastair S. "Why Should We Care about Rare Species." *Environmental Ethics* 2 (1980): 17–37.
Haak, Susan. *Philosophy of Logics.* Cambridge University Press, 1978.
Hacking, Ian. *The Emergence of Probability.* Cambridge University Press, 1975.
- *Representing and Intervening.* Cambridge University Press, 1983.
- *The Taming of Chance.* Cambridge University Press, 1990.
Hampshire, Stuart. *Innocence and Experience.* Harvard University Press, 1989.
- *Two Theories of Morality.* Oxford University Press, 1977.
Hardwig, John. "The Achievement of Moral Responsibility." *Philosophy and Rhetoric* 6 (1973): 171–85.
- "Epistemic Dependence." *Journal of Philosophy* 82, no.7 (1985): 335–49.
Hare, R.M. *Moral Thinking.* Oxford University Press, 1981.

Held, Virginia. "Reasonable Progress and Self-Respect." *Monist* 57 (1973): 12–27.

Hill, Thomas, Jr. "Servility and Self-Respect." *Monist* 57 (1973): 137–52.

Hossie, Linda. "Birders No Longer a Rare Species." *Globe and Mail*, 2 October 1990, A4.

Hudson, Stephen. "The Nature of Respect." *Social Theory and Practice* 6 (1980): 69–90.

Huizinga, John. *The Waning of the Middle Ages*. Penguin, 1976.

Hume, David. *An Enquiry Concerning the Principles of Morals*. Ed. J.B. Schneewind. Hackett Publishing Company, 1983.

Isenberg, Arnold. "Natural Pride and Natural Shame." In Amélie O. Rorty, ed., *Explaining Emotions*, 355–83. University of California Press, 1980.

James, William. *Principles of Psychology.* Volume 1. Dover, 1950.

Kant, Immanuel. *Grounding for the Metaphysics of Morals*. Hackett Publishing, 1981.

Katz, Bill. "Chasing the Ogre." *Astronomy* 14, no.1 (1986): 99–100.

Kekes, John. *Facing Evil*. Princeton University Press, 1990.

– "Moral Tradition." In Oswald Hanfling, ed., *Life and Meaning: A Reader*, 234–48. Blackwells, 1987.

Keller, Fox Evelyn. *Feeling for the Organism: The Life and Work of Barbara McClintock*. W.H. Freeman and Co., 1983.

Kymlicka, Will. "Rawls on Teleology and Deontology." *Philosophy and Public Affairs* 17, no.3 (1988): 173–90.

Landesmann, Charles. "Against Respect for Persons." In O.H. Green, ed., *Respect for Persons*, 31–43. Tulane University Press, 1982.

Langer, K. Susanne. *Philosophy in a New Key.* Mentor, 1941.

Lloyd, G.E.R. *The Revolution in Wisdom*. University of California Press, 1987.

Lovejoy, Arthur. *Reflections on Human Nature*. Baltimore, 1961.

Lukes, Steven. *Individualism*. Blackwell, 1973.

Luper-Foy, Steven. "Competing for the Good Life." *American Philosophical Quarterly* 23 (1986): 167–77.

MacIntyre, Alasdair. *After Virtue*. University of Notre Dame Press, 1984.

– *Whose Justice? Which Rationality?* Duckworth, 1988.

McKean, Kevin. "Decisions, Decisions." *Discover* 6 (1985): 22–31.

Mackie, J. *Ethics: Inventing Right and Wrong*. Penguin, 1977.

Malinowski, B. *Magic, Science, and Religion*. Doubleday, 1954.

Massey, Stephen J. "Is Self-Respect a Moral or a Psychological Concept?" *Ethics* 93 (1983): 246–61.

– "Kant on Self-Respect." *Journal of History and Philosophy* 21 (1983): 57–74.

Mele, Alfred. "History and Personal Autonomy." *Canadian Journal of Philosophy* 23, no.2 (1993): 271–80.

Moffat, Don. "What Hubble the Man Saw." *Globe and Mail*, 30 June 1990, D4.

Moody-Adams, Michele M. "Culture, Responsibility, and Affected Igno-
rance." *Ethics* 104 (1994): 291–309.
– "Race, Class, and the Social Construction of Self-Respect." *Philosophical
Forum* 24, no.1–3: 251–66.
Morillo, Carolyn R. "Doing, Refraining, and the Strenuousness of Morality."
American Philosophical Quarterly 14 (1977): 29–39.
Moyers, Bill. *A World of Ideas*. Doubleday, 1989.
Mussen, P., and Distler, L. "Identification." In S. Lee and M. Herbert, eds.,
Freud and Psychology, 305–20. Penguin, 1970.
Nathanson, Stephen. *The Ideal of Rationality*. Humanities Press, 1985.
Neely, Wright. "Freedom and Desire." *Philosophical Review* 83 (1974): 32–54.
Newton-Smith, William. *The Rationality of Science*. Routledge, 1981.
Nielsen, Kai. "Justifying Egalitarianism." *Social Research* 48, no. 2 (1981): 260–
76.
Nozick, Robert. *Anarchy, State, and Utopia*. Basic Books, 1974.
Orwell, George. "A Hanging." In Sonia Orwell and Ian Angus, eds., *The
Collected Essays, Journalism and Letters of George Orwell*, 1: 66–71. Penguin,
1968.
– *1984*. Penguin, 1949.
Parfit, Derek. *Reasons and Persons*. Oxford University Press, 1984.
Plato. *Euthyphro*.
Potok, Chaim. *The Chosen*. Simon and Schuster, 1967.
– *The Gift of Asher Lev*. Knopf, 1990.
Prescott, William. *History of the Conquest of Peru*. Allen and Unwin, 1959.
Price, H.H. "Some Considerations about Belief." In P. Griffiths, ed., *Knowledge
and Belief*, 45–8. Oxford University Press, 1967.
Putnam, Hilary. *Reason, Truth, and History*. Cambridge University Press, 1981.
Quine, W. "On Empirically Equivalent Systems of the World." *Erkenntnis* 9,
no. 3 (1975): 313–28.
Railton, Peter. "Alienation, Consequentialism, Morality." In S. Scheffler, ed.,
Consequentialism and Its Critics, 93–133. Oxford University Press, 1988.
Rawls, John. "Justice as Fairness: Political not Metaphysical." *Philosophy and
Public Affairs* 14, no.4 (1985): 223–51.
– "Kantian Constructivism in Moral Theory." *Journal of Philosophy* 77, no.9
(1980): 515–72.
– *Political Liberalism*. Columbia University Press, 1993.
– *A Theory of Justice*. Harvard University Press, 1971.
Regan, Tom. *In Defence of Animal Rights*. University of California Press,
1983.
Restak, Richard. *The Brain*. Warner Books, 1979.
Roberts, Robert. "What an Emotion Is: A Sketch." *Philosophical Review* 97
(1988): 181–209.

– "What Is Wrong with Wicked Feelings?" *American Philosophical Quarterly* 28 (1991): 13–24.

Rocco, Alfredo. "The Political Doctrine of Fascism." In Carl Cohen, ed., *Communism, Fascism and Democracy*, 333–49. Random House, 1962.

Rorty, Richard. "Philosophy in America Today." In *Consequences of Pragmatism*, 211–30. University of Minnesota Press, 1982.

Rosenberg, Morris. *Conceiving the Self*. Basic Books, 1979.

Ross, W.D. *The Right and the Good*. Oxford University Press, 1930.

Russell, Bertrand. *Autobiography*. Volume 1. McClelland and Stewart, 1967.

– *The Conquest of Happiness*. Unwin, 1985.

– *Fact and Fiction*. Simon and Schuster, 1962.

Sachs, David. "How to Distinguish Self-Respect and Self-Esteem." *Philosophy and Public Affairs* 10, no.4 (1981): 346–60.

Said, Edward. *Covering Islam*. Pantheon Books, 1981.

Schneewind, J.B. *Sidgwick's Ethics and Victorian Moral Philosophy*. Oxford University Press, 1977.

Scitovsky, Tibor. "The Desire for Excitement in Modern Society." *Kytos* 31 (1981): 3–13.

– *The Joyless Economy*. Oxford University Press, 1976.

Shaffir, William. "Chassidic Communities in Montreal." In M. Weinfeld, W. Shaffir, and I. Cotler, eds., *The Canadian Jewish Mosaic*, 273–86. J. Wiley, 1981.

Sher, George. *Desert*. Princeton University Press, 1987.

Shoeck, E. *Envy*. Harcourt, Brace and World, 1966.

Sibley, W.M. "The Rational and the Reasonable." *Philosophical Review* 62 (1953): 554–60.

Sidgwick, Henry. *Methods of Ethics*. Macmillan, 1907.

Siegel, Harvey. "Farewell to Feyerabend." *Inquiry* 32 (1989): 343–69.

Singer, Peter. *The Expanding Circle*. Farrar, Straus and Giroux, 1981.

– *Practical Ethics*. Cambridge University Press, 1979.

Smart, J.J.C. "Distributive Justice and Equality." In J. Arthur and W.H. Shaw, eds., *Justice and Economic Distribution*, 2d ed., 106–17. Prentice-Hall, 1992.

Snow, C.P. *In Their Wisdom*. Penguin, 1978.

– *The Search*. Scribners, 1934.

– *The Sleep of Reason*. Macmillan, 1968.

Steiner, George. *Language and Silence*. Atheneum, 1977.

Strawson, P.F. *Analysis and Metaphysics: An Introduction to Philosophy*. Oxford University Press, 1992.

Taylor, Charles. *Hegel and Modern Society*. Cambridge University Press, 1979.

– "Responsibility for Self." In A. Baier, ed., *Identities of Person*, 281–99. University of California Press, 1976.

– *Sources of the Self*. Harvard University Press, 1989.

Taylor, Gabriele. *Pride, Shame, and Guilt*. Oxford University Press, 1985.

Thomas, Laurence. *Living Morally*. Temple University Press, 1989.

- "Moral Deference." *Philosophical Forum* 24, no.1–3 (1992–93): 233–51.
- "Morality and Our Self Concept." *Journal of Value Inquiry* 12 (1978): 258–68.
Tolstoy, L. *Anna Karenin*. Penguin, 1954.
Tversky, A., and Kahneman, D. "The Framing of Decisions and the Psychology of Choice." *Science* 211 (30 January 1981): 453–8.
Warnock, Geoffry. "The Primacy of Practical Reason." In P.F. Strawson, ed., *Studies in the Philosophy of Thought and Action*, 214–28. Oxford University Press, 1968.
White, R.H. "Motivation Reconsidered: The Concept of Competence." *Psychological Review* 66 (1959): 297–323.
Williams, Bernard. "Egoism and Altruism." In *Problems of the Self*, 250–65. Cambridge University Press, 1973.
- *Ethics and the Limits of Philosophy*. Harvard University Press, 1985.
- "The Idea of Equality." In J. Feinberg, ed., *Moral Concepts*, 153–77. Oxford University Press, 1969.
- and Smart, J.J.C. *Utilitarianism: For and Against*. Cambridge University Press, 1973.
Wilson, E.O. *Biophilia*. Harvard University Press, 1984.
Wittgenstein, Ludwig. *Philosophical Investigations*. Blackwells, 1963.
Wollheim, Richard. "Identification and Imagination." In R. Wollheim, ed., *Freud: A Collection of Critical Essays*, 172–95. Anchor, 1974.
Wolpert, Lewis. *The Unnatural Nature of Science*. Faber and Faber, 1992.
Wood, Allen. *Hegel's Ethical Thought*. Cambridge University Press, 1979.
Woolf, Virginia. *A Writer's Diary*. Ed. Leonard Woolf. Hogarth Press, 1953.
Yanal, Robert J. "Self-Esteem." *Nous* 21 (1987): 363–79.
Young, Robert. "Autonomy and Socialization. *Mind* 89 (1980): 565–76.
- "Autonomy and the 'Inner Self.'" *American Philosophical Quarterly* 17, no.1 (1980): 35–43.
- "Egalitarianism and Envy." *Philosophical Studies* 52 (1987): 261–76.
- *Personal Autonomy: Beyond Negative and Positive Liberty*. Croom Helm, 1986.
Yovel, Yirmiyahu. *Spinoza and Other Heretics: The Adventures of Immanence*. Princeton University Press, 1989.

Index